From a Watery Grave

To Boyd Henry,

Thank you for your
interest in La Belle!

Jim Bruseth

9/14/05

LE COMTE DE VERMANDOIS

From a Watery Grave

THE DISCOVERY AND EXCAVATION OF LA SALLE'S SHIPWRECK, *LA BELLE*

JAMES E. BRUSETH *and* TONI S. TURNER

TEXAS A&M UNIVERSITY PRESS
COLLEGE STATION

The paper used in this book meets the minimum requirements of the
American National Standard for Permanence of Paper for Printed Library Materials,
z39.48-1984. Binding materials have been chosen for durability.
∞

Unless noted otherwise, illustrations are courtesy the Texas Historical Commission.

Library of Congress Cataloging-in-Publication Data

Bruseth, James E.
From a watery grave: the discovery and excavation of La Salle's
shipwreck, La Belle / James E. Bruseth and Toni S. Turner. —1st ed.
p. cm.
Includes bibliographical references and index.
ISBN 1-58544-347-6 (cloth : alk. paper) —ISBN 1-58544-431-6 (pbk. : alk. paper)
1. La Salle, Robert Cavelier, sieur de, 1643-1687.   2. La Belle
(Frigate)   3. Shipwrecks—Texas—Matagorda Bay.   4. Matagorda Bay
(Tex.)—Antiquities.   I. Turner, Toni S. II. Title.
F352.L35 2004

2004012105

917.64'13204—dc22

Dedicated to the following current and former members of the
Texas Historical Commission for their wonderful support:

JOHN LISTON NAU III, *current chairman*

JEAN ANN ABLES-FLATT	FRANK W. GORMAN
BRUCE T. AIKEN	DAVID A. GRAVELLE
THOMAS E. ALEXANDER	ALBERT F. "BOO" HAUSSER
GAIL LOVING BARNES	EILEEN JOHNSON
JANE COOK BARNHILL	THOMAS E. KROUTTER, JR.
BOB BOWMAN	ARCHIE P. MACDONALD
J. P. BRYAN	MAMIE L. MCKNIGHT
JAN F. BULLOCK	CARL MCQUEARY
DIANE D. BUMPAS	SUSAN MEAD
SHIRLEY W. CALDWELL	JOHN E. PRESTON
CHRIS CARSON	JUAN F. SANDOVAL
LAREATHA H. CLAY	ROSE T. TREVIÑO
HAROLD COURSON	LINDA VALDEZ
T. R. FEHRENBACH	CLINTON WHITE
WILLIE LEE GAY	FRANK D. YTURRIA

Contents

Foreword

In September, 1933, a powerful hurricane hit the Texas coast around the mouth of the Rio Grande. This storm (they were then unnamed) was one of the worst of the century in terms of tidal flow. Seawater was driven inland over the low marshes and salt flats, in some places as far as twenty miles, and considering an average rise in elevation of one foot per mile, this indicated a tide of perhaps twenty feet. Fortunately there was very little development along the coast at that time, and only about a dozen people died. Near the gulf, however, reinforced concrete highways were twisted and torn up, new shallow inland lakes were created where small shrimp boats fished for years afterward, and saltwater species such as redfish and tarpon were introduced into freshwater *resacas* around the city of Brownsville. More important, the south arm of Brazos de Santiago Pass, about four miles north of the Rio Grande, which had silted up by the 1880s, was blown open. The Brazos Island of history books was again an island, as South Bay of the Laguna Madre was now open to the gulf.

As soon as temporary roads were restored I went to the area to fish with my grandfather. A short distance inland, the pass revealed a marvelous sight: hundreds (perhaps thousands—I was eight years old) of pilings ran out into the water from the south shore; there were roadways and wagon tracks in uncovered clays leading to the Rio Grande. No one, even at the local newspaper, had any idea what these were. Shortly afterward, we went by boat to the north part of Brazos Island just across from Port Isabel. Here was another incredible sight—rows and rows of tent pegs, more ruts and tracks, and much scattered debris. I found several heavy conical musket balls and a brass or copper button from a uniform coat. Other people found bottles, mid-nineteenth-century silver coins, even a set of leg irons. None of us who found this site knew what it was, and, alas, it was thoroughly looted. The area was soon sand-filled once again and, like the pilings, disappeared beneath coastal muck.

I think this was the beginning of my interest in history and archaeology, two disciplines that are, or should be, always intertwined. Much later, when I uncovered old documents, I realized that the pilings represented the many piers to which cargo was lightered and then taken by a short rail to White's Ranch for loading on steamboats running upriver. Here the U.S. Army during the Mexican War of 1846–48 was supplied.

The tent pegs on Brazos Island were remnants of a Union camp during the Civil War, when federal troops held the island, and Confederates held Port Isabel and the shore. Thousands of soldiers landed and bivouacked there during and after the war. And these relics were completely covered by shifting sands in the hurricane of 1867, which also destroyed settlements at the mouth of the Rio Grande. (They were partly uncovered again by a hurricane in the 1960s, but there was not much left.)

Public collecting from a historical site on public land could not happen today. Texans are much more conscious of our history. And in fact, we do not wait for storms to uncover the past; we use documents and whatever evidence we have to hunt it down. The search for *La Belle*, the only seventeenth-century French ship to survive in North America, may not have reached an audience as large as *The Hunt for Red October*, but to those fascinated by the triumphs, failures, and agonies of our forebears, it is just as thrilling—and vastly more significant.

One forlorn wreck in Matagorda Bay is telling us much we may have guessed but never really knew. La Salle's doomed venture is now a story that will never die.

As former chair and member of the Texas Historical Commission, I am gratified—but not proud—to have played a small part in this venture, the saving of *La Belle.* Our Texas archaeologists did the hours of work, suffered the years of frustration, and the glory is theirs. But we should all be mindful that sciences need sup-

port, not just from aficionados but also from citizens and state. I am proud of the support that Texas and Texans have provided in getting to the bottom (so to speak) of what was once only a romantic tale.

James Bruseth and Toni Turner have created a splendid book, scientifically, historically, and visually. I believe this book, as well as *La Belle,* will become a Texas treasure, inspiring future seekers as a long-forgotten mass of rotting pilings on the Texas coast once inspired me.

T. R. FEHRENBACH,
Commissioner Emeritus, Texas Historical Commission

Preface

In addition to being the senior author of this book, I directed the excavation of *La Belle* for the Texas Historical Commission from October, 1996, to April, 1997. I worked seven-day weeks and twelve-hour days but had one of the most fascinating archaeological jobs in the world. I also directed the research into the artifacts recovered from the wreck. My wife and second author of this volume, Toni Turner, helped with excavation and fundraising, edited manuscripts, and gave lectures to members of the public who visited the cofferdam.

We have written this book for a general audience, recounting the story of *La Belle*'s shipwreck in 1686, discovery in 1995, and excavation in 1996 and 1997. While technical facts are explained in lay terms, all of the latest research and interpretations related to the vessel as of the date of this publication are included. This is the second in a series of volumes on La Salle's ship *La Belle*. The first, Robert Weddle's *The Wreck of the* Belle, *the Ruin of La Salle,* published in 2001, described the explorer's expedition to Texas and the tragic circumstances surrounding the loss of his ship. Future volumes will report the results of analyses of *La Belle*'s hull and cargo and will be written by researchers who have collaborated for several years on the project. Their contributions, many referenced in this book, will be for a more academic audience.

Seldom is it the case in North American nautical archaeology that there are sufficient funds to excavate an entire shipwreck in a single field season. More often, a team of marine archaeologists works underwater and retrieves artifacts one by one over several short seasons. In most cases, a significant portion of the wreck remains submerged and unexcavated after the project ends. The excavation of *La Belle* was quite different: the entire wreck was recovered in one major effort.

We had good reasons for choosing this method. Miles away from the nearest coastal town and the watchful eyes that come with it, the wreck would have been vulnerable to vandalism between field seasons. The remains of *La Belle* already had survived, miraculously, for more than three centuries in near-pristine condition, despite extensive oil exploration and drilling in Matagorda Bay and the proximity of a deep, manmade intercoastal canal that supports heavy ship and barge traffic along the Gulf Coast. We could not leave her to the vagaries of fate again, so we felt compelled to recover the entire shipwreck in one long field season.

From the beginning we knew the costs of a complete excavation would be high and that constant challenges would test our decision. Our resolve remained strong as we faced each one with commitment and ingenuity. We knew the excavation would be only a part of the entire project and that large sums of money would be required to preserve what fate had left for us. From the beginning, therefore, we budgeted funds for artifact conservation. Of the six million dollars expended on this project, more than two million will be used to preserve the remarkable artifacts that survived three centuries in a watery grave.

As this book reveals, our decision to excavate the entire shipwreck at once yielded invaluable information that would have been difficult to discern from a series of field seasons. The system of numbers carved into the hull timbers, for example, led us to understand that *La Belle* was essentially a "ship kit"—a conclusion that might not have been possible had we conducted several small-scale excavations. The entire collection of artifacts, the totality of what remained in *La Belle*'s cargo holds, tells us much about the goals of La Salle's colonial enterprise. If we had recovered these objects piecemeal, season by season, our interpretations might have been hindered.

An especially difficult decision was determining exactly how to excavate *La Belle.* It was only after considerable discussion that we decided to build a cofferdam around the vessel and pump out the water inside so that we could work in nearly dry conditions. Nautical archaeologists from the United States and abroad provided guidance on this issue. Some were supportive, others uncertain, and a few were downright hostile. Critics raised concerns about the high cost, about whether the cofferdam could function in rough seas and inclement weather, and whether the artifacts inside the structure would degrade from drying out too much. Solutions were found for all these potential problems.

The State of Texas appropriated public monies, and we secured additional resources from other public and private sources to complete the project. Archaeologists toiled during turbulent weather and developed methods to keep the crew safe while the excavation continued. To prevent artifacts from drying out, water hoses were installed inside the cofferdam. The recovered objects were kept wet, carefully wrapped, and transported to the project laboratory in Palacios, Texas.

The task was enormous, but a traditional underwater excavation would have been even more difficult. While the depth of the water at the wreck site was only twelve feet, visibility was poor—on most days, virtually zero. Nautical archaeologists routinely deal with such poor conditions during field projects, but even the best will inadvertently damage fragile artifacts and miss small objects. We are convinced that the decision to use a cofferdam was the best way to proceed. Ultimately, the results presented in this and other volumes will enable others to judge our success.

We hope the readers of this book will enjoy the story of our efforts to find and recover La Salle's wrecked ship. For the many hundreds of people who helped with the excavation—and the millions who followed our progress in the media—we proudly present our results.

JAMES E. BRUSETH,
Texas Historical Commission

From a Watery Grave

Chapter One

INTO A WATERY GRAVE

For want of an anchor the ship was lost; for want of a ship the colony was lost.
—ROBERT S. WEDDLE, *The Wreck of the* Belle, *the Ruin of La Salle*

A frigid north wind battered the French ship *La Belle* as she lay anchored in an uncharted bay in the northern Gulf of Mexico. Pacing the deck, Capt. Pierre Tessier anxiously scanned the horizon. La Salle had promised to return in ten days, but more than a month had passed.[1]

It was February, 1686, almost two years since Robert Cavelier, Sieur de La Salle, had sailed from France with four ships—*La Belle, l'Aimable, Le Joly,* and *Le Saint-François*—and three hundred crew and settlers to establish a colony in the New World. They had built a small compound known as Fort St. Louis about thirty miles away from where *La Belle* now lay anchored.[2] But the expedition's main purposes were to find the mouth of the Mississippi River, establish a permanent settlement, and open the continent to France for trade with the Indians and the export of furs. Invading the Spanish silver mines to the west was another—but secret—part of the French plan. Success would bring glory to King Louis XIV, vast territories to France, and great wealth to La Salle. But *La Belle* was the expedition's last surviving vessel, and now even she was in danger.[3]

In January, La Salle had taken twenty men overland to locate the Mississippi, leaving Tessier in command of *La Belle* with orders to stay anchored. When La Salle had found the Mississippi, Tessier would sail the ship to the river, bringing the cargo for a new colony.

As the gale steadily increased, Tessier's anxiety deepened. He was not the original captain of *La Belle;* La Salle had only recently assigned him this position. On leaving the French port of La Rochelle, the ship's captain had been the experienced Daniel Moraud. Tessier was only the second mate. Moraud died along the Texas coast a few months after making landfall from eating prickly pear fruits; he had not removed the spines and suffocated when his throat became swollen. Upon Moraud's death, La Salle gave command of *La Belle* to Elie Richaud, formerly the ship's pilot. Richaud, along with five other men on a reconnaissance of the shoreline, was attacked and killed by Karankawa Indians in late 1685. Tessier was thus the third captain of *La Belle* and the least experienced, which only added to his anxiety.[4]

Drinking water was running low, which jeopardized the crew's very survival. Tessier directed his five best sailors to go ashore for water. They loaded the only

HOSTILE KARANKAWAS

When La Salle landed on the Texas coast in 1685, he found the area inhabited by Karankawa Indians. For centuries, these indigenous people had lived along the coast, from today's Galveston Island to Corpus Christi Bay. They were nomads, collecting wild plants, catching fish, gathering shellfish, and hunting animals such as deer. Their dwellings were small huts made with poles placed in the ground and drawn together at the top. Hides and mats covered the poles, providing windbreaks and protection from rain.[1]

Karankawa men were exceptionally tall, well built, and muscular. Most of the time, they went naked, their only adornment being small pieces of cane inserted through their nipples or lower lips. Women wore a small skirt of Spanish moss or animal skin, but their upper bodies remained uncovered. Both sexes decorated their bodies with tattoos that formed lines and animal figures.[2]

Initial French encounters with the Karankawas were friendly. La Salle's explorations of the Great Lakes and Illinois provided years of experience in dealing with native peoples, and he knew the advantages of quickly establishing amicable relationships with them. But because of the ignorance of some members of his 1684 expedition, relations with the Karankawas soured. After landing on the Texas coast, La Salle needed Indian canoes to move cargo from ship to land. He sent a small envoy of men to a nearby Karankawa village to trade for canoes. The soldiers entered the village with guns drawn, frightening the Indians away. With the village abandoned, the Frenchmen stole animal hides and canoes, rather than trading for them as La Salle had always been careful to do. When the Karankawas returned to their camp, they discovered the theft and interpreted it as a declaration of war.[3] From that time forward, the Karankawas sought revenge, ferociously attacking members of La Salle's party and eventually killing many of the colonists.

Karankawa campsite along the Texas coast. *Illustration by Charles Shaw*

Notes

1. Robert A. Ricklis, *The Karankawa Indians of Texas: An Ecological Study of Cultural Tradition and Change*, pp. 1–10.
2. W. W. Newcomb, Jr., *The Indians of Texas from Prehistoric to Modern Times*, pp. 63–65.
3. William C. Foster, ed., *Joutel Journal*, pp. 93–94.

remaining longboat with wooden barrels and rowed toward land. Late in the day, the crew of *La Belle* saw the longboat attempting to return. The men in the small boat strained at the oars, but were unable to make progress against the strong wind. At dusk the ship's crew urged Tessier to attach a lighted torch to the top of the mast. Instead, he placed a lighted candle in the ship's lantern on the deck. It was quickly extinguished by the wind, and the longboat disappeared into the darkness.

At dawn there was no sign of the longboat, and the crew feared that Karankawa Indians had attacked the five men. Now that *La Belle*'s best sailors and only longboat were lost, Tessier knew that conditions could only worsen as water and supplies ran out. Nevertheless, they waited, hoping in vain for the longboat to return.

Desperate to preserve their dwindling rations, the crew began to kill and eat pigs they had planned to use for breeding in the colony. They tried to make bread with seawater, creating an inedible mess. Tessier controlled the supplies of brandy and wine, including a large barrel of Spanish wine meant for religious sacrament; he drank greedily and remained in a stupor. Some crew members, close to death from thirst, also drank wine, hoping for relief. But dehydrated further by the alcohol, several died, and chaos reigned.

In February, 1686, the crew of *La Belle* attempts to sail across Matagorda Bay to get supplies from the Fort St. Louis colony. As a strong storm blows in, they lose control of the ship.
Illustration by Charles Shaw

The crew was in a quandary: disobeying La Salle's orders to stay anchored would trigger his infamous temper, but waiting for the leader's return could spell doom. Tessier, though impaired by alcohol, finally comprehended that La Salle's instructions must be disregarded. He decided to sail to the other end of the bay, where they could join the colonists at Fort St. Louis. It was the crew's last hope for salvation.

Resolute, Tessier ordered the anchor pulled. But as *La Belle* began to sail, a ferocious cold front blew in from the north. Without skilled sailors to harness the wind, the ship lurched out of control and was thrust south across the bay. Tessier ordered the anchor released, but against the strong winds all efforts proved useless. Normally, a second anchor would have been deployed to help stop the ship's drift, but the other anchor had been lost. As the ship was blasted stern-first, or backward, its single anchor scraped hopelessly at the shallow bay bottom, gouging a narrow groove into the sand. Helpless, the crew could only watch as *La Belle* finally slammed aground at the southern end of the bay. She lay a quarter mile offshore, listing to starboard and resting in twelve feet of water.

At nightfall the winds diminished and the waters calmed. But exhausted and in totally unknown waters, the crew could not free the ship or escape to dry land.

The next day they constructed a crude raft from planks and barrels. Two men boarded the raft to go ashore, but it soon began to break up. One man drowned; the other managed to land. He briefly searched for water but soon gave up and tried to swim back to the ship. Overcome by exhaustion and cold, he also drowned. A new, more solid raft was constructed, which successfully carried several men ashore, where they finally found fresh water. The remaining crew disembarked. Tessier, however, remained on board for several more days under the pretense of helping to offload all of the cargo. In reality, he was finishing off a barrel of brandy.

The new raft was small and difficult to maneuver in rough seas, but it was adequate for daily returns to the ship to retrieve cargo. The crew managed to salvage some of La Salle's papers and clothes, barrels of flour, casks of wine, glass beads, and other trade items, but most of the cargo lay too deep under the water. Finally, a strong southerly wind drove the ship's hull deep into the bay's muddy bottom, entombing the remaining cargo. Only the rear deck remained above water, with her torn sails flapping in the gulf winds.

Two of *La Belle*'s crew attempt to go ashore after building a raft out of barrels and planks.
Illustration by Charles Shaw

Of the twenty-seven people originally assigned to the ship, only six survived: Captain Tessier, a priest, a military officer, a regular soldier, a young servant girl, and a small boy. They were now trapped on part of a peninsula at the eastern end of the mainland, and the only means of escape was to walk around the bay to join the others at Fort St. Louis. The Karankawa Indians were a constant threat, however, and would spare no chance to kill them.

For three months the six castaways remained on the peninsula, hunting waterfowl, catching fish, and collecting oysters from the shallow waters. They used flour rescued from *La Belle* to make bread and retrieved some barrels of wine, which they drank to dull their misery.

Then one day a small boat washed ashore, an Indian canoe La Salle had lost earlier in a storm. It now offered a glimmer of hope for the stranded survivors. They could now paddle directly across the bay to Fort St. Louis without fear of encountering Indians en route. Determined, all six piled into the canoe for the trip across the bay and up the creek leading to the fort, seeking the safety and comfort of their compatriots. As they neared the settlement and heard voices, the cast-

aways called out, "Who goes there?" The response was the code word, "Versailles." They knew they had indeed reached the French colony. Finally, they thought, their ordeal was over. But *La Belle* was lost, and with her, La Salle's principal means of escape.

THE PLACE OF THE BROKEN SHIP

The Spanish Crown had begun searching for evidence of a French incursion nearly a year before *La Belle* sank, after one of La Salle's own crew members had revealed much about the expedition to Spanish officials. The young man, Dénis Thomas, unwittingly stumbled right into the middle of the struggle between the French and Spanish empires for control of the New World.

Born to a peasant family in Longueville, France, Thomas had served as a page for one of the king's advisers, and through this position learned about La Salle's expedition. Excited by prospects of adventure and fortune, Thomas enlisted as a member of the expedition.[5] During the two-month voyage across the Atlantic, Thomas became friends with one of La Salle's servants and gained inside information about the fa-

Pass Cavallo, the entrance into Matagorda Bay from the Gulf of Mexico. *La Belle* successfully entered the bay here, but *l'Aimable* was lost. *Photograph by Alan Govenar, courtesy Documentary Arts*

mous explorer's goals. The reticent La Salle confided in only a few trusted men, and Thomas was not part of this inner circle, but his chance alliance with the servant made him privy to its secrets.

On his way to the New World, La Salle had stopped at the rough-and-tumble Caribbean port of Petit Goäve, part of today's Haiti. At Petit Goäve, Thomas and other French colonists mingled with local inhabitants, as well as with pirates, or freebooters. Henri Joutel, one of La Salle's lieutenants and chronicler of the expedition, described Petit Goäve as a place where "the air was bad, the fruit the same, and there were a great many women worse than the air or the fruit."[6] Freebooters told Thomas of the perils that awaited La Salle in the Gulf of Mexico. Adding to the young man's anxiety was the constant bickering between La Salle and Taneguy Le Gallois de Beaujeu, the captain of *Le Joly,* who by order of Louis XIV was in command while the expedition was at sea. La Salle's authority would not commence until they reached the New World.

Thomas decided he would be better off with pirates than with La Salle, so he joined the crew of a captured Spanish vessel, *Nuestra Señora de Regla,* where

his shipmates were Spaniards, mulattoes, Negroes, and French expatriates.[7] He did not realize he had joined forces with two of the most infamous pirates of the Caribbean: Michel de Grammont of France and Laurens de Graff of the Netherlands.

Shortly after setting sail, Thomas found himself involved in a ruthless pirate attack on the coastal Mexican community of Campeche. Twelve pirate ships collected at Cabo Catoche, at the tip of present-day Yucatan, with plans to raid, plunder, and pillage. On July 6, 1685, the ships entered the town's harbor and disgorged hundreds of pirates. Local inhabitants, alerted to an impending attack, had moved their valuables to nearby Mérida or into the surrounding jungle. The invaders, disappointed that their invasion would not yield anticipated riches, unleashed six weeks of devastation upon the town and its people. Several local inhabitants were hanged.

Some of the pirates, including Dénis Thomas, decided to join another ship headed for Petit Goäve and ultimately France. But along the way that ship was captured by the Spanish fleet and returned to Spain's control. Thomas and 119 of his shipmates, now subjects of

La Salle's Fort St. Louis colony was established along a river (today's Garcitas Creek) flowing into Lavaca Bay. His settlement was located about thirty miles north of the Gulf Coast on high ground that could be defended if attacked by pirates, Spaniards, or Indians. *Illustration by Charles Shaw*

the Spanish Crown, were taken to Veracruz and interrogated. Thomas claimed that he was unaware he had joined a band of freebooters and had only wanted to return home. In an effort to save his life, the young man confessed what he had learned from La Salle's servant. He told his inquisitors that four ships had sailed from France to establish a fortress and build a New World colony at the mouth of the Mississippi River. Thomas also divulged another secret: La Salle hoped to reach the rich Spanish silver mines west of the Mississippi.[8]

This latter fact was extremely important. During the late 1600s, Spain obtained a significant portion of her New World wealth from silver deposits in northern Mexico. Each year the king eagerly awaited shipments of the Crown's share of the riches, and the Spanish economy became heavily dependent on these annual infusions. Spain knew that Louis XIV coveted the silver mines of Nueva Vizcaya, and now they had proof from Thomas that the French king was colonizing Spanish territory in the New World. How much longer would it be before the silver mines were directly threatened?

Thomas's revelation of La Salle's intent was a fatal

mistake: once he had divulged this information, he was no longer of any value to his captors, and he was summarily hanged. His intelligence was hurriedly conveyed from the Viceroy of New Spain to Madrid. The War Council of the Indies met in special session and urged Spain's prompt action to "pluck the thorn which has been thrust into the heart of America."[9] The Spanish ultimately dispatched eleven expeditions by land and sea, from both Florida and Mexico, to search for the French invaders.

One of the expeditions was led by Captains Martín de Rivas and Pedro de Yriarte, who set sail in two ships on December 25, 1686, to find La Salle. A narrative of the voyage, written by the pilot, Juan Enríquez Barroto, begins at the port of Veracruz and continues as they sailed along the coast from Mexico toward Florida, as the crew searched for signs of French intruders. Before sunrise on April 4, according to Enríquez Barroto, the captains dispatched canoes to explore a bay located midway between Mexico and Florida. Local Indian guides assisted in the search. About three miles from the two Spanish ships, the canoes entered Matagorda

Route of La Salle's expedition to the Gulf of Mexico. *Illustration by Roland Pantermuehl*

Bay, and on the south side they discovered a "broken ship." The three fleurs-de-lys on her stern told the Spaniards they had indeed found a French vessel. They took two swivel guns from the deck, and, searching the shore, found wooden barrels of gunpowder, ruined by rain, and other broken barrels.[10]

The next morning, the Spanish party reentered the bay to examine the ship more carefully. All of the rigging was still intact, although many pieces were beginning to rot. Five cannons remained, still on their carriages and lashed to the deck; these were taken to Veracruz. The ship's anchor and some cordage were salvaged and the masts fashioned into oars.

The Spaniards also located the onshore campsite of the ship's survivors, where they found another gun carriage and some sailcloth, along with a large smith's bellows, a cooper's plane, and pages from books written in French.

Spain had finally found *La Belle.* They named the location Navío Quebrado, the place of the "Broken Ship."[11]

PAGES FROM *LA BELLE*'S LOG

Although *La Belle* lay wrecked along the Texas coast, her influence was soon to be felt in the interior reaches of northern New Spain. On April 10, 1689, Governor Juan Ysidro de Pardiñas Villar de Francos sat in his quarters at the Presidio of San Francisco de Conchos in Nueva Vizcaya near today's Parral, Mexico. Four Indian chiefs from the Jumano and Cíbolo nations— identified as Don Juan Xaviata, Miguel, Cuis Benive, and Muygisofac—had come to meet with the governor and deliver some papers. Xaviata was head of all the Jumanos and Cíbolos, while the other three were

Engraving showing Petit Goäve in 1786, a century after La Salle's expedition stopped at the Caribbean island. Entitled *Vue du Port de Lacul du Petit Goäve,* it is based on a drawing made by Pierre Ozanne in 1786. *Illustration courtesy Musée national de la Marine*

chiefs of individual bands. Governor Pardiñas interrogated them, and their statements still survive in the archives of Seville.[12] The chiefs handed over four pages with handwriting in French and a picture of a ship with notations, also in French. All the items were carefully wrapped in a neck cloth of lace.[13] Pardiñas, unable to read French, was oblivious to the fact that the Indians had just handed him pages from *La Belle's* log and a picture of another ship, possibly *Le Joly.* Yet he recognized the items to be more proof of French activity in the northern frontier of New Spain.[14]

How portions of *La Belle's* log, which recorded the ship's progress as she sailed across the Atlantic toward the Mississippi River, ended up in a remote Spanish post is another fascinating part of this tale. Captain Tessier must have rescued the log from the wrecked ship—it was probably among the dampened papers taken back to the Fort St. Louis settlement.[15] The log remained at the French colony for nearly two years, until Karankawa Indians attacked the settlement in the winter of 1688–89.

For several years before the fall of Fort St. Louis, Spain had been receiving information about French activities from the Jumano and Cíbolo Indians. As the

Spaniards' trusted allies, they carried messages and mail between remote Spanish settlements and occasionally served as auxiliary scouts and troops. The Jumanos in particular were legendary traders and middlemen among the Southern Plains Indians and Spanish settlements of northern New Spain, bartering goods over an area covering much of Texas and the eastern part of New Mexico.[16]

In 1687 the Jumanos and Cíbolos informed the Spaniards living in missions in the La Junta region of today's Texas Big Bend that Moors—the term used by the Indians to describe Europeans—were trading with the Tejas (Caddo) Indians of eastern Texas. According to Muygisofac, "They called these men Moors because they brought coats or breastplates of steel, and helmets on their heads. They [the Frenchmen] visited these Indians there many times and gave them axes, knives, beads, copper kettles, and sometimes clothing, and made gifts to the women of ribbons and other things."[17]

The Indians also reported that the Moors lived in wooden houses on the water, an apparent reference to *La Belle* when she was anchored in Matagorda Bay. The Spaniards realized that the Indian chiefs were describing members of La Salle's expedition, probably including La Salle himself, during their exploration of the land west of Matagorda Bay in 1685. The chiefs said the interlopers were even traveling up the Rio Grande to within two hundred miles of La Junta. What is more, they had asked how far it was to the silver mines of Parral, how good the road was, and how many soldiers were guarding the mines. The Indians' declarations provided additional evidence of La Salle's secret mission to assess the logistics of invading the Spanish silver mines.

In late 1688 or early 1689, the Jumanos and Cíbolos went on reconnaissance for Spain in the eastern and coastal regions of Texas. They visited many Indian bands, including the Karankawas, native inhabitants of

CARIBBEAN PIRATES

When La Salle left France in 1684, the Caribbean was rife with roving freebooters in search of plunder. During times of war, these privateers carried official "letters of marque" from European monarchs giving them legal authority to attack and ransack enemy ships. During times of peace, freebooters were considered to be pirates, and they continued to pillage and plunder, illegally attacking ships of their former enemies. Although pirates preyed on the burgeoning trade among Europe, the Americas, and Africa, their primary targets were the Spanish treasure fleets that carried New World riches back to Spain. The Spanish Crown had a long-standing policy of extracting gold, silver, and gems from the New World. In fact, the Spanish economy had become highly dependent on the exploitation of New World riches and suffered when shipments were lost to pirates.

By the sixteenth and seventeenth centuries, the easily accessible sources of plunder were exhausted. To overcome the reduction in revenues from treasure fleets, ambitious pirates increasingly turned their attention to coastal Spanish communities. Pirates could net as much from a raid as from a Spanish treasure galleon, and the coastal settlements were subjected to repeated attacks over time. Inhabitants would often hide their valuables, but the pirates quickly realized that wealthy individuals could be captured and held for ransom to obtain hidden riches. Incredible sums of wealth were stolen during a successful raid, and the bounty was distributed among all participants. Spanish military ships traversed the Caribbean searching for pirate ships. Interception meant a quick interrogation and long imprisonment at hard labor. Less fortunate prisoners were condemned to a public beheading.[1]

Many of the pirates in the Caribbean were French buccaneers, originally hunters brought to pursue the wild herds of cattle and swine inhabiting what is now Haiti. As the herds were exterminated because of this intense hunting, the buccaneers turned their attention to raiding the seafaring trade.[2]

One of La Salle's plans to establish a French colony at the mouth of the Mississippi involved the use of more than a thousand buccaneers to seize the entire province of Nueva Vizcaya, including northern portions of today's Mexico and southwestern portions of the United States. The goal was to gain control of the Spanish silver mines of Parral, Cuencamé, Sombrerete, San Juan, and Santa Barbara. Ultimately he and the king decided against it, questioning the reliability of freebooters.[3]

Notes

1. Jenifer G. Marx, "Brethren of the Coast," in David Cordingly, ed., *Pirates: Terror on the High Seas, from the Caribbean to the South China Sea*, pp. 36–57.

2. Ibid., p. 38.

3. Robert S. Weddle, *Wilderness Manhunt*, pp. 19–23.

Pirates prepare to raid a coastal community. *Illustration by Charles Shaw*

The Jumano Indians search for evidence of La Salle and his men. *Illustration by Charles Shaw*

the area around the Fort St. Louis colony. The Karankawas told them that all the French had been killed, except some who were off trading with the Caddos of East Texas.[18] The Karankawas possessed European clothing taken as spoils and were "still having dances in celebration of having killed the strangers."[19] They gave Don Juan Xaviata the papers and the picture of a ship they had taken from the French settlement. Xaviata carefully wrapped them in a French lace neck cloth.

On the way back to the Spanish settlements at La Junta, Xaviata and his Indian colleagues encountered Gen. Juan de Retana camped on the Pecos River. He was on a mission to attack renegade Indians and gather information on French activities in the area. Xaviata showed the papers to Retana, who asked the chief to carry them, along with a letter he composed, to Governor Pardiñas at Parral.

The four pages of *La Belle*'s log are on two sheets of paper, each measuring 12¼ by 8 inches. Each page contains writing on the front and the back. One sheet of paper covers the time periods of October 1–2 and November 25–26, 1684.[20] These log pages describe the movements of *La Belle* as she sailed to and from Petit Goäve, including observations of wind direction,

weather conditions, and depth of water for anchorage. The pages of the other sheet of paper, reproduced and translated below, were written in January, 1685, when *La Belle* was anchored off the coast of Texas waiting for *Le Joly* to arrive.[21]

JOURNAL OF JANUARY 17, 1685

The same day at 6 A.M. the wind was north and the Aimable set a signal fire. Then we manned the windlass, hove the anchor, and set sail, and took our course to the southwest three leagues, then sounded forward, as above, and found seven fathoms, sand and mud. At 9 P.M. the wind died down and we were obliged to anchor, and anchored in seven fathoms, sand and mud. Then at noon I took the altitude, [latitude] 27 degrees 45 minutes, which I know is the [unintelligible] of the equinoctial [?] line. Wednesday. At 2 P.M. we set sail to bring ourselves near the Aimable, and the wind was south, light wind, and our longboat went aboard and Monsieur de La Salle got into it to go to land, but as the sea was too high he could not land and returned aboard the said ship and ordered a cannon to be fired to bring in their longboat, which had gone into a little river there, and also ordered us to take up our anchor and go forward and we went forward but met it as it was coming. Then we returned to anchor near the Aimable, and they told us that they had gone a league and a half into the river and had found no fresh water. The 18th of the same, Wednesday, at 7 A.M. Captain Aigron's longboat came aboard, and his people got into our longboat to go and search for a man who had remained on shore the evening before, and the boatswain of the longboat told Captain Moraud that Monsieur de La Salle had told him to tell him that he wished to talk to him and to me also. Therefore we embarked [page ends]

JOURNAL OF JANUARY 18, 1685

[next page begins] in the said longboat with some of our people who laid us aboard, and when we had come to him Monsieur de La Salle asked us if we had kept our reckoning from our departure from Cape San Antonio, and also asked for our altitude taken yesterday noon. That of Captain Moraud was 27 degrees 30 minutes and mine 27 degrees 45 minutes, and the Sieur de La Salle asked the advice of the said Captain Moraud and mine, and acknowledged that he had made a mistake and that he was behind their ship and the said Sieur de La Salle and Captain Aigron agreed with my point, and we had a council all together to see whether we should continue our course to the Madeleine to decide better as to affairs, but the said Sieur de La Salle would not go there, seeing that he had

Le mesme   a 6 heure du matin le vint est toit nord et
l'aimable a mis le haut don nous auons mis
a tire et nous auont le ... l'ancre et mis a la
Sonde a los de uent   voille et nous auons ... le Cap au surrout
Coumme sis dessud   jusques que 9 heure que le Calme ne nous a pris
treuue 7 brasse sable   et nous auont esté obligé de mouille et nous a
vasard   vont mouille par 7 brase sable vasard
ensuite a midy jay pris hauteur de 27
degré 45 minute que je suis et loingne de
la ligne qui est nord que saille le tout le mesque
...

a 2 heure apres midy nous auont mis a la
ville a selle fin de nous mettre aupres de
l'aimable et le vent est toit sud petit vend
et notre Chalouppe est allé a bord et monsieur
de Lasalle saiy en barque de dent pour alle
a taire mais coumme la mer est toit trop grande
il niy a pas put de valle et saiy retourne a
bord du dict nauire et a fait tire un coud de
Canon a selle fin de faire venir leur Chalouppe
qui auoit entré de dent une petite riuiere
qui est toit la et mesme nous a fait coumendemens
de uu l'ancre et valle à l'ande vent et
pour luy somme allé mais nous l'auont ran
contre par les chemin quelle venoit don
nous somme retourne mouille aupres de
l'aimable et mesme il nous ondict quil a
voit entré une lieus et de miy a l'ande den
et quil nauoit point treuue deau douste

Le 18   du dict demesque diy a 7 heure du matin
la Chalouppe du Chapitaine est grond et
venut a bord et saiy jean se sont en barque dent
notre Chalouppe pout alle cherche un houmme
qui auoit thaiy le te le soit a taire et le
patron de Chalouppe a dict au Chapitaine
morand que monsieur de Lasalle luy auoit
dict de luy dire quilluy faut parle et
moiy aussy don nous somme enbarque

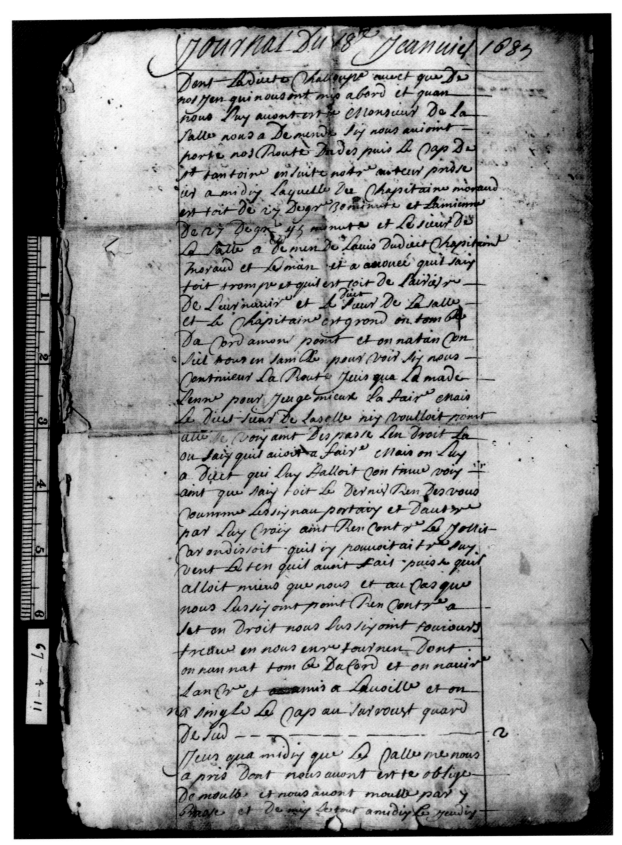

Page from the log of *La Belle*, dated January 18, 1685. *Photograph courtesy Center for American History, University of Texas, Austin*

passed the place where he ought to be, but he was told that it was necessary to continue, seeing that that was the last rendezvous as the signals indicated, and that others in his company believed that they should meet the Joly, for it was said that she might be there, considering the time that had gone on, for she went better than we, and in case we should not find her at that place we should anyhow find her as we returned, on which there was no agreement, and we hove anchor and set sail and took our course southwest-quarter-south till noon when the wind died down, whereupon we were obliged to anchor, and anchored in 7 fathoms and a half. All this at noon on Thursday.

LOST TO HUMAN MEMORY

La Belle had been wrecked during a winter storm in 1686. She lay partially submerged at the bottom of the bay. The Spaniards discovered her location a little more than a year later, and had salvaged items from the ship. Even four pages from her log had miraculously turned up in the spring of 1689 at a remote Spanish settlement in northern New Spain. But all the attention paid to *La Belle* was about to end. For the next three centuries, her exact location was lost to human memory.

La Belle lay mired in Matagorda Bay, with only her stern above water. Waves crashed over her deck, and winds tattered her sails. The lower portion of the ship gradually settled into the bay's sandy bottom until a little more than a third of her hull was covered. The upper two-thirds became the target of seawater and marine decay. Tiny teredo worms invaded the hull's wooden timbers, riddling them with small holes until they were so weak that waves and currents washed them away. Dissolved calcium carbonate and magnesium hydroxide, natural chemicals in seawater, precipitated over iron cannon balls, axe heads, bar stock, and other ferrous items, forming concrete-like encrustations. With time, smaller iron objects rusted completely away, leaving only encrustations that were nearly perfect molds of the artifacts.

More durable metal objects—pewter plates, cups, bowls, kettles, and candlestick holders—slowly shifted downward as the wooden boxes and barrels containing them disintegrated. Thin layers of encrustation formed on them. Other items, such as ornate bronze cannons, became incorporated into dense concretions around iron objects.

Human corpses still on board *La Belle* were consumed by fish and microorganisms. Only one skeleton was preserved; it rested on a large coil of anchor rope deep inside the ship's bow. A few bones from another person were entombed in the sediments that covered the wreck.

As the silts and sand settled in the bottom part of the hull, they sealed the remaining cargo and lower timbers in an anaerobic environment. Reduced oxygen levels preserved wood from the ravages of teredo worms and decay by marine bacteria. Other items were also spared the destruction caused by seawater-borne bacteria as they lay entombed at the bottom of the bay. The ship and her cargo became a time capsule from a grand—but doomed—colonial enterprise. *La Belle* now rested in a watery grave, waiting for her twentieth-century rediscovery.

Chapter Two

LA SALLE'S GRAND DREAM

In the name of the most high, powerful, invincible, and victorious Prince, Louis the Great, by the grace of God, King of France and Navarre, fourteenth of the name, I, this ninth day of April one thousand six hundred and eighty-two, do now take, in the name of His Majesty and of his successors to the crown, possession of this country of Louisiana, its seas, harbors, ports, bays, adjacent straits, and all nations, peoples, provinces, cities, towns, villages, mines, minerals, fisheries, streams, and rivers.

—ROBERT CAVELIER, Sieur de La Salle, April, 1682

Less than four years before *La Belle* was lost on the Texas coast, La Salle, in a vast marshland with no one to hear him but a small band of followers and some curious local Indians, had claimed possession of one-third of the North American continent for France. After a long and arduous journey, he had finally discovered where the mouth of the Mississippi River emptied into the Gulf of Mexico.

The French claim in the New World now extended from the upper reaches of Canada to the shores of the Gulf of Mexico, encompassing savannas, forests, deserts, and plains. The land was watered by innumerable rivers, streams, and creeks and populated by thousands of American Indians who knew nothing of this moment or its implications.

A DRIVEN MAN

Scion of a wealthy family of merchants, La Salle was born in 1643, baptized a short time later, and grew up in Rouen, a major port on the River Seine in Normandy.[1] Early in his life, La Salle joined the Jesuit priesthood, as did many French boys from well-to-do families. Entering the monastery meant La Salle must relinquish his share of the family's fortune, for he was expected to make the church paramount. Trained in the Jesuit Order, he became a teacher.

La Salle's quiet and introspective temperament, however, did not suit the vocation of teaching unruly schoolboys. He appealed to his Father Superior to be sent to a mission in China, where he could experience the excitement of remote parts of the world. His request was denied. Undaunted, he then petitioned to go to Portugal to teach mathematics; this request was also refused. With this rejection and after twelve years as a Jesuit, La Salle submitted his resignation.[2]

La Salle then decided to travel to New France, or today's eastern Canada, to join his elder brother, the Abbé Cavelier, a priest of St. Sulspice in Montreal. In the spring of 1666, at the age of 23, La Salle thus made his first journey to the New World. Despite its unforgiving climate, the colony of New France was a bustling place, though its remoteness often weakened the rule of law. Opportunities for entrepreneurs were abundant. European powers had long sought a water pas-

La Salle discovers the mouth of the Mississippi River and claims for France all of the land it drains, about one-third of the United States. *Illustration courtesy Historic New Orleans Collection, accession no. 1970.1*

sage through the New World to China and the East Indies for trade. The St. Lawrence River, leading to the Great Lakes and beyond, seemed a likely route. There was even talk of a great river that might traverse the continent and discharge into the Gulf of California.

The young La Salle was intrigued by the wealth and prestige that awaited the explorer who might discover such a route across North America. The conditions would be harsh, to be sure: there would be hostile Indians, severe winters, and uncertain food supplies. Nevertheless, he began to devise a plan—and met considerable opposition. The Jesuits, who had built a series of missions in the Upper Great Lakes, controlled the region through their religious emissaries and profited from the fur trade with the Indians, although they could not admit that profit was a motive in their endeavors. La Salle appeared to be a threat to the Jesuits' monopoly over trade.[3]

The merchants of New France were even more alarmed at his intentions. Discovery of a new water route through the continent might interrupt the trade in furs and hides that flowed through Montreal and Quebec. The merchants did not wish to see their rewarding enterprise disrupted by this brash young Norman with grandiose ideas. These two groups, Jesuits and merchants, were to become the "enemies" about whom La Salle lamented many times during moments of despair: "I am utterly tired of this business; for I see that it is not enough to put property and life in constant peril, but it requires more pains to answer envy and distraction than to overcome the difficulties inseparable from my undertaking."[4]

North American rivers and lakes were the seventeenth-century equivalent of modern highways, and knowledge of their locations could be turned into great monetary gain. Louis Joliet and Father Marquette, who had discovered the Mississippi River in 1673, were the first to understand the relationship of that river to the Great Lakes. They observed that the Mississippi, flowing southward, probably emptied into the Gulf

La Salle's baptismal record from the Bibliothèque Municipale in Rouen, France.

of Mexico, rather than the Gulf of California. However, Joliet and Marquette never reached the Mississippi's mouth.[5]

La Salle, who by this time had already begun searching for a transcontinental water route, received news of the Joliet-Marquette expedition with great interest. He formulated a plan to chart this potential watercourse through North America. If the Mississippi flowed into the Gulf of Mexico, it might be possible to establish a warm-water port at the mouth of the river. Furs and hides could be transported downstream, allowing the riches of Canada and the Great Lakes to be transported to France year-round. Traders could avoid the cold climate of eastern Canada and the icebound streams and lakes that made commerce impossible in winter. Moreover, France could control the land along the Mississippi, creating a vast empire that would keep the English and Dutch in the east and the Spanish in Mexico.

The realization of this grand dream would require a new series of forts along the river and substantial financial backing. La Salle had previously secured private funding to establish forts at various points along Lakes Michigan, Erie, and Ontario. But he was a poor manager, and each time a series of mishaps had eliminated the profits he promised his backers. Adding to his difficulties, his Jesuit detractors constantly undermined his credibility in Montreal and Quebec.

There was another problem: La Salle's own personality. He often lapsed into a mysterious sickness, described as a "moral malady."[6] He probably suffered from periods of depression and might today be diagnosed as manic-depressive.[7] This chronic debilitation fed La Salle's arrogant and demanding nature, which in

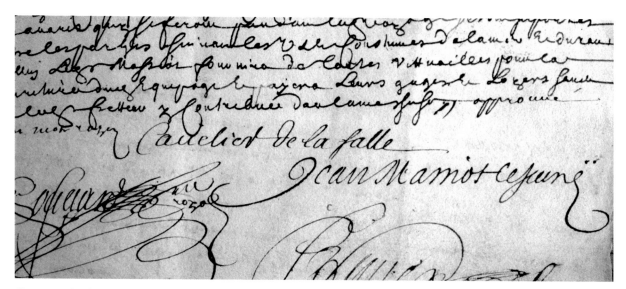

Signature of Robert Cavelier, Sieur de La Salle, before he received the title of Sieur from the king. *Photograph by John de Bry*

turn created a recurring inability to inspire and direct his men amid the challenges of exploring the wilderness. His failings were so severe that during a trip along the Ohio River in 1679 one of his servants tried to kill him by mixing hemlock into his salad. La Salle was sick for more than forty days.[8] From that time on, he carried an antidote with him to protect against poisonings.

Though in 1682 he had traveled down the Mississippi River and found its mouth, La Salle knew his plan would be met with skepticism in France. His only choice was to present his case to the king himself. He traveled back to France in 1683 and petitioned Louis XIV to establish a colony where the Mississippi River met the Gulf of Mexico. In an effort to foil his plan, La Salle's enemies had written to France that he was unfit for future explorations in the New World.[9] La Salle tried to get support from merchants in Rochefort and La Rochelle, but his reputation for leading failed enterprises in New France preceded him. Finally, he headed to Paris to enlist the support of two abbés, Claude Bernou and Eusèbe Renaudot, who enjoyed the favor of the French court. They agreed to lobby on La Salle's behalf.[10]

Spain had declared war on France the preceding October, and tensions between the two countries could not have been higher. La Salle was counseled that an expedition through the Gulf of Mexico would attract more royal support than a return to the Mississippi River mouth by way of New France and the St. Lawrence River. The French king was angry with Spanish opposition to foreign ships traveling in the Gulf of Mexico. French vessels violating this zone were cap-

tured and their crews imprisoned.[11] La Salle's effort would be a bold statement against Spain's efforts to control the gulf.

Thus, from the point of view of the French monarch, the timing was just right for such a mission, but it was even more propitious when one considered Spain's current role in the New World. Spain had ignored Nueva Vizcaya, what is now northern Mexico, since the early explorations of Pineda, Cabeza de Vaca, and De Soto had failed to find gold, silver, or other wealth there. Spain had also lost control of the seas with England's defeat of the Spanish Armada in 1588 and had difficulty monitoring significant portions of its territorial claims. This was especially true of territories north of today's Mexico between Florida and New Mexico.[12]

It was against this backdrop of international incident and intrigue that La Salle presented his plan to the king in 1683. He proposed a three-pronged approach. First, he would establish a fort at the mouth of the Mississippi River to maintain the French claim to Louisiana. Second, he would establish trade with thousands of Indians and convert them to Christianity. Finally, he would establish a permanent colony, a base from which the future invasion of Spain's Nueva Vizcaya could be launched.[13]

For the French Crown, the colony was a critical part of La Salle's plan. While Spain had been shipping gold, silver, and other treasures from the New World, France had been forced to content itself with beaver pelts from its Canadian colonies. Louis saw his op-

Artist's concept of La Salle's house in Lachine, near the city of Montreal. *Illustration courtesy Musée national de la Marine*

portunity to capture some of Spanish King Charles II's wealth.

Several variations on La Salle's proposal were discussed, some involving the use of French buccaneers to help invade Nueva Vizcaya and seize control of the silver mines. The king finally granted La Salle the authority to "command . . . all the lands of North America that may hereafter be submitted to our [French] rule, from Fort St. Louis on the Illinois River to Nueva Vizcaya." [14] Louis also gave La Salle substantial support for the expedition, including two ships rather than the one he had originally requested. Specifically, La Salle was granted the naval gunship *Le Joly* and a *barque longue* (light frigate) christened *La Belle.* As it turned out, these two ships did not possess enough cargo space for such a venture, and La Salle was forced to lease two other vessels, the frigate *l'Aimable* from La Rochelle ship owner Jean Massiot and a small ketch, *Le Saint-François,* from François Duprat, also of La Rochelle.[15] The king's grant included full crews, a hundred soldiers, and funds to hire carpenters, masons, coopers, and other skilled workers to establish his colony.[16] The expedition included about three hundred persons in all.

Some supplies, such as goods to trade with the In-dians, were not provided by the king, which meant that La Salle and his men had to buy them. The explorer had persuaded twenty thousand Shawnee, Illinois, and Miami Indians to settle around Fort St. Louis des Illinois, which he had established in 1682.[17] La Salle's plan was that these Indians would hunt and trap in the northern Great Plains and Great Lakes and bring the furs and hides to the fort for trade, where he would ship them down the Mississippi River to the settlement he envisioned on the Gulf of Mexico, and then onward to France. From the warm gulf port, France could import goods year-round, a distinct advantage over the ports of Montreal and Quebec, where the St. Lawrence River was iced over half the year. The medium of exchange that would drive all this would be the glass beads, brass pins, finger rings, iron knives, and hatchets they purchased to trade to the Indians.

DESTINATION: A NEW WORLD

La Salle set sail from La Rochelle, France, on July 24, 1684, to fulfill his dream of a colony at the mouth of the Mississippi River—and to enrich himself.

Robert Cavelier, Sieur de La Salle, looks over his shoulder at a map of the North American continent, as if planning his expedition to colonize the mouth of the Mississippi River.
Illustration by Pierre Gandon, courtesy Musée national de la Marine

On January 1, 1685, after a long and difficult journey across the ocean, La Salle's expedition sighted land along the Gulf Coast, somewhere in today's Louisiana west of the Mississippi. By this time, only three vessels remained: *Le Joly, l'Aimable,* and *La Belle.* The *Saint-François* had been captured by Spanish privateers off the western coast of Hispaniola as the ship traveled from Port de Paix to Petit Goäve.

La Salle had been warned about strong easterly currents that carried ships towards the Bahamian

Louis XIV contemplates La Salle's proposal to establish a French colony at the mouth of the Mississippi River. *Illustration by Howard Pyle entitled* La Salle Petitions the King for Permission to Explore the Mississippi, *from the February, 1905, issue of* Harpers Monthly. *Illustration courtesy Delaware Art Museum*

Channel. Upon sighting land, he concluded that they had not made enough westward progress and were in fact east of the Mississippi. He decided to travel west, following the Gulf Coast as closely as possible.[18]

For the next two and a half weeks the ships continued to sail westward, turning toward the southwest as they progressed. La Salle remained certain that the Mississippi lay in this direction. Measurements of latitude were taken daily to help chart their progress, but longitude—a time-dependent measurement—could not be accurately calculated until the eighteenth cen-

tury. Consequently, there was no accurate method to determine exactly how far west they were traveling—a problem La Salle recognized. In addition, an astrolabe La Salle suspected to be faulty had hampered measurements of latitude during his 1682 journey down the Mississippi River, so those earlier calculations were erroneous as well. To complicate the situation further, some period maps showed the Mississippi flowing into the Gulf of Mexico through what is now central Texas. Despite these problems, La Salle believed the Mississippi River lay farther to the west, and he in-

Starved Rock, Illinois, where La Salle established his Fort St. Louis des Illinois in anticipation of trading with the Indians along the Mississippi River.

structed Captain Beaujeu to continue sailing in this direction.

Finally, they noticed that they were moving more southwest than west, and suspected they might have passed the Mississippi. La Salle and Beaujeu quarreled about their location, but La Salle remained resolute that they were near one of the western branches of the great river. The relationship between the two men had deteriorated to the point that they were communicating only through official letters couriered back and forth; their deep mutual antipathy may be seen in a letter La Salle wrote when Beaujeu wished to return to France rather than assist in landing the colonists:

[Y]our longboat does not give me time to reply to your letter with so much consideration as you have devoted to writing it, though the way in which you vent your spleen in the letter suggests that you wrote it rather more hastily than its length would require.

It is no fault of mine, Monsieur, if you have not already provided for the safety of His Majesty's ship; but I know on what grounds you ask me for pilots to take it into this river which I never intended that it should enter, and more than I wished to stop it at this shore. You may take it where you think fit.[19]

On January 17, 1685, La Salle determined it was time to land his men, explore the coast, find the river, and locate a place to establish the colony. He was probably near Cedar Bayou and the western end of today's Matagorda Island in Texas.[20] After several days of surveying the surrounding countryside, the expedition's chronicler Henri Joutel noted, "The country did not seem very favorable to me. It was flat and sandy but did nevertheless produce grass. There were several salt pools. We hardly saw any wild fowl except some cranes and Canadian geese which were not expecting us."[21]

Early in February, La Salle ordered Joutel to disembark with 120 to 130 men and march up the coast to find a large river that he was convinced would be the west branch of the Mississippi. Joutel complained that the men had little or no military experience: "Truthfully, although we had 120 to 130 men with us, 30 good men would have been better and would have done more and perforce eaten less, to which end they were without rival. . . . these were all men who had been taken by

The port of Rochefort in 1762. Photograph of a painting by Joseph Vernet entitled *Vue du port de Rochefort (detail). Courtesy Musée national de la Marine*

The port of La Rochelle in 1762. Photograph of a painting by Joseph Vernet entitled *Vue du port de La Rochelle (detail). Courtesy Musée national de la Marine*

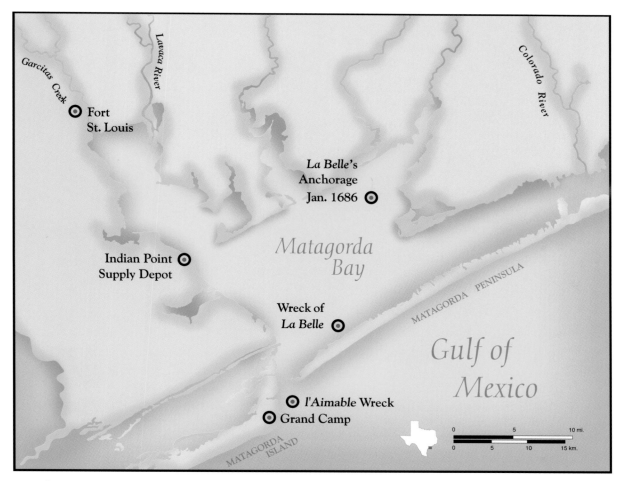

Map of Matagorda Bay showing the locations of the French camps, Fort St. Louis, and the wreck of *La Belle*. Illustration by Roland Pantermuehl

force or deceit. In a way, it was almost like Noah's Ark where they were all sorts of animals. We likewise had men of different nationalities. The soldiers had been recruited by the lower ranking officers of the navy, who received a half pistole [five francs] for each man, by whatever means possible."[22]

The party eventually encountered what they thought was a large river, which was actually Pass Cavallo, today's name for the entrance into Matagorda Bay. The three vessels arrived shortly afterward, and La Salle came ashore to inspect the terrain. He found a location on the western side of Pass Cavallo suitable for establishing a temporary camp, called the Grand Camp, and ordered *La Belle* and *l'Aimable* to come through the pass. On February 16, the ship's pilots made a sounding and determined that the two vessels could enter. They marked the entrance with buoys to guide the two ships away from hazardous sandy shoals.

La Belle came through the pass without difficulty

about two in the afternoon and anchored inside Matagorda Bay. La Salle ordered that cargo be unloaded from *l'Aimable,* the expedition's main supply ship, which was five times larger than *La Belle,* so that she could also enter the pass. Eight iron cannons were removed from the ship and taken ashore to the temporary camp. On February 19 *l'Aimable*'s Captain Aigron was satisfied that adequate cargo had been unloaded, although much remained on board. According to Joutel, "On the 20th, La Salle ordered the captain to approach the bar, adding that when the sea was high, he should signal to him to be towed. La Salle also ordered the pilot of *La Belle* to help the captain of the *Aimable* with what he had to do as that ship had already entered. But the captain sent the pilot back, telling him that he was capable of bringing the ship in without him."[23]

When the water level was sufficiently high, La Salle signaled for the ship to enter the pass. At about the same time, he was told that local Karankawa Indians

La Salle's ships *La Belle* (left), *Le Joly* (middle), and *l'Aimable* (right) at the entrance to Matagorda Bay in 1684. Note that *l'Aimable* has run aground. Photograph of a painting entitled *La Salle's Expedition to Louisiana in 1684*, by Théodore Gudin. *Courtesy Rèunion des Musées Nationaux/Art Resource, New York*

had taken some of his men hostage. La Salle was now compelled to go search for them. He traveled about a league and a half (about three miles) until he found the Indian village, but before entering it he could see *l'Aimable*'s sails, indicating that she was beginning to enter the pass. She appeared to do so incorrectly, however, running too close to the shoals. La Salle was greatly concerned, but he was powerless to influence the situation. Soon a cannon was fired, indicating distress aboard the ship. Next *l'Aimable*'s sails were furled, confirming his fear that a disaster had occurred. La Salle met with the Indians, retrieved his men, and returned to assess the damage to his supply ship.

L'Aimable was grounded hard against a sandbank. Upon questioning the captain and crew, La Salle grew suspicious that the captain, Aigron, had intentionally run the ship aground. Aigron was unhappy with La Salle's efforts to find the Mississippi, believing that the explorer had missed the river and was taking the expedition into uncharted areas that would result in failure

of the colony. La Salle concluded that Aigron had deliberately steered the ship past the buoys marking the safe entry and directly onto a sandbank. Once the ship was stuck, the captain could have thrown out an anchor and freed the vessel. Witnesses stated that, instead, the captain ordered the ship to sail forward until she was firmly grounded on the shallow sandy bottom. There was now no hope of saving the ship.[24]

According to Joutel, "we learned how the captain had disgraced himself. The incident made one conclude that the mischief must have been by design or premeditated act. Four buoys had been placed and one only had to steer by them. Moreover, a sailor was in the topmast for seeing better. Although the sailor continually called out 'to luff sail,' the ill-intentioned captain called out to the contrary and gave the command to bear down until he saw he was on the sandbanks."[25]

L'Aimable, a large private merchant vessel, contained much of the planned colony's provisions. La Salle prepared to unload as much cargo as possible, but

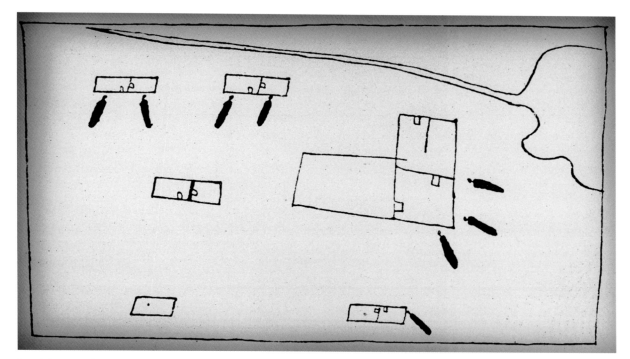

Spanish map of Fort St. Louis in 1689 showing the eight French cannons. The map is included in an expedition narrative written by Alonso de León, *Relacion y Discursos de Descubrimiento*. Western Americana Collection, Beinecke Rare Book and Manuscript Library, Yale University

the ship was far from shore and he had only small longboats. The crew could remove cargo when the waters were calm. But *l'Aimable* broke apart one night during a period of heavy seas, and in the morning the buoyant cargo was found floating in the water.

In early March *Le Joly*'s captain, Beaujeu, decided to return to France. He had orders only to accompany La Salle to the New World and unload his ship's cargo. Once this had been accomplished, his job was done. Beaujeu was impatient to leave the wild country and the arrogant explorer with whom he often quarreled, and a number of the colonists decided to join him. La Salle asked Beaujeu to ensure that supplies would be sent back to assist his colony. On March 14, *Le Joly* departed with 120 of the original 300 colonists, leaving La Salle with a diminished number of men and greatly compromised provisions for building a settlement. La Salle's request for more supplies was delivered to officials in France, but it was never honored.[26]

With only *La Belle* and 180 colonists, La Salle began to seek a more permanent location for his fort. He sought a safe site where he could leave many of the colonists while he searched overland for the Mississippi. When he found the river, he would build his sec-

ond and final settlement. La Salle and a few men left the temporary camp near Pass Cavallo in late March, 1685, and began searching along the western side of Matagorda Bay for a more suitable site for a fort. He found a creek that he called "the River of the Bison" (now known as Garcitas Creek) flowing into the northwestern part of today's Lavaca Bay. On a high, flat rise on the western side of the creek, about four miles upriver from the bay, he began construction of the temporary settlement, Fort St. Louis, where he would begin colonizing the Gulf Coast.

Provisions from *l'Aimable* and *Le Joly,* together with cargo from *La Belle,* were moved to a supply depot about midway between the pass and the Grand Camp. From the depot they were transported by canoe upriver to the fort. Wood suitable for buildings was not readily available, so La Salle commanded his men to travel a league inland and bring back trees of suitable size. This proved difficult work, and several men died from the exertion. Finally La Salle resorted to salvaging timbers from *l'Aimable* to build the fort.

A two-story structure similar to buildings La Salle had constructed in Canada was erected. It was divided into four rooms: one for La Salle, another for the priests, a third for the officers of the expedition, and a

THE CANNONS OF FORT ST. LOUIS

Shortly before the wreck of *l'Aimable* in March, 1685, La Salle had eight iron cannons removed from the cargo hold to lighten the ship. These cannons, weighing between seven hundred and twelve hundred pounds each, were carried from the shore near Pass Cavallo to Fort St. Louis on Garcitas Creek, where they were deployed to guard the colonists. They were fired to repel Indians and to commemorate holidays and special events, such as La Salle's departures to locate the Mississippi River.

The cannons are clearly identified on a Spanish map based on sketches made by Alonso de León when he discovered the remains of Fort St. Louis in 1689, several months after the Karankawa Indians had killed the French colonists. De León buried the cannons in a pit, intending to dig them up later and use them to arm a planned Spanish presidio at the site. Thirty-two years passed before Spaniards returned to establish Presidio Nuestra Señora de Loreto y la Bahía, however, and by that time the location of the cannons had been forgotten.

They remained buried for 307 years, until discovered by an employee of the Keeran Ranch near Victoria, Texas. Shortly thereafter, at the invitation of the First Victoria National Bank— trustee of the ranch—a team of archaeologists from the Texas Historical Commission excavated and removed the remarkably well-preserved cannons for cleaning and exhibition. The successful recovery of these cannons represents one of the finest archaeological discoveries in Texas during the twentieth century.

The discovery of the cannons also finally ended a controversy about the actual locations of Fort St. Louis and Presidio La Bahía. Arguments have been made that the French fort and subsequent Spanish presidio were built farther up Garcitas Creek or even along the Lavaca River in neighboring Jackson County. Clearly, no logical argument can now be made for their location anywhere else but on the Keeran Ranch in Victoria County.

Archaeologist Curtis Tunnell stands by the newly excavated French cannons at Fort St. Louis.

fourth, the upper story, for supplies. Smaller structures were erected to house other members of the expedition. *L'Aimable*'s eight cannons would help fight off Karankawa Indian attacks.[27]

With the settlement established, La Salle again concentrated on finding the Mississippi. Now realizing that the river almost certainly had to be toward the east, he organized an exploration party. He left supplies for the colony on *La Belle*, along with all of his personal possessions and those of his men. He instructed her captain to proceed as far up the bay as possible, where he should lay anchor and wait for La Salle's return. The exploration party, meanwhile, would travel along the shore and head east to find the Mississippi.[28]

La Salle expected to be gone about ten days; instead he was absent for more than two frustrating months. The Indians he encountered along the way knew nothing of the great river. In fact, these native peoples did not even speak the languages he had heard along the Mississippi on his earlier travels. La Salle traded for horses and food with the Caddo Indians and returned to Fort St. Louis, where he was devastated to discover that his sole remaining ship had been lost in a storm.

La Belle had contained all the remaining supplies to build his final New World colony. With his grand dream of a French settlement on the Gulf of Mexico in great jeopardy, La Salle's only recourse now was to go overland to his settlement at Fort St. Louis des Illinois

HENRI JOUTEL, FAITHFUL LIEUTENANT AND CHRONICLER OF THE EXPEDITION

Henri Joutel, a trusted member of La Salle's expedition, was an astute observer, and his journal provides a riveting account. From leaving France in 1684 to the final journey in 1687, Joutel kept notes during his travels in the New World, writing extensively and colorfully about his observations. He details dozens of plant and animal species and identifies numerous Indian tribes. Though always faithful to and supportive of La Salle, Joutel occasionally comments on the explorer's autocratic ways: "La Salle was interested only in his opinion, having said as much to me several times, as well as to others, and had had no intention of bringing advisers along with him."[1]

The son of a gardener on the La Salle estate outside of Rouen, Joutel had known La Salle as a boy. In fact, they were probably childhood companions. In 1684, when La Salle was soliciting support for his expedition to the Mississippi River, Rouen was abuzz with gossip about the young Cavelier's success in the New World and his plans for yet another, even bolder journey. By then Joutel had sixteen years of military experience, which prepared him well for La Salle's disciplined and demanding command.[2]

Joutel was one of only six men with La Salle at the time of his assassination who returned to France. After the murder, Joutel and the five others followed wilderness trails, sought guidance from Indians, and eventually arrived at the Mississippi River in present-day Arkansas. From there they traveled upriver to the Great Lakes and east to Quebec, from where they departed for France.

Once home, Joutel prepared a manuscript chronicling La Salle's effort to colonize Texas. Originally published in French, the portion of the journal pertaining to Texas has been translated and published in English.[3]

Notes

1. William C. Foster, ed., *Joutel Journal*, p. 103.
2. Ibid., pp. 24–27.
3. Ibid., pp. 24–29.

La Salle meeting the Cenis (Caddo) Indians of eastern Texas. George Catlin painting entitled *La Salle Received in the Village of the Cenis. Illustration courtesy National Gallery of Art, Paul Mellon Collection, Washington, D.C., #1965.16.340*

La Salle and sixteen of his men leave Fort St. Louis for Canada in search of help. *Illustration by Charles Shaw*

La Salle's men, disaffected with their leader, ambush and kill him near today's Navasota, Texas. *Illustration by Charles Shaw*

and up to Canada to get supplies—a journey of twelve hundred miles.

MURDER ON THE TRAIL

On January 12, 1687, La Salle and sixteen men departed the small settlement on Garcitas Creek to obtain supplies from Canada. It was to be the explorer's last expedition.[29]

Remaining at Fort St. Louis were twenty men, women, and children—a meager fragment of the more than 180 who had stayed to help build the settlement. Disease and Indian attacks had taken the rest. The survivors would be stranded on Garcitas Creek for two years, waiting in vain for La Salle's return with the desperately needed provisions. In late 1688 or early 1689, the Karankawas would launch a final attack on the vulnerable outpost, killing almost all the remaining colonists and kidnapping several children.

In March, 1687, La Salle and his overland party reached a spot near today's Navasota, Texas, where they crossed the River of the Canoes and camped. During La Salle's previous trip, he had buried food supplies at a crossing a short distance downstream. He gave orders for some of his men to go and recover the stores because hunting was lean this time of the year. The men found the food, but it was spoiled. Luckily, La Salle's trusted Shawnee Indian hunter, Nika, shot two buffalo while returning to their leader. The men stopped to smoke the meat and sent word to La Salle.

As the men prepared to eat the portions that could not be smoked, La Salle's nephew, Colin Morenger, instructed them that he would control the remaining food and would decide who would eat what portion. For the dispirited men who had endured countless hardships and depredations, this was the final insult, and they plotted to kill Morenger. Revenge was planned by five men: Duhaut, Liotot (the expedition surgeon), Hiems, Tessier, and L'Archevêque. Later that night, they murdered Morenger, Nika, and La Salle's servant, Saget.

The murderers had accomplished their immediate plan, but they knew that La Salle, still at the other camp and waiting for the buffalo meat, would exact punishment. The five planned yet another murder: the assassination of Robert Cavelier, Sieur de la Salle. They knew that La Salle would soon come looking for them, and they waited in ambush.

Within a few days, a gunshot warned the men that La Salle was nearby. Duhaut and L'Archevêque crossed the river on a trail that La Salle would follow and waited in the bushes. As the explorer approached, L'Archevêque stepped into view. La Salle asked where Morenger was, and L'Archevêque replied that he had drifted away. Before La Salle could respond, Duhaut, who was hidden from view, fired a musket shot into the explorer's head, killing him.

At the age of 43, after twenty years of conquering and colonizing the wilderness of North America, the great explorer lay dead. La Salle's killers took his possessions, even his clothing, and left his body "to the discretion of the wolves and other wild animals."[30]

Chapter Three

A MONUMENTAL DISCOVERY

For a century and a half, historians wrote about La Salle's expedition to Texas, noting that the ill-starred explorer had lost two ships. Archaeologists, keenly aware of the missing vessels, were eager to track them down. But finding sunken ships in large bodies of water is a difficult challenge under the best of circumstances. It can take many years, and even the most painstaking efforts may well end in failure. Furthermore, until positioning systems and magnetic-detection devices were developed in the 1970s, the equipment used to look for sunken ships was fairly primitive.

At about the same time that technology for undersea searches was improved, Kathleen Gilmore, an archaeologist at Southern Methodist University, published a landmark study that made it seem just possible that La Salle's ships could be located.[1] Gilmore had analyzed artifacts from the Keeran site in Victoria County, Texas, the presumed location of La Salle's Fort St. Louis. These specimens came from a 1950 excavation sponsored by the Texas Memorial Museum, which had been commissioned to investigate the site to determine whether it might be the French colony. The

museum's archaeologists had obtained several thousand items, most of them apparently Spanish, but no report on the findings was ever completed. Adding to the confusion was the fact that archaeologists in the 1950s were as yet unable to distinguish accurately between French and Spanish colonial artifacts. In North America, the field of historical archaeology—the study of archaeological sites from time periods for which we have written records—was a nascent discipline, and researchers were only then working out which types of artifacts were associated with which nations and time periods.

By the time Gilmore performed her analysis in the 1970s, historical archaeology had advanced considerably. She was able to determine that some of the Keeran artifacts, such as green glazed and tin-enamel glazed ceramics, were identical to specimens found at French and French Canadian sites of the same time period. This made it more likely that Keeran might be La Salle's lost colony.

Gilmore also examined historical accounts of the La Salle shipwrecks—records left by the French colo-

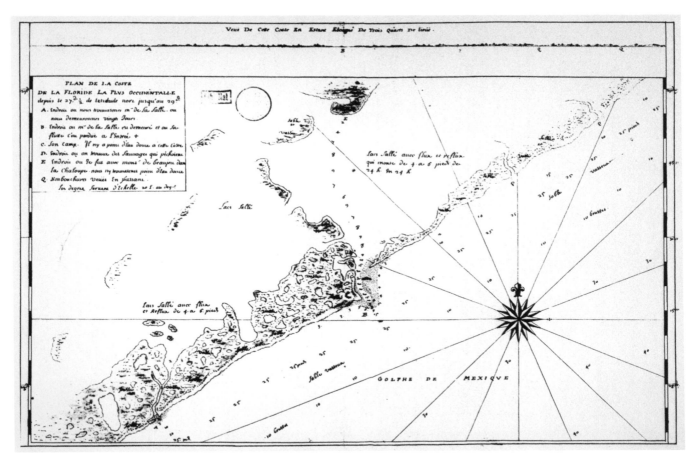

Map made by La Salle's engineer, Minet, of the Gulf Coast around Matagorda Bay, entitled
Plan de la Coste de la Floride la plus occidéntale. Courtesy Center for American History, University of Texas, Austin

nists as well as those of the Spanish soldiers who later searched for La Salle. She developed general guidelines suggesting where researchers should look for the sunken vessels, and this provided an important impetus for marine archaeologists with the Texas Historical Commission to begin the search for *La Belle* and *l'Aimable* in the late 1970s.[2]

MAPS PROVIDE CRITICAL CLUES

Only a few historical maps of the area were known to exist, but Texas Historical Commission archaeologists suspected that other maps, not yet recognized for their significance, might be found in French archives. They contacted Sister Mary Christine Morkowski, an independent researcher in medieval philosophy from San Antonio, who was planning a trip to France in 1977, and she graciously offered to look for La Salle materials in Paris. Her efforts were rewarded when she found original copies of maps made by La Salle's engineer, Jean-Baptiste Minet, that clearly indicated where the French colonists had landed on the Texas coast. Minet's assignment was to help fortify any settlements the explorer established and to map bays and rivers around them. Recording geographical features of the largely uncharted land was important on all expeditions; the colonial power with the best maps had a distinct advantage in the struggle over New World territory.

Minet had lost confidence in La Salle shortly after landing on the Texas coast in 1685 and eventually sailed back to France on *Le Joly* with the similarly disaffected Captain Beaujeu. The engineer took with him his maps, as well as his journal of the expedition. Since Minet left before *La Belle* sank, his maps do not depict

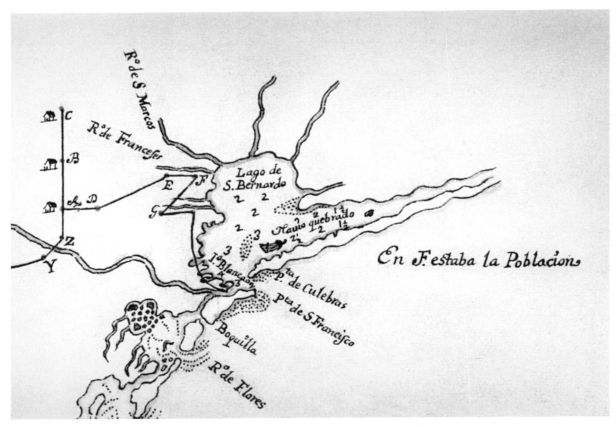

Close-up of a portion of a map made by Carlos de Sigüenza y Góngora based on sketches made during Alonso de León's 1689 trip to San Bernardo Bay (today known as Matagorda Bay) to find Fort St. Louis. Note the depiction of *La Belle* as *Navío Quebrado*, or "Broken Ship," and the location of the French settlement, labeled *F. Courtesy Center for American History, University of Texas, Austin*

the location of the wreck. He had observed the sinking of *l'Aimable*, however, and he recorded Pass Cavallo and Matagorda Bay in considerable detail, including the location of *l'Aimable*. The maps Sister Morkowski found plainly showed that La Salle made landfall in today's Matagorda Bay and not farther down the coast near Aransas Pass, as at least one scholar had suggested.[3] In addition, they allowed detailed comparisons between the Matagorda Bay of today and that of 1685.

Historical maps had been found by other researchers in European archives that provided additional important information. One was a map made in 1689 by Carlos de Sigüenza y Góngora, who was given the title of Royal Cosmographer of Mexico. Sigüenza created the map in Mexico City based on sketches done by Gen. Alonso de León during one of the eleven Spanish expeditions to find La Salle's colony.[4] The map shows

a large segment of southern Texas, including Matagorda Bay (then called Lago de San Bernardo), as well as the locations of the French colony and *La Belle*, labeled Navío Quebrado, or "Broken Ship." A 1716 map made by the French mapmaker Le Maire, undoubtedly based on Sigüenza's 1689 version, shows *La Belle* wrecked off the northern shore of today's Matagorda Peninsula, with her masts erect and sails blowing in the wind. These maps were especially critical to the search for *La Belle* since they actually showed the location of the wreck.

An additional map, drawn in 1690, further established the general whereabouts of the wrecks. Members of de León's expedition had located and burned the remains of La Salle's colony and saw what they thought were buoys placed in the bay by the French. Officials in New Spain, understandably alarmed, ordered Captain Francisco de Llanos to sail to Matagorda

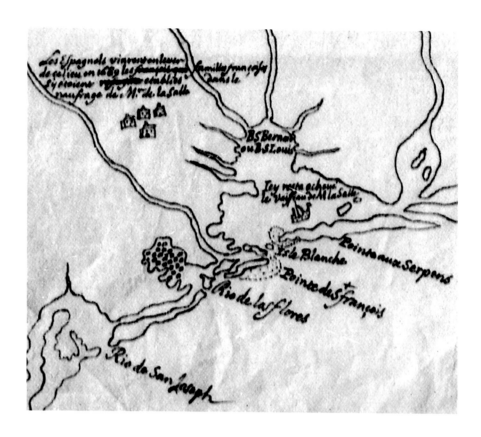

Untitled 1716 map of the northern Gulf Coast by François le Maire. *Courtesy The Newberry Library, Chicago (original in Bibliothèque Nationale de France)*

Bay and remove the buoys to thwart any new French attempt to settle the area. Mapmaker Manuel Joseph de Cárdenas y Magaña, who was part of that three-month voyage, drew one of the most detailed maps of Matagorda Bay and the rivers flowing into it, especially one he labeled Rio de los Franceses, on which Fort St. Louis was situated. The map even shows the location of the Fort St. Louis colony.

With these maps in hand, Barto Arnold, then the State Marine Archeologist working for the Texas Antiquities Committee, in 1978 proposed a ten-week search for La Salle's sunken ships. Arnold contacted geomorphologist Robert A. Morton of the University of Texas to help determine where the landforms of Matagorda Bay would have been in the late 1600s. Coastlines undergo continual changes due to ocean-wave action, storms, and the flow of inland rivers. Morton carefully examined the historical maps and overlaid them on modern maps, focusing on two areas.[5] He studied where the Sigüenza map showed the wreck of *La Belle* and determined that this part of Matagorda Bay had moved relatively little north-south and that the principal axis of movement had been parallel to the coast, or northeast-southwest. The entrance to

Pass Cavallo has probably retained about the same width over the past several centuries, slowly shifting to the southwest as Matagorda Island's eastern shore migrated southwest. *La Belle* was thus postulated to be about two hundred yards from Matagorda Peninsula. Morton charted three "probability" zones in Matagorda Bay, areas where he thought *La Belle* most likely rested.

The geomorphologist also tried to pinpoint the position of *l'Aimable*, which Minet had shown wrecked in Pass Cavallo. Maps from the mid-nineteenth century indicated that the western side of the pass had slowly migrated to the southwest. In fact, the U.S. Corps of Engineers reported that a Civil War fortification, Fort Esperanza, had been washed into Pass Cavallo in the late 1800s.[6] The Matagorda Lighthouse, a beacon for ship traffic into the bay and the port town of Indianola, was moved during the same period because it was also in danger of washing into the pass. On the basis of all this evidence, Morton determined that Pass Cavallo had definitely been moving to the southwest over the past few centuries. He proposed two probable locations for *l'Aimable*, both in the Gulf of Mexico more than a mile from today's shore.

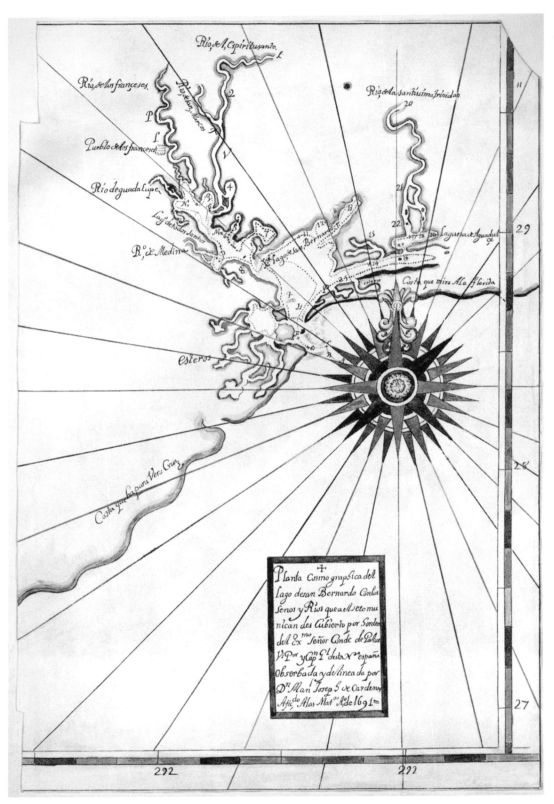

Manuel Joseph de Cárdenas y Magaña's 1690 map of the Matagorda Bay area. *Courtesy Center for American History, University of Texas, Austin (facsimile of the original in the Archivo General de Indias, Seville)*

Finding an offshore shipwreck is far more complicated and requires much more elaborate equipment than identifying an archaeological site on land, when crews of archaeologists fan out over the terrain, searching the ground surface for artifacts or other evidence of past human settlement. One of marine archaeology's most effective tools is the magnetometer, a remote-detection instrument similar to a highly sensitive metal detector. Modern magnetometers use sensors that measure proton precession or excited cesium gases to record minute amounts of magnetism.

The principle behind the magnetometer is that all land, including the seabed, has a natural magnetic susceptibility from the interaction of the earth's magnetic field with iron-rich particles in the soil. Modifications in this natural magnetism, such as the presence of a sunken vessel with large amounts of iron, cause disruptions in the earth's magnetic field, which the magnetometer records. Modern instruments can detect 1/1,000,000 of the magnetic force required to move a compass needle, making them very sensitive. Shipwrecks almost always contain ferrous metal: spikes or bolts holding wooden timbers together, iron from the ship's fittings, or cargo in the ship's hold.

To find shipwrecks, a magnetometer sensor is sealed in a watertight container and dragged behind a boat. A cable connects the sensor to a receiver on the boat that records the strength of the signal, measured in nanoteslas, the standard unit of measurement for magnetic fields. As the magnetometer sensor passes through water, it periodically sends back readings of the local magnetism. Modern equipment provides readings at the rate of about ten per second, whereas older models record about one reading per second. When a magnetometer moves over a wreck site containing metal, it records a much higher signal, indicating that ferrous materials are located below. Although the principle is relatively straightforward, using a magnetometer to find a wreck is complicated by the fact that our coastal waterways are littered with modern shipwrecks and ferrous trash such as discarded pipe, cables, and other debris.

Arnold started his magnetometer survey in the summer of 1978 over the high-probability zones defined by Morton's geomorphological study. With what was then state-of-the-art positioning equipment using microwave-based land-reference points, he mapped changes in the seabed magnetism, termed *magnetic anomalies,* with one-meter accuracy. Arnold used the Texas Antiquities Committee's research vessel, R. V. *Anomaly,* a thirty-two-foot-long boat specially built for conducting magnetometer surveys and named to reflect its purpose. Its aluminum hull is nonmagnetic so that it cannot influence the magnetometer sensors.

Arnold guided the *Anomaly* in parallel transects across Morton's high-probability zones, traversing each transect at the relatively slow speed of four to six miles per hour. Magnetism was recorded on the receiver's paper strip chart.[7]

To cover large areas in less time, Arnold also performed a magnetic survey from a helicopter. The

The Texas Historical Commission's boat, the R. V. *Anomaly,* as the crew investigates a shipwreck in Matagorda Bay. *Photograph by Alan Govenar, courtesy Documentary Arts*

helicopter could survey shallow waters and land, unlike the boat. Altitude was difficult to control accurately, however, and some wreck sites with weak signals were missed.[8] Unfortunately, though several other shipwrecks were found in the high-probability zones, *l'Aimable* and *La Belle* were not located.

Over the next seventeen years, a lack of state funding resulted in only minimal attempts to search for La Salle's ships.

THE 1995 SEARCH FOR *LA BELLE*

During the 1990s the Texas Antiquities Committee merged with the Texas Historical Commission, and Arnold became part of the commission's Archeology Division. He met with division director James Bruseth, senior author of this book, on a spring afternoon in 1995 to discuss how the marine archaeology program could better fulfill its mission to locate and preserve

the state's most important historic shipwrecks. There was little likelihood of increased state funding, so we decided that securing private money for any new undertakings would be crucial. The best way to raise funds was to embark on a project that would arouse considerable public interest.

The 624 miles of Texas coastline are filled with a remarkable array of shipwrecks, including sixteenth- and seventeenth-century Spanish galleons loaded with gold and silver, La Salle's *La Belle* and *l'Aimable*, eighteenth-century pirate ships carrying booty from nefarious activities, sailing schooners that transported arms for use in the fight for Texas independence from Mexico, and steamships that brought immigrants to Texas. After considerable discussion, we decided that we would focus on La Salle's lost ships.

Arnold knew that *l'Aimable* was probably in the treacherous waters of Pass Cavallo, or possibly in the Gulf of Mexico. A recently constructed channel from Matagorda Bay to the Gulf of Mexico had caused drift-

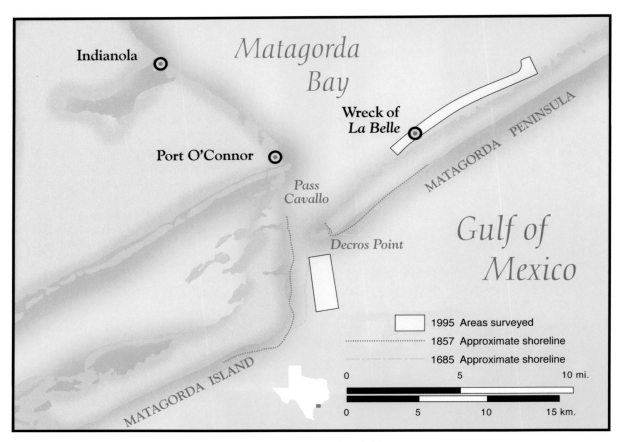

Map of Matagorda Bay showing 1995 magnetometer survey areas and probable movements of the shoreline in the past three hundred years. *Illustration by Roland Pantermuehl*

ing sand to partly fill Pass Cavallo, making water travel even more difficult. If by chance *l'Aimable* could be found, she would be hard to excavate, especially since she might be buried under many feet of sediment. *La Belle* might be under a large amount of bay silt, but at least she would be within the relatively calm and shallow waters of Matagorda Bay. For these reasons *La Belle* was considered the better candidate.

Grants were received from the Trull Foundation of Palacios, the Kathryn O'Connor Foundation of Victoria, and the Texas Department of Transportation's Intermodal Surface Transportation Efficiency Act (ISTEA) program, a federal highway initiative to spend tax dollars on promoting attractions that can be viewed by the traveling public. With this financing, we were ready to begin the search for *La Belle*.

Work commenced in June, 1995. The first month would focus on a magnetometer survey and the second on evaluating the results. Since the 1978 surveys, electronic surveying equipment had continued to improve. Modern technology includes a Global Positioning System (GPS), which uses satellites to accurately track positions on the water. The NT200D model provided by Trimble Navigation, Inc., was capable of receiving U.S. Coast Guard transmissions that correct for the military's degradation of satellite signals to protect national security. Onboard computers supplied by Compaq Computer Corporation correlated the GPS data with readings from a Geometrics model 866 magnetometer. Armed with these advanced tools,

Arnold and his crew began to target several areas of interest.

La Belle was thought to be sunk near the southern shore of Matagorda Bay, so the survey was concentrated there. Since the crew and expensive equipment would already be on the water, the researchers decided to investigate other historical sites as well. Particularly intriguing was Indianola, a port established in 1843 to receive German immigrants. For some time in the mid-nineteenth century, this bustling community was the entry point for most Texas settlers, but it was abandoned after hurricanes pounded it in 1875 and 1886. The town had largely eroded into the bay, and sometimes its ghostly remains could be seen in the shallow waters off the coast.[9]

By the end of June, the survey work in Matagorda Bay had recorded thirty-nine magnetic features that required further investigation. Although a magnetometer can find spots of unusual magnetism, divers must then determine what is actually causing each anomaly. Arnold carefully studied the magnitudes and overall shapes of the anomalies, and then he prioritized them, with the ones most likely to be a ship the size of *La Belle* at the top of the list.

The crew maneuvered the R. V. *Anomaly* to the first of these sites, and a team of divers entered the water and began to search for anything that protruded from the bottom of the bay. Diving in the murky coastal waters of Texas is dangerous, and the first dive is always a cause for anxiety. A diver never knows what

Diver preparing to investigate a magnetic anomaly in Matagorda Bay. Underwater visibility is typically very poor in the bay, and divers must use their sense of feel to identify a wreck.

might be waiting at a potential wreck site. If an anomaly turns out to be a relatively modern wreck, for example, scuba gear can get tangled in nets or rigging. Although the water was shallow, only about twelve feet deep, churned sediments made visibility virtually nil. Since they could not see, the divers had to feel the bottom with one hand and with the other hold onto a guide rope linked to a surface buoy.

After a short time, they resurfaced and reported that a wreck was buried almost entirely beneath the mud at the bottom of the bay. Without some effort to remove sediments and directly examine the vessel, it would be impossible to determine exactly what they had. They decided to insert a large pipe, called a *prop-wash deflector,* over one of the propellers of the *Anomaly* to propel the water outflow downward, thus blowing a small hole in the sediments on the bay bottom. Divers could then examine a portion of the wreck. Using a prop-wash deflector is a trade-off: it can easily disturb fragile remains, but it is often impossible to determine what a magnetic anomaly represents without it.

As they began the blowing operation, the divers found artifacts almost at once. First they recovered a wooden plank. This was not entirely encouraging, however; the presence of wood usually indicates that a wreck is relatively recent, since wood does not normally preserve well in the warm waters of the gulf. Marine teredo worms (actually a type of mollusk) normally bore through submerged wood and eventually weaken it until it simply disintegrates. But then the divers brought up exciting finds—lead musket balls, which are known to date back at least 150 years. Often called *lead shot,* they were used in flintlock muskets, which were phased out as more sophisticated guns were developed during the mid-nineteenth century. This meant the wreck was probably not recent after all.

Master diver Chuck Meide then led a second team into the water. As he felt his way along the bay's bottom, Meide encountered a large metal object, and as he examined it further, he realized that it formed a loop. He thought it might be a cannon's dolphin, or lifting handle. But could it be? This would be a remarkable find because cannons often bear markings with important clues about a ship's origin. What were the chances of discovering a cannon on the very first day of diving to explore the very first anomaly? As Meide searched the muddy bottom in the vicinity of the metal loop, he found another metal loop not far away, parallel to the first. These *had* to be the lifting handles of a cannon, he thought. Then as he probed further, he found the muzzle end and was even able to insert his hand into the bore. At the other end he found the round ball called the *cascabel.* Meide rushed to the surface to tell Arnold and the crew, who began to cheer.

Other artifacts were brought to the surface: a brass buckle, ceramic jars, a stack of pewter plates, small brass bells, brass pins, glass beads, small finger rings, a sword hilt, and staves from wooden barrels. Barrels were often used to store cargo in early ships. Everything pointed to a historic wreck, yet no conclusive ev-

Artifacts, intended for trade with the Indians, found on *La Belle* during the 1995 field investigations.

idence linked it to La Salle. For that, the artifacts would have to be examined carefully, and—more importantly—the cannon had to be recovered from the muddy waters below.

Unfortunately, the cannon could not be removed immediately. It was solid bronze and weighed several hundred pounds, and its underside was attached to the wreck by a dense, concrete-like mass formed from calcium carbonate and other suspended sediments in seawater. Divers would have to painstakingly remove the concretion so that lifting straps could be inserted under the cannon. This would take days to accomplish.

ARTIFACTS PROVIDE THE EVIDENCE

Arnold transported the artifacts found on *La Belle* to the Corpus Christi Museum of Science and History. Here they were cleaned and made ready for analysis by conservators with the museum's Ships of Discovery program. Relatively few French colonial sites in Texas have been investigated, which meant that there were not many artifacts available for comparison—the same problem Gilmore had encountered with the Keeran site materials more than two decades earlier. Artifacts from archaeological sites outside the state would have to serve instead.

Of particular interest were several ceramic jars, most of which still contained their contents. Small seeds and black greasy substances, mixed with mud

and seawater, could be seen on close inspection. These containers were apparently not for serving food, but for storing something intended for later use. Their distinctive white color, straight sides, and slightly outflaring lips should make them easy to compare with artifacts from other French colonial sites.

One of the best sources of French artifacts is the "Tunica Treasure," a huge assortment of colonial objects excavated from Tunica Indian graves near Angola, Louisiana. During the late-seventeenth and eighteenth centuries, the Tunica Indians occupied critical points along the lower Mississippi River where they could control the flow of French goods from the north. The Tunicas were expert middlemen in trade between the Europeans and Indian cultures along the lower Mississippi, and they amassed great riches themselves.[10] To maintain their wealth even after death, the Tunicas placed personal possessions in graves to accompany the deceased on the journey to another world.

In the late 1960s a Tunica cemetery discovered and excavated by a local pothunter—a person who indiscriminately digs in Indian graves to obtain artifacts, usually to sell—yielded thousands of artifacts, many of French origin. Digging in Indian burials is highly offensive to Native Americans today, but over the past 150 years many collections were obtained in this way. The Tunica artifacts were studied by Harvard archaeologist Jeffrey Brain, who published several reports on his analysis.[11]

The white ceramic jars from the Matagorda Bay

Ceramic vessels, a strainer without a handle, a hook for a metal vessel, and a pewter plate found on *La Belle* during the 1995 field investigations.

shipwreck were nearly identical to Tunica jars from the late 1600s and early 1700s. The containers represented the earliest variant of French faïence, a tin-glazed earthenware that when fired in a kiln gains a lustrous, opaque white outer surface; later versions of the pottery were decorated with blue designs.[12] These jars are known to be apothecary containers and were used to carry medicines to the New World.

The evidence was mounting, but indisputable proof that we had found La Salle's ship was still absent. The cannon had to be raised soon: its markings would almost certainly settle the issue.

Retrieving the famous French explorer's cannon would also create enormous publicity. Already word had spread, and dozens of sightseeing boats were buzzing around the site. A team of divers had been working long hours to prepare the cannon. They had chiseled narrow slits through the concretion beneath it so lifting straps could be slipped through, a task made all the more difficult in water of near-zero visibility. Kingfisher Marine of Port Lavaca generously provided the project with a barge and a large crane that could be used to extract the cannon.

On a warm July day in 1995, with the public and

A bronze cannon is lifted from the bay in July, 1995, by a barge and crane provided by Kingfisher Marine of Port Lavaca, Texas. *Photograph by Alan Govenar, courtesy Documentary Arts*

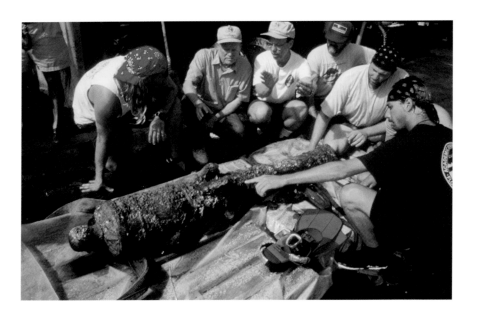

La Salle's bronze cannon is seen for the first time in 309 years.

Insignia on the cannon of le Comte de Vermandois, admiral of France from 1669 to 1683.
The Count of Vermandois gained his position and title because he was the son, though
illegitimate, of Louis XIV.

LOÜIS DE BOURBON.
Comte de Vermandois, Amiral de Fr.ce
Né a St. Germain en Laye le 2.8bre 1667.
Mort a Courtray le 18.9bre 1683.

A Paris chez Odieuvre, Md d'Estampes rüe Danjou Dauphine la deuxieme Porte Cochere.

Engraving of a young le Comte de Vermandois. *Illustration courtesy Musée national de la Marine*

LA SALLE'S OTHER LOST SHIP, *L'AIMABLE*

The excitement surrounding *La Belle*'s discovery caused many people to ask whether *l'Aimable* could also be located. (The Texas Historical Commission had searched unsuccessfully for the vessel in the late 1970s.) The National Underwater Marine Agency (NUMA), an organization created by author Clive Cussler to search for historic shipwrecks, offered to resume the search in 1997. If NUMA found the ship, it would turn the information over to the Texas Historical Commission for further investigation. Cussler hired two experienced underwater archaeologists, Wes Hall and Ralph Wilbanks, to search for *l'Aimable.*

Airborne magnetic surveys, conducted by World Geoscience, Inc., of Houston, and boat-driven magnetic surveys were completed, covering ten square nautical miles. The surveys identified sixty-six magnetic targets, eighteen of which were probable shipwrecks and the rest miscellaneous pieces of debris. From December, 1997, until August, 1999, a team of divers investigated all the potential wreck sites, often assisted by marine archaeologists from the Texas Historical Commission.

All but one were determined to be recent shipwrecks. The magnetic anomaly that could not be eliminated had a signature of 560 nanoteslas, consistent with a shipwreck containing three to five tons of ferrous metal. Since historical documents indicate that *l'Aimable* sank holding many of the supplies for the colony, including an iron forge and most of the cannonballs, an anomaly of that size was close to what would be expected.

NUMA archaeologists investigated the wreck, which was deeply buried in the sandy bottom of the Gulf of Mexico almost a mile from shore. Initial probes ten feet down found nothing. Divers then sunk a probe twenty-five feet below the bottom of the gulf but again failed to encounter the magnetic anomaly. The wreck was simply too deep to detect.

It is entirely possible that the wreck is *l'Aimable,* since all other possible shipwreck sites have been located and ruled out. But only a very dangerous and costly excavation that can uncover more than twenty-five feet of sand will determine whether La Salle's supply ship has been found.

Notes

Much of the information in this feature is based on Ralph L. Wilbanks, Wes Hall, and Gary E. McKee, "Search for *L'Aimable,*" National Underwater Marine Agency Priority Data, Texas Historical Commission Antiquities Permit no. 1852.

The bronze cannon discovered on *La Belle* during the July, 1995, field investigations.

media representatives watching, the marine archaeologists made their last dive to secure the lifting straps and connect them to the crane's cable. Then the order was given to start raising the line. This had to be done as slowly and gently as possible—it would be a disaster to damage the priceless cannon. Very gradually, the slack cable tautened, and then there was a slight jerk as the cannon broke free. The cable continued to rise, and ever so slowly a beautiful bronze cannon emerged from the water and was lowered onto the barge. Archaeologists and media people crowded around, vying for the best view. They saw elaborate decorations and

Close-up of the cannon's lifting handles, cast in the shape of leaping dolphins.

an inscription bearing the words, "LE COMTE DE VER-MANDOIS." The cannon was unmistakably French.

Researchers, naturally, quickly focused on the Count of Vermandois, and learned that he was the child of Louise de la Vallière, mistress of Louis XIV. Her relationship with the king, which began around 1661, resulted in the births of five children, three of whom died in infancy. Two lived longer, and one of them was Louis de Bourbon, born October 2, 1667.[13] In recognition of Louise de la Vallière's service, the king legitimized this child in February, 1669, by conferring upon him the title le Comte de Vermandois. The two-year-old boy was further designated admiral of the French fleet. He died in 1683 at the age of 16.[14]

This was the final confirmation we needed. In 1683 and 1684, when La Salle was securing supplies for his expedition, cannons for use on *La Belle* would have borne the admiral's insignia. After 309 years of secret rest on the bottom of Matagorda Bay, it was clear that *La Belle*'s watery grave had been discovered.

Chapter Four

EXCAVATION INSIDE
A COFFERDAM

After nearly seventeen years of searching, we had finally found *La Belle*. She was hailed as "one of the most important shipwrecks in North America" and her discovery as a monumental archaeological find.[1] But along with the fanfare came the realization that critical issues had to be addressed immediately. First, should a full excavation be attempted, or should only a portion of the ship be recovered?

A full excavation would require major commitments of time and money, and although time was not an issue, money certainly was. A complete excavation, in which *La Belle* and all of her contents would be removed, would be costly. The State of Texas provides only a small part of the funding for the Texas Historical Commission's marine archaeology program, so private funds would have to be raised.

A partial recovery would be less expensive. If we chose this option we would excavate the wreck over a period of years, in short seasons, normally during the summer months when weather conditions are optimal for diving. A portion of the vessel would be investigated each summer. But when the excavation was over, significant portions of the wreck would remain below

the waters of Matagorda Bay, vulnerable to the destructive forces of hurricanes and the malicious pursuits of treasure hunters. *La Belle* had survived, almost miraculously, for more than three centuries. Could we leave her to the vagaries of fate once more?

As long as *La Belle* had lain undiscovered on the bottom of Matagorda Bay, she was protected. Once detected, she was in jeopardy. The Texas Historical Commission had already received an anonymous letter threatening to find and plunder the ship before commission archaeologists could excavate her. Although state antiquities laws protected *La Belle,* and local law enforcement officials had been told about the need to monitor the area, she lay miles from populated land in a remote part of the bay.

Treasure hunters could do serious damage, because when shipwrecks are looted, the artifacts are rarely analyzed; they are simply sold to private collectors, and invaluable information about the past is lost. Even worse, some treasure-hunting schemes have more to do with bilking unsuspecting investors out of their money than with recovering ancient artifacts.

Scientific archaeology, by contrast, is concerned

with what the wreck and its contents reveal about the past. Unlike treasure hunters, archaeologists consider the *information* as important as the objects, although an important goal is to see the artifacts studied and displayed in museums. To draw the sharpest possible contrast between scientific archaeology and treasure hunting, any investigation of *La Belle*—whether a full excavation or a phased recovery—would demand the highest standards.

Another significant challenge for any investigation would be the murkiness of the bay's water. Marine archaeologists are accustomed to these "dark water" excavations, and many are adept at them, but even the most experienced face nearly overwhelming odds when they cannot see what they are doing. Small objects are inevitably lost, and especially fragile artifacts, such as the delicate organic remains of cloth or wood, can be easily damaged.

Weighing heavily on the decision about how best to excavate *La Belle* was her enormous historical significance. This was not just another wreck off the coast of Texas, but the oldest French shipwreck discovered in the Western Hemisphere up to that time. Furthermore, she belonged to La Salle, whose efforts to establish a French colony significantly shaped the history of the state. The ship's recovery was thus uniquely important, and a partial excavation began to seem inadequate.

Early in the planning, an alternative to a traditional underwater excavation had been proposed: surround *La Belle* with a cofferdam, a huge steel circumferential structure, so that the interior could be emptied of water and the wreck excavated as if she were on dry land. Cofferdams are routinely built for bridge construction. The advantage of such an approach was obvious: archaeologists could see what they were excavating. With the water gone, they could recover artifacts from the bay floor with the same degree of precision as in land excavations. Even the smallest and most fragile objects could be retrieved for study and display.

If we chose to pursue this plan, it would be the first attempt in North America to excavate a shipwreck in dry conditions inside a cofferdam. A cofferdam had been built around an eighteenth-century ship from the Battle of Yorktown in Virginia, but only to clear murky water; the excavation itself took place underwater.[2] Dry-land cofferdams had been built to investigate shipwrecks in Europe, but none of these ships had been as large as *La Belle*.[3]

To build a cofferdam would also be very expensive. Several marine-construction firms estimated that it would cost about $700,000, given the anticipated dimensions of *La Belle*—about sixty feet long and twenty-five feet wide. Excavation and analysis would cost another $1–1.3 million, bringing the total to nearly $2 million. This was a huge sum for an archaeological project, and considerable debate occurred within the Texas Historical Commission about the best way to proceed. A meeting to discuss the issue called by the commission's chair, John Nau, included commissioners and noted historians T. R. Fehrenbach and Archie MacDonald, former executive director Curtis Tunnell, Archeology Division Director James Bruseth, and State Marine Archeologist Barto Arnold.

After much discussion we decided that a cofferdam excavation, while costly, would provide the best method of retrieving *La Belle* and her precious cargo. We realized that not everyone in the scientific archaeological community might agree. Some would view the cofferdam as an untested methodology that would create new problems. The wreck could become too dry inside it, which would cause artifacts to deteriorate from dehydration. Ironically, the same seawater that had entombed *La Belle* for three centuries was now indispensable to her preservation. Despite these concerns, we felt confident that ways could be found to keep the artifacts from drying out. Clearly, the benefits of a cofferdam excavation—allowing for the careful recovery of small and fragile items—far exceeded those of a traditional partial underwater recovery.

With that major decision behind us, the next hurdle was raising the money. Texas philanthropists had indicated support for the project, but only on the condition that the state provide a sizable share of the funds. Fortunately, the Texas Historical Commission had a powerful ally in Bob Bullock, the lieutenant governor who also had a long political career as a Texas legislator and state comptroller. We were also fortunate to have the support of then-Governor George W. Bush. Success for us depended greatly on the support we received from these two leaders of our great state.

Bullock had a passion for Texas history. He had already lent his support to several Texas Historical Commission programs, and he recognized that *La Belle* presented a great historical find and a wonderful opportunity to gain new information about early Texas history. Bullock readily offered to solicit support from the legislature for the excavation.

The Texas Legislature meets only every two years, however, and the last session had just ended in June, 1995, one month before *La Belle* had been discovered.

Cofferdam and the R. V. *Anomaly* on a foggy morning in 1997.

Once a legislative session is over, it is extremely difficult for funds to be appropriated. But without them *La
Belle* would be in jeopardy for at least two more years,
and as the initial public excitement about the discovery
waned, fundraising might become more difficult.

Bullock, working with John Nau, managed to per-
suade legislators to reallocate unspent funds from the
Department of Criminal Justice to the project. Reallo-
cation does take place from time to time, but it is rare
and usually reserved for state emergencies—not archaeological projects. In the fall of 1995, Texas leaders,
including Governor Bush, approved the reappropria-
tion of $1.75 million for the excavation. With this state
money in hand, we could now begin to seek private
matching funds.

Meanwhile, *La Belle* had to be protected from vandalism. An emergency grant from Houston Endowment, a private foundation, allowed us to hire a local
boat captain to check the site daily, and also paid for
a small staff to work with engineers on plans for the
cofferdam.

Texas' philanthropic community continued to respond generously to the need for financial help. The
late Dennis O'Connor, a businessman from Victoria,

Texas, donated a gift of stock. Houston Endowment
provided a large additional grant for construction of
the cofferdam. Dallas-based Meadows and Summerlee
Foundations and other foundations throughout Texas
also supplied much needed financial support to aug-
ment the state appropriations. The Texas Historical
Commission could now start making plans for the cofferdam construction.

The design firm selected was G&W Engineering in
Port Lavaca, Texas. Their engineers had extensive experience in marine work and were familiar with building cofferdams for the construction of bridges and
highways. After analyzing the project and talking with
us, the engineers proposed a large octagonal structure
consisting of two rows of sheet piling filled with sand
to form the walls. Using computers, they calculated the
force of Matagorda Bay's waters against the cofferdam
walls. The force would be enormous even under normal conditions, and this structure would have to survive storms, perhaps even a hurricane. The slightest
break in the walls would be catastrophic if the waters
of the bay rushed in over the archaeologists working
inside.

By early 1996 we were worried: the design pro-

The sheet piling of the cofferdam was driven into the bay bottom by a giant vibrator. It took only a few minutes for each sheet to be driven into place. *Photograph by Stephen Myers*

cess was taking longer than anticipated. Funding for the boat captain guarding the site was running out, and the increasing media attention made it more likely that vandals would find the wreck. Furthermore, it was important that the excavation start soon so that work could take place in the spring, when chances of a hurricane were lowest. Although the cofferdam would be built to handle such a storm, a direct hit could cause damage and shut down the project for a long time.

Finally the plans were ready and a call for bids went out. We selected a New Orleans contractor, Kostmeyer Construction, on the basis of their low estimate and past experience in building cofferdams. In May, 1996, a few months later than planned, construction of the cofferdam began. The new start date meant that construction would continue into the hurricane season, but this was a risk we would have to tolerate; further delay was impossible. Expenses had soared to

Cofferdam sheet piling as it is being driven into the bed of Matagorda Bay. *Photograph by Stephen Myers*

nearly $1.5 million, an amount more than double the initial estimate. The extra costs were incurred because a cofferdam built for a shipwreck excavation was considerably different from an ordinary cofferdam. The steel sheet pilings that would form the walls, for example, would have to penetrate forty feet into the bed of the bay to prevent water pumped out of the cofferdam from seeping under the wall and back into the structure. This would require 57-foot-long pilings, which had to be specially milled in a Pennsylvania steelyard and shipped to Matagorda Bay. And unlike conventional cofferdams, this one would have to be freestanding—not attached to another structure or to the shoreline.

Final plans called for an elongated, octagonal structure. Two concentric walls of sheet piling would be separated by a 33-foot gap filled with sand, with steel tie rods linking together the inner and outer walls. The pilings would be .37 inch thick, 3 feet wide, and would extend about 5 feet above the waterline. On the outside, the cofferdam would measure 178 feet long and 131 feet wide. The inner wall would leave an ample 82 by 53 feet of workspace around the ship's hull. A steel

cover would be built over the interior of the dam to provide shelter for the crew and to protect the exposed wreck as excavation proceeded.

CONSTRUCTION BEGINS

Three large barges hauled the sheet piling and all the equipment to the site, where a 100-foot-long crane stood ready. The crane used a huge vibrator, attached to the top of the pilings, to drive them 40 feet into the silty bay bottom. It took a surprisingly short time, only a few minutes, to place each piece.

The engineers knew that the cofferdam could not be made completely watertight—the cost of such a structure would have been astronomical. In fact, they warned us that it *would* leak and, furthermore, that they could not predict the rate of leakage. Some estimates suggested that water might enter faster than it could be removed, which would eliminate the possibility of working in a relatively dry interior. But the engineers' best guess was that the leakage would be slow enough for sump pumps in the bottom of the coffer-

Construction of the cofferdam in July, 1996. The walls were made of interlocking steel sheets driven into the bottom of Matagorda Bay. The barge to the right contains construction equipment and materials.

Sand was dumped into the wall of the cofferdam to form a seal around the interior. Water nevertheless leaked through the sand but at a manageable rate.

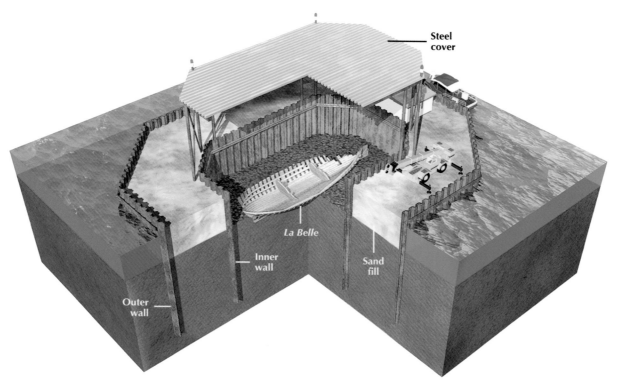

Cut-away view showing the internal construction of the cofferdam. *Illustration by Clif Bosler, courtesy Fort Worth Star-Telegram*

Completed cofferdam with the R. V. *Anomaly* docked at the southern end. © *1997 Kay Chernush*

dam to keep up. They made no guarantees, however, and we spent many sleepless nights worrying about it.

By August, 1996, construction was complete and a suction pump eight inches in diameter, driven by a diesel engine, began to pump out the water. After several days of pumping, the bottom of Matagorda Bay was revealed for the first time in untold millennia. The pumps strained to keep up with the water rushing in from numerous leaks that appeared along the cofferdam's walls. But after a few days, the sand in the walls began to compact, slowing the rate of leakage enough so that four electric sump pumps, one in each corner, could easily keep the bottom dry. The cofferdam was working.

A WRECK EXPOSED

What would we find once the waterlogged remains of *La Belle* were exposed for the first time in more than three centuries? How much of the ship's cargo might still exist, and what condition would the ship's remains be in? Another, perhaps even more disturbing, question loomed: Would the artifacts recovered from the excavation be worth the cofferdam's cost, now approaching $2 million? Although we had retrieved several artifacts during testing the year before, there was no guarantee that the excavation itself would be productive.

Indeed, the remains of *La Belle* looked decidedly unimpressive at the beginning of the excavation. The

bottom of the cofferdam was a blanket of mud, with only a few objects visible, mostly some broken barrel staves. Although we had planned for three months of excavation, it looked like that might be more than we really needed.

As we began excavating, we were finding few artifacts in the layers of mud that covered the wreck. The mud was from farming during the late 1800s to middle 1900s, which had eroded the soil into the rivers and creeks that fed into Matagorda Bay, depositing the sediments on the bottom and decreasing the depth of the already shallow water.

Yet as the team continued digging patiently through the mud, artifacts finally did begin to appear: some lead shot—bullets for La Salle's flintlock muskets—and fragments of rope. On wrecks in warm waters such as those in the Gulf of Mexico, rope and other perishable items normally are not well preserved, so we started to feel more optimistic about what might lie below. As we peeled off the layers, one-meter square of mud by one-meter square, the outline of a ship began to take form.

Gradually, we began to realize that something extraordinary had happened to *La Belle*. Mud had encapsulated the bottom of the hull, resulting in exceptional preservation. Her cargo was largely intact, still contained in wooden barrels and boxes, many of which were exactly where La Salle and his men had loaded them into the ship more than three hundred years before. Unlike the cargo of many wrecks, where the ship is broken apart and its contents spilled to the bottom

Excavation inside the cofferdam as *La Belle* is just beginning to be uncovered. The R. V. *Anomaly* is in the background. *Photograph by Robert Clark*

of the sea, this cargo remained largely contained within the ship. We now suspected that what we were going to find would be extremely significant to North American archaeology.

METHODS OF THE ARCHAEOLOGISTS

The archaeological work proceeded in two main areas: inside the dam around the wreck where excavation took place (called the excavation pit), and on top of the cofferdam wall where support activities were carried out. Inside the pit, some workers excavated while others labored to keep water out. The sump pumps operated twenty-four hours a day, seven days a week. They were set in fifty-five-gallon drums perforated with holes to help prevent loose sediments from clogging them, but the intake pipes clogged anyway, necessitating constant maintenance, repair, and replacement.

Like conventional excavations on dry land, this one took place within a grid, a coordinated system with numerical designations that divides the site into one-meter squares. When artifacts are removed, they can thus be identified as coming from a specific square meter. In some instances the artifacts may be plotted to their exact position, again using the grid to triangulate the precise coordinates. The location of each artifact is called its *provenience,* and the recording of this information is imperative to modern archaeology. The grid coordinates were posted on the inside walls of the cofferdam for easy reference. As in dry-land excavations, sediments were removed in 10 cm (4 inch) increments, or levels. When a finer provenience was deemed necessary, we divided the one-meter squares into 50 cm (20 inch) quadrangles, or quads.

The crew collected all the sediment in buckets and transported it to the cofferdam wall for processing. Large artifacts, and features such as barrels, boxes, and clusters of related artifacts, were piece-plotted with a Sokkia SET5E Electronic Total Data Station (TDS) with an SDR33 Electronic Field Notebook for recording and downloading readings to computers. This instrument was donated to the project by the Sokkia Corporation. Some large objects, such as intact barrels and boxes, were encased in plaster and removed in their entirety, to be opened and carefully examined after the field-work was completed.

As the dig progressed and overlaying sediments were removed, it became increasingly difficult for the excavators to avoid standing on the fragile remains of

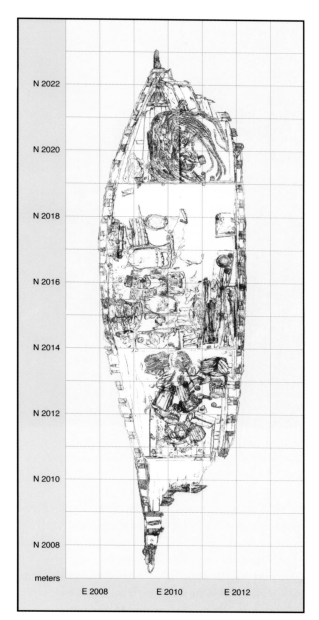

A grid of one-meter squares (each 39.4 inches on a side) over the wreck ensured accurate recording of the locations of all artifacts. *Illustration by David Johnson*

the ship and its cargo. To remedy this, we positioned large aluminum boards on wooden blocks at each side of the wreck and over the excavation squares. We could then lie on the boards to excavate the artifacts below. A drawback was that we were forced to constantly reach down into the excavation squares, which could become terribly uncomfortable after a while.

Meanwhile, on top of the cofferdam wall, other crew members emptied the buckets of sediment from the excavation onto mesh screens and sprayed the sed-

Inside the cofferdam the crew was able to excavate in one-meter squares, just as they would at archaeological sites on land. *Photograph by Stephen Myers*

A Sokkia SET5E Electronic Data Station was used to precisely map all artifacts.

iments with pressurized water to expose small objects that the excavators might have missed. To salvage even the tiniest artifacts, the sediments were washed through mesh screens of an eighth of an inch or finer. All artifacts were bagged and labeled according to the provenience of the excavation square from which they came. A large crane positioned on top of the wall removed heavy or fragile artifacts and transported equipment into and out of the excavation.

Also on the wall, beyond the water screens, a small building housed the field office and a bunk for the night guard. Initially, the field office was on a large barge located adjacent to the cofferdam, but the barge broke loose in a storm. After this, the building and equipment on the barge were moved to the cofferdam wall.

At first security guards were hired to watch the cofferdam at night, but eventually staff archaeologists performed this duty to reduce costs. Next to the office was a large steel trailer enclosing two diesel engines; these drove a large generator that provided a constant stream of electricity. At least one of the engines had to be run-

ning at all times, because the electricity powered the pumps: if we lost electrical power, the interior of the cofferdam would begin to fill with water, excavations would be interrupted, and the exposed artifacts could be damaged. There were occasional power outages during strong storms, but we could usually resume work within a few days.

As expected, one of the most pressing challenges was preventing the waterlogged artifacts from drying out. We installed a high-pressure pump on the cofferdam to provide a constant source of seawater to all parts of the structure. Inside the excavation pit, hose bibs were connected to garden hoses that were always within a few meters of the wreck. As a result, the artifacts could be kept wet at all times.

Another challenge was the cofferdam's distance from project headquarters, more than fifteen miles away in the town of Palacios, a trip by boat of an hour and fifteen minutes. This would have been a logistical concern for a traditional underwater excavation as well, but it was especially difficult to be that far away

Archaeologists screened all of the mud over and inside the wreck to find tiny artifacts like beads, pins, rings, and bells. © *1997 Kay Chernush*

The wall of the cofferdam held a small portable building that served as an office. Screens, also on the wall, were used to wash the excavated sediments to recover small artifacts.

and in the middle of the bay. All supplies and tools had to be brought to the site in advance, and any unexpected requirements caused delays.

Operating the cofferdam was expensive—about $100,000 per month—so to make the most of the time the Texas Historical Commission archaeological team labored seven days a week, twelve hours a day, in all but the worst weather. The crew could work safely inside the cofferdam during inclement weather, but getting there was sometimes another matter. As luck would have it, during the excavation season of 1996–97, the Matagorda Bay area experienced a record number of cold fronts, and each created extremely rough seas. When we rode to and from the cofferdam during these

storms, huge waves crashed over the R. V. *Anomaly*, soaking the entire crew.

On one memorable boat ride during December, 1996, we were taking *National Geographic Magazine* writer Lisa Moore LaRoe to the wreck site. We were delighted that the magazine was doing a story about the project, and despite the inclement weather, we were anxious to get her to the cofferdam. As we left the Palacios headquarters in the R. V. *Anomaly*, waves from Matagorda Bay began crashing over the bow of the boat. We continued on, though, undaunted: we had driven in waves like this before. After an hour, we noticed that the water had taken on an ominous green-gray color and looked as if it was almost boiling under

To avoid damaging the delicate cargo, archaeologists excavate from boards suspended over the wreck. *Photograph by Stephen Myers*

the unrelenting winds blowing across the bay. This we had not seen before. We finally made it to the cofferdam, but we were able to dock only after several attempts, each hampered by the high seas. We made our way into the excavation pit as the cold winter winds intensified and the bay's waves crashed even harder over the cofferdam. Conditions were too difficult to attempt any excavation, but LaRoe was at least able to see *La Belle*'s remains.

On the return trip we were heading directly into the north wind, and now the waves were slamming hard onto the *Anomaly,* each wave jolting the crew inside the cabin. Then the worst possible thing happened: we lost one of our two engines. At least we thought that was the worst. The boat continued running on just one of its diesel engines, but we would travel only half as fast. Then, to our horror, the other engine quit! Now only the angry forces of nature propelled us. Our equipment manager, Bill Pierson, quickly climbed down into the engine bay to get the engines going, and after some coaxing, they started back up. We traveled a few miles—and they stopped again. We radioed headquarters to send help, and they contacted the U.S. Coast Guard, who immediately inquired if we were sinking. Our excited response was not yet, but we needed help! The Coast Guard told us to call back when we *were* sinking—a response that undoubtedly reflected the agency's shrinking federal budget.

Pierson kept working with the engines and luckily got one of them running again. This time it kept going

long enough for us to limp back to the Palacios headquarters. When we finally docked the *Anomaly,* LaRoe jumped to shore, kneeled down, and kissed the earth, thankful for having survived the fury of a storm on Matagorda Bay.[4]

We faced yet another obstacle in early December, 1996: project funds were about to run out. The high costs of operating the cofferdam had used much of the project's funds, and more money was urgently needed or everything would shut down. The cofferdam pumps would be silenced, and the excavation pit would begin to fill with water, once again reclaiming *La Belle.*

Rescue came from an unexpected source. Mobil Oil Exploration, hearing about our project and the possibility of a shutdown, generously stepped forward with a $250,000 donation. George W. Bush, Bob Bullock, and Texas Speaker of the House Bob Laney were present at the ceremony in the state capitol building when Mobil Oil handed over the check to the State of Texas. Without a doubt, this contribution saved the project. Other emergency funds were provided by the Cullen Foundation, Trull Foundation, and Diamond M Foundation.

REMOVAL OF THE HULL

The next issue we had to address was how to remove *La Belle*'s hull. After more than three centuries of immersion in seawater, the ship's greatest enemy now was

HEADQUARTERS IN PALACIOS

Every major archaeological project needs a headquarters where artifacts recovered in the field can be stored, preliminary analysis can take place, and stabilization of fragile items can begin. Initially, we intended to headquarter in the town closest to the cofferdam, Port O'Connor. The facilities available there, however, did not have enough space for a laboratory and large crew. We were then contacted by Roberta Ripke, representing the community of Palacios. City officials there embraced the project with open arms and offered a number of incentives to locate in their community. The most important, provided by Matagorda County Navigation District Number One, was a rent-free headquarters building located directly on Matagorda Bay. The building even had several boat slips and a docking facility that would accommodate our thirty-two-foot-long vessel, the R. V. *Anomaly.*

This building needed work, however. Junk was piled everywhere, and significant repairs and modifications were required to make it serviceable. But the free space was tempting. Also, archaeologists often prefer to use older buildings that are not in the best condition. The cleaning, storing, and analyzing of artifacts—especially marine artifacts—can be a dirty business. Much water is used to keep the artifacts wet, various chemicals are employed to stabilize them, and the cleaning process can leave behind a great deal of debris. In a somewhat dilapidated, as opposed to pristine, building, archaeologists can go about their business without worrying about damaging anything.

The headquarters building was large enough so that the crew's accommodations could be built upstairs, which meant that they would not have to rent houses. This kept costs down, and the round-the-clock presence of crew members also increased the security of the priceless *La Belle* artifacts stored in the building.

The town of Palacios was a wonderful host. The city provided, in addition to a headquarters building, fresh water free of charge. County commissioners helped with myriad other needs, and townspeople came by to donate furniture, equipment, and other necessities. Without the assistance of the people of Palacios, the excavation of *La Belle* would have been far more difficult.

The Palacios headquarters, an old boat marina, was provided free of charge by the Matagorda County Navigation District Number One to help conserve project funds.

air. Whatever strategy we chose, all the wood would have to remain wet, even while being transported more than two hundred miles away to the Texas A&M University Conservation Research Laboratory in College Station.

Determining the best method of hull removal is a common dilemma in marine-recovery projects. Recently, the CSS *H. L. Hunley,* a forty-five-foot-long, steel-hulled submarine, sunk during the U.S. Civil War, was raised intact and transported to shore. The Swedish *Vasa* and the British *Mary Rose* were also raised intact. This is what Fred Hocker, one of our project consultants and a professor in the nautical archaeology program at Texas A&M University, proposed for *La Belle.* The plan entailed digging below the hull and positioning wooden supports. Because the sand under the ship was unconsolidated and unstable, much like a sand castle buffeted by waves, placing the supports would be complicated. First the marine archaeologists would spray jets of pressurized water under the hull from the port to starboard sides in several places and thread straps through the resulting tunnels. The straps would position and cradle the hull. Further excavation would then be required to build a support cradle that would hold the straps. The cradle would have to be strong enough to bear the weight of the entire lift, estimated at several tons.

We consulted the project engineers about the feasibility of this method. David Gann, owner and chief engineer of G&W Engineering, inspected the hull, us-

Large diesel engines ran twenty-four hours a day, seven days a week, providing electrical power to keep the mechanical systems operating on the cofferdam. Without the diesel engines, the cofferdam would have filled with water. *Photograph by Bill Pierson*

ing the tip of his pocketknife blade to probe the timbers. After an hour he concluded that the timbers, although they appeared to be structurally sound, would not be able to support themselves during a move, let alone support the weight of the overlying timbers. Only a solid cradle that entirely encased the bottom of the hull would prevent it from breaking apart. But such a device, he said, could easily cost as much as the cofferdam—another $2 million. Then there was the problem of transporting the hull to Texas A&M. The cofferdam's cover would have to be removed, and a large crane on a barge would lift the hull and its cradle from the bottom of the bay and take them to Port Lavaca. There they would be loaded onto a large trailer. The most difficult part would be the two-hundred-mile journey from Port Lavaca to College Station. Unless the ship was enclosed in a vibration-free chamber, the fragile timbers would be rattled into unrecognizable wooden mush. The special chamber, of course, would demand yet another considerable expense.

The other option for removing *La Belle* was to disassemble her in much the same way as she was originally put together, only in reverse. The timbers could

then be moved individually, which would greatly simplify shipment, since most of them were small enough to be hauled back to the Palacios headquarters in the project boat. The larger pieces could be stored on the cofferdam and transported back on a barge at the end of the project.

Another advantage of dismantling *La Belle*'s hull was that we would be able to examine all the timbers, some of which would otherwise be obscured by exterior or interior planking. We might be able to trace the sequence of construction and identify intricacies of manufacture—the carpenter's tool marks, details of how the timbers were fastened together, and the type of wood used for different timbers. We could also excavate the sand beneath the hull and find artifacts that might have become lodged under the vessel when it wrecked.

The disadvantage of this approach would be a longer field season. At this point, in early 1997, the cost of the ship's excavation now exceeded $3 million, and dismantling the vessel would take another two to four months, at a cost of $100,000 a month. The ship would have to be reassembled later, and that would require

*T*he first call came in to the lab at 2:00 one October morning. It was archaeologist Layne Hedrick's turn to be night guard at the cofferdam. The archaeologist with guard duty stayed overnight in the field office, which was then on a sixty-foot-long barge tied up to the cofferdam. During the night, a strong cold front had blown in, creating torrential rains and huge waves. Storms were normal occurrences during the fall and winter months, and the cofferdam had been designed to withstand them. But this storm was different.

Hedrick, calling from a cell phone, said the north wind was creating six- to eight-foot-high waves that were crashing unrelentingly over the barge, smashing into the office where he huddled and causing one of the two moorings that secured the barge to sway. We urged him not to panic and to simply wait it out, since the mooring timbers were driven deeply into the bay floor.

About thirty minutes later, Hedrick called back, shouting that one of the two moorings had broken free and the southern end of the barge was drifting out into the bay and then immediately slamming back into cofferdam. If this continued, the barge might be punctured and sink. Now greatly alarmed, we told him to put on a life jacket and immediately move onto the cofferdam for safety. He threw on a raincoat, grabbed a life jacket, and headed out the building. Just as he neared the small bridge that connected the barge to the cofferdam, a huge wave lifted the barge high into the air, knocked Hedrick off his feet, and tossed the bridge into the bay. He ran back into the office building and immediately phoned back with an SOS. We told him to stay in the building and that we would try to get him help. By now it was 3:00 in the morning. Who would venture out into a severe night storm to rescue him?

A short time later Hedrick phoned again with the worst news yet. The barge had entirely broken loose of the remaining mooring and was now floating freely in the bay. Heavy rain was pounding the craft and huge waves were crashing over it. We desperately began calling for help.

Fortunately, Kingfisher Marine based in Port Lavaca sent out a tugboat to rescue the archaeologist. They found the barge but could not attach to it because the seas were too rough. They told Hedrick that they would watch him during the night and retrieve the barge in the morning. By daybreak the winds had died down and the rain had stopped. The tugboat caught hold of the barge and towed a waterlogged and very tired archaeologist back to shore. He was finally safe. The episode set the project back $30,000, but it left everyone with a new appreciation of the furious storm that sank *La Belle* in 1686.

An archaeologist on the cofferdam watches an approaching storm. *Photograph by Bill Pierson*

even more time and funds. But on balance, this option would probably be less expensive than moving *La Belle* in one piece.

After careful consideration of both options, we decided to dismantle *La Belle* timber by timber. Financial backing for moving the entire vessel in one piece prob-ably could have been found, but the possibility of catastrophic damage to the ship was too great.

Since few shipwrecks in the world have been completely dismantled, not many archaeologists possess the necessary expertise. We sought advice from Peter Waddell, an archaeologist for the Canadian govern-

After the wreck was completely mapped, each hull timber was removed and labeled with an orange tag.

Automotive jacks, nylon wedges, and cats-paw chisels were among the many different tools employed to remove timbers from the hull.

ment, who had dismantled a Basque whaling vessel, the *San Juan*, from Labrador Bay in Canada.[5] Waddell spent a couple of weeks in Texas, where he assisted in identifying the necessary tools and training the crew.

The disassembly of *La Belle* began in February, 1997. The first step was to make detailed drawings and photographs of all the timbers in place. This would provide a record of exactly how the hull looked in the sediments, and it would also enable conservators to follow a master plan that would show where each timber should go when they reassembled the ship. Next, all the timbers were marked with numbers. Plastic cattle-ear tags, bright orange with black numerals, were chosen for this because they would be durable in seawater and also easy to read. They would be fastened to the timbers with small stainless-steel nails. We had a difficult time convincing the purchasing staff at the Texas Historical Commission that we needed cattle-ear tags for a shipwreck excavation, but we finally prevailed and the ear tags were ordered.

After three centuries in seawater, many of the iron bolts and pins holding the timbers together had rusted away, but some had turned into dense concretions that permeated the wooden timbers around the fastening holes. The trick would be to break apart these concretions without damaging the wood. Other timbers were fastened together with treenails—wooden pegs—and would require a different method of disassembly: the treenails would have to be sawn in two.

We used a wide variety of tools to separate the timbers: special pruning saws with ultra-thin blades imported from Japan; nylon wedges made at a local machine shop; thin strips of steel that were inserted between timbers and hammered; automotive bottle jacks modified by adding a *z*-shaped metal appendage to pry timbers apart; carpenters' cats-paws; and even sledge hammers. Some fasteners were still intact and very stout, especially those deep within the hull that held large frames to the keel and keelson. For these, a line from a large crane on the cofferdam wall was lowered into the excavation pit and attached to the timber with a strap. The line was slowly pulled up until the bolt broke and the timber was freed from the wreck.

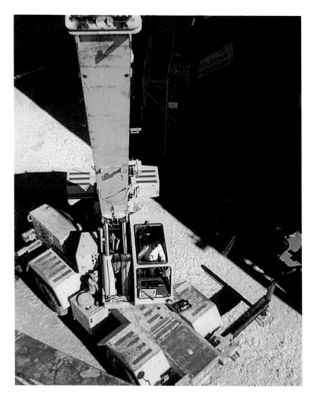

A large crane is used to lift heavy objects from the excavation pit to the wall of the cofferdam. *Photograph by Bill Pierson*

A crane is used to loosen heavy timbers.

Like the artifacts, the timbers had to be kept moist at all times. We constantly wet them with hand sprayers and hose-end sprinklers as we excavated and covered parts of the hull we were not working on with burlap and fiberglass cloths. As the timbers were removed, they were placed in plastic-lined wooden vats filled with bay water, where they rested until they were ready for transport back to headquarters. So great was the need for wooden vats that a team of carpenters worked nonstop building new vats during the disassembly. By

On April 3, 1997, archaeologists removed the last timber of *La Belle*, ending the vessel's watery entombment at the bottom of Matagorda Bay. Shown from left to right are Layne Hedrick, Chuck Meide, Bill Pierson, Toni Carrell, Greg Cook, James Bruseth (project director), and Henry Thomason.

the end of the project, the entire wall of the cofferdam was covered with vats of *La Belle*'s hull timbers.

The dismantling went well. In April, 1997, after little more than two months, we had removed nearly four hundred timbers. Most of the hull wood was removed intact, although a few unusually stout timbers were difficult to separate and broke during removal. The breaks were sharp, though, and could be repaired so that in the end the damage would not be apparent. All timbers underwent preliminary cleaning at the Palacios headquarters, where sediments and concretions still adhering to the timbers were cleared away and drawings were made of each. They were then shipped to the lab at Texas A&M.

The decision to remove the hull timber by timber began to pay dividends when we found noteworthy artifacts under the ship, including some very large pieces of sailcloth that had become entangled beneath the bow. Rarely do archaeologists find major portions of a shipwreck's sails. Unfortunately, any effort to remove segments of the now-fragile cloth caused it to dissolve into unidentifiable pieces, so it could only be viewed in its original location. Careful drawings and photographs would be the only record of *La Belle*'s sails.

In the end, the cofferdam had worked beautifully. It was surely one of the most extraordinary aspects of the excavation. The structure allowed us to recover many remarkably preserved materials—even brain tissue from a human cranium and insect parts—that would have been damaged or impossible to collect otherwise. By any measure, use of the cofferdam was in the best interest of *La Belle* and constituted a milestone in U.S. scientific archaeology.

Chapter Five

THE BEAUTIFUL VESSEL

Was *La Belle* truly a beautiful ship, as her name asserts, or were her christeners simply given to hyperbole? To explore this question, and many others, we examined her hull and the remains of her sails, masts, and rigging and searched the marine archives of France. A distinguished French naval historian recreated the vessel on paper, and, on the basis of his drawings, an artist constructed scale models. We now possess important clues about the ship's structure and appearance.

The fact that about 40 percent of *La Belle*'s hull was preserved is not only fortunate but remarkable when one considers that when ships founder they often break apart and become scattered over large areas. The upper part of the ship, which remained above the bay floor, was destroyed by storms, waves, worms, and bacteria. About three-fourths of the starboard hull was preserved, while only a small portion, to the turn of the bilge, remained on the port side. When we discovered the shipwreck, it was listing 21 degrees to starboard and pitched 1.7 degrees slightly downward towards the bow. After we adjusted for this tilt, the preserved hull measured 52 feet 3 inches long and about 13 feet wide.[1] This

compares with an original length of 54 feet 4 inches and a width of 14 feet 9 inches.

Nearly one-quarter of the ship's rigging elements were preserved, in an array comparable to those of larger, well-known rigging collections from shipwrecks such as the *Mary Rose* and the *Vasa*. Catharine Inbody Corder, a graduate student in nautical archaeology at Texas A&M University, identified almost 150 items, the most numerous being 42 blocks.[2] These were essentially pulleys to raise and lower the yards and sails and to hoist cargo in and out of the ship. The blocks occur in several shapes. Most common are single-sheaved blocks with one internal pulley. Others, called *fiddle blocks* because of their resemblance to a violin or fiddle, consist of a large and a small block joined end-to-end. Also found were double-sheaved blocks with two pulleys side-by-side, a Dutch lift block for adjusting the yards in a vertical plane, and a rare pendant block, so named because it was suspended from a line of rigging called a *pendant*.

We recovered twelve deadeyes, which are similar to blocks but without moveable pulleys. They were part

La Belle as she looked under full sail. *Illustration by Charles Shaw*

of the ship's standing rigging and secured the masts to the sides of the ship. A rope, called a *shroud,* extended down from the mast to a deadeye at deck level on the ship. Another rope, the lanyard, connected the deadeye to another deadeye a few feet down on the outside of the hull. The lower deadeye was connected with a metal strap, known as the *chain plate,* to the hull of the ship through a wooden channel. The tension on the masts was adjusted by tightening the lanyard connecting the two deadeyes. In addition to the deadeyes, concretions were found that contained molds of the chain plates that attached to the hull. A single crosstree—a short, flat piece of wood used to spread and secure the topmast shrouds—was also recovered. Still attached were a futtock and deadeye strap, parts of the rigging that held the topmast in place.

Other rigging elements include several parral trucks, basically large wooden beads. They would be wrapped around the masts and attached to the yards and served as ball bearings to allow the yards to move up and down the masts as they were raised and lowered. We even found one parral rib, a thin piece of wood that fit between the beads to keep them properly lined up while in use. Other items include five thimbles that prevented rope from chafing, a topmast fid that helped support the housing of the topmast, a variety of cleats, various metal rings, and bolts used to secure lines.

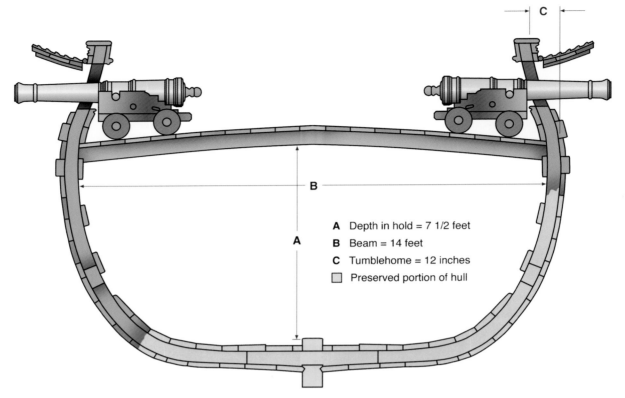

A Depth in hold = 7 1/2 feet
B Beam = 14 feet
C Tumblehome = 12 inches
☐ Preserved portion of hull

Cross-sectional view of the hull showing the portions of the vessel found during excavation. *Illustration based on figure 24 in Glenn P. Grieco, "Modeling La Belle: A Reconstruction of a Seventeenth-Century Light Frigate"*

CLUES FROM THE ARCHIVES

In addition to the physical evidence, archival documents revealed much about the vessel. John de Bry of the Center for Historical Archaeology in Florida made the most important archival find in Rochefort, the small town on the west coast of France where *La Belle* was built. Inside a dusty book in the city's marine archives, he located a handwritten page dated 1684 and titled "Proportion of a *barque* named *La Belle* that was built at the port of Rochefort during the months of May and June 1684, of 40 to 45 tons." This was an official order approving the construction of *La Belle* and listing her major dimensions: a maximum beam of 14 *pied de roi* (14 feet 9 inches) and an overall length of 51 *pied de roi* (54 feet 4 inches). The document was drafted shortly after the completion of *La Belle*.

These measurements tell us that the length of the hull that remains today is only slightly smaller than it was originally. The capacity, or the amount of cargo the ship could carry, was listed in the order as 40 to 45 tons. But a recent analysis by J. C. Lemineur, a French histo-

rian who specializes in mathematically modeling the hull capacities of old ships, indicates that *La Belle*'s hold might have been closer to 47 to 52 tons.[3]

At the bottom of the document are the signatures of the Rochefort *conseil de construction*, four carpenters and four senior naval officers who approved the construction of new vessels.[4] The master shipwright in charge of building the vessel was Honoré Mallet, who signed with his initials, *HM*. The person responsible for the design of *La Belle* is thought to be Pierre Masson, a son-in-law of Mallet who signed with his last name.[5] Others who penned their signatures to the document include master carpenter Jean Guichard; the La Rochelle naval *intendant* Jean Gabaret; naval squadron commander François Colbert de Saint-Mars; and ship captains Alexandre-Adrien Chambon, Chevalier d'Arbouville, and Barthélemy d'Aralle, Chevalier de Perinnet.[6]

In later times, shipwrights used models or detailed line drawings to direct the construction of a ship, but in the late 1600s all that was required was a document that stated the vessel's critical dimensions. From these

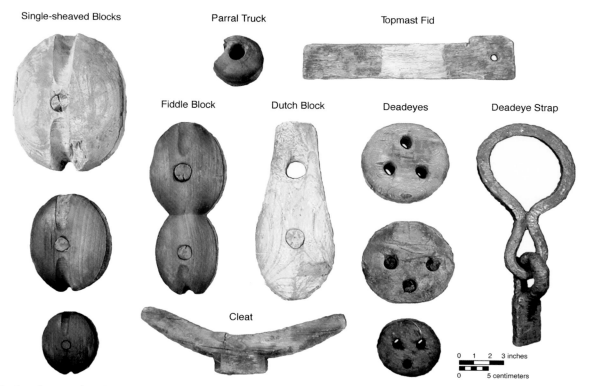

Single-sheaved Blocks   Parral Truck   Topmast Fid

Fiddle Block   Dutch Block   Deadeyes   Deadeye Strap

Cleat

0   1   2   3 inches
0   5 centimeters

Rigging elements found on *La Belle. Illustration courtesy Catharine Inbody Corder*

alone, shipwrights could build a complete vessel; minor details of design or function were left to their individual discretion. General rules had to be followed, however, and France was at that time attempting to exert more control over shipbuilding. A series of official regulations was issued about ship design and construction. Shipbuilding councils were established in each royal shipyard, and they met regularly to oversee the construction of new vessels. At the beginning of each year, the councils reviewed proposals from shipwrights for the construction of new ships. If a proposal was deemed acceptable, the council issued an official approval for construction. When completed, a document was drafted that identified the ship by name, listed its major measurements, and was signed by the council members.[7] This is precisely the document de Bry found in the Rochefort archives confirming the construction of *La Belle.*

A BARQUE LONGUE

On the basis of *La Belle*'s measurements, the French naval historian Jean Boudriot undertook a study to

recreate her on paper and in detailed scale models.[8] Boudriot has researched early French ships for more than forty years and is considered by many to be the leading authority on the topic. The discovery of the document with *La Belle*'s measurements was a key factor in his decision to take on the task. Boudriot thought that without this information any reconstruction would have been unacceptably speculative, because, as he saw it, too little of the upper part of the ship remained for an accurate reconstruction to be made on the basis of the archaeological evidence alone.

After studying historical documents concerning ships similar in shape or style, including *corvettes, petite frigates,* and *chattes,* Boudriot proposed that *La Belle* was a *barque longue,* a particular style of sailing ship that generally had three masts. The rear, or mizzenmast, was rigged fore-and-aft, while the mainmast and foremasts were square-rigged. From his examination of the only surviving plan for a *barque longue,* which was in the Danish royal archives, and from his years spent studying the Rochefort shipwrights, especially Pierre Masson and Honoré Mallet, Boudriot drew various views of *La Belle.* From these,

Dry dock in Rochefort, France, similar to the one where *La Belle* was assembled in 1684.

master model builder Bernard Frölich constructed two models of *La Belle,* one at 1:48 scale and another at 1:24.[9]

The drawings and models convince us that she was indeed a beautiful vessel, a sleek three-masted sailing ship with a draft of about eight feet. In France she might have been used to unload large vessels off the Atlantic coast and carry supplies into the shallow Charente River to the Rochefort docks. But she was also well suited for navigating the shallow bays, rivers, and coastlines of the New World, which made her ideal for La Salle's expedition.

Boudriot and Corder's work reveals that *La Belle's* mainmast was situated slightly aft of the center of the ship and connected to the bottom of the hull at the midship frame (a hull frame in the widest part of the ship). The foremast was located near the bow and connected to the hull bottom at the stem. Both of these masts had two sails, each square-rigged, an arrangement whereby the sails hang from spars, or yards, which themselves are attached perpendicularly to the mast. The mizzenmast had a triangular lateen sail, suspended from a yard attached diagonally to the mast. A bowsprit ex-

tended from the bow over the water and held another small square sail. The combination of a lateen and square sails made *La Belle* highly maneuverable.

The masts were held in place by standing rigging, consisting of large rope stays, back stays, and shrouds, that connected the masts to each other and to the ship's sides. When properly adjusted, the standing rigging held each mast firmly in place as the unfurled sails harnessed the wind. Running rigging, a series of ropes and blocks (pulleys), allowed *La Belle's* sails to be raised, adjusted, and lowered. Each sail would have been carefully trimmed for optimal performance. Given the relatively small number of sails, a minimal crew of trained sailors could have handled the vessel easily in all but the worst weather.

La Belle had only a single deck, so movement of the crew and passengers was limited. Six three-pound cannons were on deck, each on its own wooden carriage and strapped to the ship's side with the muzzle pointing out through a gun port. Even though *La Belle* was not built for battle, most ships of the time had to be ready for enemy attacks. A small covering over the bow formed the forecastle. Under this overhang, a

Proportion d'une barque Nommée *la belle* qui a esté construitte au port de Rochefort durant les mois de may et Juin 1684 du Roi de 40 a 45 Tonneaux.

Armement

Longueur de la quille portant sur terre . . . . 45 Piés
Longueur de l'estrave a l'estambot . . . . 51 P
Largeur de droit en dedans . . . . 14 P
Hauteur de l'estrave . . . . 12 P
Hauteur de l'estambot . . . . 11 P ½
Hauteur d'arcasse a de long . . . . 9 P 4 Pouces
Hauteur du fond de Cale . . . . 7 P 3 Pouces
Largeur des estrave . . . . 4 P 6 Pouces
Largeur de l'estambot . . . . 4 P 6 Pouces
Creux a la Maistresse varangue . . . . 9 P 4 Pouces
Hauteur de la ligne du bau mou en milieu . . . . 6 P 3 Pouces
Hauteur de la ligne du fort devant . . . . 9 P 4 Pouces
Hauteur de la ligne du fort darriere . . . . 13 P 6 Pouces
Hauteur du Clair en droitte ligne du maistre bau . . . . . . 7 P ½
Abaissement du son milieu . . . . 12 Pouces
Bauissement son Estrave . . . . 3 Piés 2 Pouces
Hauteur de la façon devant . . . . 4 Piés 6 Pouces
Hauteur de la façon d'arriere . . . . 3 P 6 Pouces

Fait a Rochefort le quinziéme Decembre 1684.

Major measurements for *La Belle* as approved by shipwrights in Rochefort, France. Before the middle of the eighteenth century, these measurements—rather than detailed drawings—were often the only direction needed by shipbuilders. An English translation of this document is on the next page.

small galley provided space for cooking. Just aft of the forecastle was the windlass, a large winch-like device that raised and lowered two anchors, which were located along either side of the bow, and helped raise and lower the ship's sails. The middle portion of the ship held a longboat, which provided the crew's only transportation ashore while she lay at anchor. Aft were the tiller for steering and the bridge where the ship's captain directed operations. In the very rear was the poop, a small upper deck.

COMPARTMENTS FOR CARGO, STORAGE, AND CREW

The ship had five compartments below deck. In the front was the bow compartment—measuring 11 feet

Proportion of a barque named *La Belle* that was built at the port of Rochefort during the months of May and June 1684, of 40 to 45 tons.

Firstly

1.	Length of the [footprint of the] keel on the ground	*45 feet*
2.	Length from stem to sternpost	*51 feet*
3.	Breadth	*14 feet*
4.	Length [height] of stem	*12 feet*
5.	Length [height] of sternpost	*11 feet 1/2*
6.	[Wing] transom	*9 feet 4 inches*
7.	Height [depth] of hold [from top of keelson]	*7 feet 3 inches*
8.	Rake of stempost	*4 feet 6 inches*
9.	Rake of sternpost	*1 foot 6 inches*
10.	Flat of master floor	*9 feet 4 inches*
11.	Height of the line of extreme breadth amidships	*6 feet 3 inches*
12.	Height of the aft line of extreme breadth	*9 feet 4 inches*
13.	Height of the forward line of extreme breadth	*13 feet 6 inches*
14.	[Depth of] hold in straight line with master beam [to top of floors]	*7 feet 1/2*
15.	Tumblehome amidships	*12 inches*
16.	Tumblehome [offset between max. beam and wing transom]	*3 feet 2 inches*
17.	Height of narrowing of the forward tail frame	*5 feet 6 inches*
18.	Height of narrowing of the aft tail frame	*3 feet 6 inches*

Done at Rochefort the fifteenth of December 1684

GABARET
HM [Honoré Mallet]
GUICHARD
P. MALLET
COLBERT de ST. MARS
MASSON
LE CHEVALIER dePERRINET
LE CHEVALIER D'ARBOURVILLE

English translation of the document shown on previous page. The numbers at left were not part of the original document.

5 inches long, 12 feet wide at its widest point, and 7 feet high—which contained the hawser, or anchor rope, and was accessible from up top through a deck hatch. The rope, coiled in the center of the hold, could be easily uncoiled when the ship's two anchors were lowered. The bow compartment also served as the crew's cramped sleeping quarters; their hammocks would have hung from the deck above, and wooden platforms may have served as bunks.

Immediately aft, separated from the bow compartment by a bulkhead, was the main hold, measuring 16 feet 5 inches long, slightly less than 14 feet wide, and about 7.5 feet at its highest. It was accessible from another hatch on deck. Here the ship's cargo was stored.

The goods were mostly in barrels and boxes, stowed so tightly that they interlocked and could not move independently of the ship, a distinct advantage in rough waters at sea. At the rear of this hold was a small locker enclosing the two pumps for removing water from the bilge. The handles for operating the pumps were on deck immediately aft of the main mast. Especially heavy cargo, such as cannon balls or lead shot, were stored as ballast outside the locker in the deepest part of the hull, supplementing the stone ballast also deposited there.

The aft cargo hold, separated by a bulkhead from the main hold, was located to the rear of the main hold. It was about 10 feet long and 12 feet wide, with its height

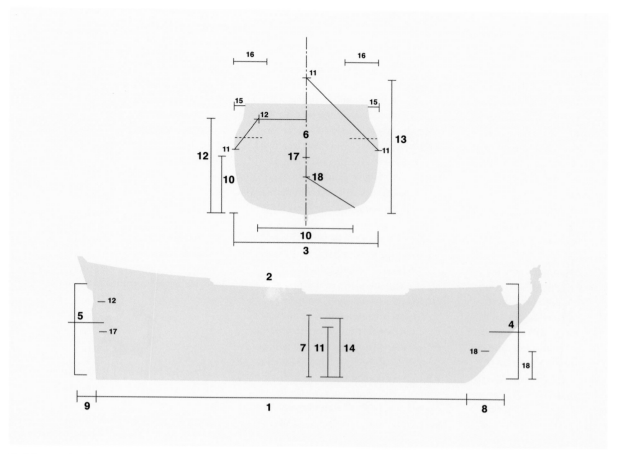

Position on the ship of *La Belle*'s major measurements (numbers correspond to those in the translation of the historical document approving the ship's construction shown on facing page); after Boudriot, 2000.

at 7 feet. Here provisions such as cured meat, water, and wine were stored. A hatch from the deck above gave access to the cargo.

The lazarette, a small hold in the stern, stored spare weaponry, including gunpowder. It measured about 9 feet in greatest length, about 12 feet in greatest width, and between 5 to 7 feet in height, a result of the marked curvature of the rear of the hull as it narrowed and rose toward the stern.

The lazarette's hatch opened into the stern cabin immediately above, a small room thought to be about 6 feet long and 5 feet high, which would have been furnished with a hammock for sleeping and a small table for charting the ship's course and keeping the daily log. This cabin would have been occupied by the ship's captain.

La Belle was small, designed to carry only crew and cargo, with no special accommodations for pas-sengers. Any aboard during her journey across the Atlantic would have been confined to the deck in all but the worst weather, when they might seek the shelter of the forecastle or climb into one of the holds to sit on cargo if space permitted. This ship was built to maneuver in shallow waters, not to transport people upon the high seas.

THE SHIP KIT

The archaeological remains of the hull provide much information about how *La Belle* was designed and built. Among the more intriguing characteristics of the ship were the roman numerals followed by a letter carved into the side of the keel and onto many of the major framing timbers. It became clear that these alphanumeric designations represented a systematic number-

By the summer of 1997, *La Belle* had been dismantled and shipped to College Station, and millions of dollars had been raised and spent on the recovery. Then, unexpectedly, the French government filed an official claim for the ship and its contents. France argued that official documents declared *La Belle* to be a royal naval vessel owned by the king in 1684 and that she therefore remained a possession under the control of the French government.

Two documents found in the dusty archives of the port city of Rochefort support this claim. Both are official listings of the vessels belonging to King Louis XIV. One dated 1688 lists *La Belle* as a *barque longue* of fifty tons and six cannons. A notation to the left of the entry states that the ship "is in Mexico under the command of Mr. De La Salle." Another document prepared a year later also describes *La Belle* as having a capacity of fifty tons and six cannons but adds that she was built by "H. Mallet" and had a draught of seven feet (7.5 feet in modern English measurement). A notation to the right reads, "Mr. De La Salle took her to Mexico from where she has not yet returned." One on the left adds that the "crew is not indicated because the pilot who has just returned said that she no longer exists."[1] The latter entry undoubtedly refers to *La Belle*'s third captain, Pierre Tessier, who after participating in the murder of La Salle in 1687, walked to Quebec and boarded a ship for the return to France, where he provided information about the loss of *La Belle*. Obviously, though, he kept his involvement in the murder a secret.

The International Law of the Sea, the legal authority governing how nations use and respect the world's major bodies of water, gives ownership of official naval vessels to the flag nation—the country for which a ship flies a flag. Armed with these historical documents and international law, the French government filed its claim with the U.S. State Department. The State Department forwarded the claim to the governor of Texas, whose legal team, together with members of the Texas Historical Commission, assessed the claim and considered how to address the French assertion of ownership. In the closing days of the Clinton administration, Secretary of State Madeleine Albright conceded the claim in favor of France, setting the stage for the development of an international treaty. Negotiations took place in 2000 and 2001, culminating in a meeting in Paris among officials of the Texas Historical Commission, the Texas Attorney General's Office, the U.S. State Department, and members of the French government. This meeting resolved the issue in favor of French ownership and became the basis of an international accord settling the dispute. The agreement, signed in the Treaty Room of the U.S. State Department on March 31, 2003, gives title to France, some oversight to the Musée national de la Marine in Paris, but relinquishes day-to-day control in perpetuity to the Texas Historical Commission. A traveling exhibit of artifacts for France is encouraged, as are scholarly exchanges between U.S. and French researchers.

The accord refers to an accompanying administrative agreement, which contains a number of stipulations about the curation, care, and exhibition of *La Belle* artifacts and publications about them. One stipulation, important for this book, is that any publication about *La Belle* must include the following statement: "Property of France from the collection of the Musée national de la Marine located in Paris, France." The museum's logo, shown below, must also appear.

Thus, this book has just complied with the terms of the international agreement.

Was the treaty advantageous to Texas? Perhaps the answer is best stated as follows: The agreement obeys the conventions of international law and settles in an amicable manner the final title and control of *La Belle*. The ship sailed to the New World amid international contention, and she has been resurrected against a new dawn of contention. But this time the dispute was resolved by the order of law and not the might of a conquering power.

Note

1. John de Bry, "Fleshing Out the Cultural History of *La Belle* and the La Salle Expedition (1684–1687): Archival Research in French Repositories," on file at Texas Historical Commission.

ing system. *La Belle* had been divided into four quadrants, with the main mast as the center of the four parts. The forward portion of the keel, from the main mast to the bow, was assigned roman numerals followed by the letter *A* for the French word *avant,* or front. From the mast to the rear of the keel, the roman numerals were followed by a *D* for *derrière,* the French word for rear or aft. Roman numerals labeled the ship's frames, sometimes called "ribs" by lay people, with the main mast in the center of the ship as the starting point

Drawing of *La Belle* by the French naval historian Jean Boudriot, who conducted extensive research into the *barque longue* ship type and the master shipwright, Mallet, who was responsible for building *La Belle. Courtesy Jean Boudriot, www.ancre.fr*

and having an asterisk (*) designation for the midship frames. From the main mast to the bow, the frames were numbered from I to XI and from I to XVII from the main mast to the stern. A letter *T* for *tribord* and a *B* for *babord* were also put on some frames to designate them as belonging to the starboard or port sides of the ship, respectively.

Of the hundreds of shipwrecks around the world, very few have been labeled in this manner. Although this numbering system seemed fairly straightforward, exactly how it related to the ship's construction was unknown. Once again, we returned to archival sources to shed some light on the matter. Bernard Allaire, a professional archivist in Bordeaux who has spent considerable time among French archives, searched the naval archives of Rochefort. There he found a dispatch dating from 1684 that stated that four *barques longues* were in port at that time.[10] Two were seaworthy, but they had been reserved to patrol the waters against pirate attacks on French shipping vessels. A third was needed for another purpose, but there was an unassembled *barque longue,* the dispatch declared, that could be used by La Salle.

Other historical documents Allaire found indicate that La Salle intended to load the pieces of this vessel onto one of his other ships, *Le Joly,* and carry it as cargo across the ocean. Yet another document from the

French archives referring to *barques longues* suggests that only major frame timbers were transported, with other elements such as planking to be made from locally available wood sources. "We will only have to carry in bundles the members of the *barques longues* staying in the said Islands [Caribbean] to be planked with pear tree from America after their arrival," the document states.[11]

More than likely, the frames of the vessel would have been accompanied by the ship's rigging. In fact, La Salle had six years earlier shipped rigging for the construction of two vessels to Canada and then transported the materials up the St. Lawrence. One of the ships, the *Griffon,* was constructed on Lake Erie; the other was to be built along the Illinois River, but was never finished.[12]

In this case, however, the ship that would carry the unassembled parts, *Le Joly,* was already fully loaded with supplies for the colony. Either another, larger ship would have to be made available to carry the unassembled ship or it would have to be put together. The question of whether a ship like *La Belle* could make an ocean voyage must have been posed, judging by a passage in another document Allaire found: "We, the undersigned officers of the port and Royal Pilots, unanimously agree that a bark of 40 to 50 tons, put in good condition, can easily make the crossing from the coast of

Model of *La Belle* built by Bernard Frölich. *Photograph courtesy Jean Boudriot, www.ancre.fr*

France to that of Canada, with its load well-distributed, especially in the season we are entering now. . . ."[13]

So the evidence suggests that *La Belle* began as a shipbuilder's "kit," like that for a model.[14] The roman numerals and letters on the timbers were labels to assist in the ship's later assembly. This finding was fascinating, although Allaire's subsequent research showed that this situation was not unique. Some eight years after *La Belle* had been in the Rochefort shipyard, yet another *barque longue* lay in labeled pieces, awaiting assembly.[15]

But why would La Salle have wanted to transport an unassembled ship? Would it not have been preferable to take an intact ship that could transport not only itself but also cargo for the colony, instead of one that would be cargo itself? Part of the answer may lie in

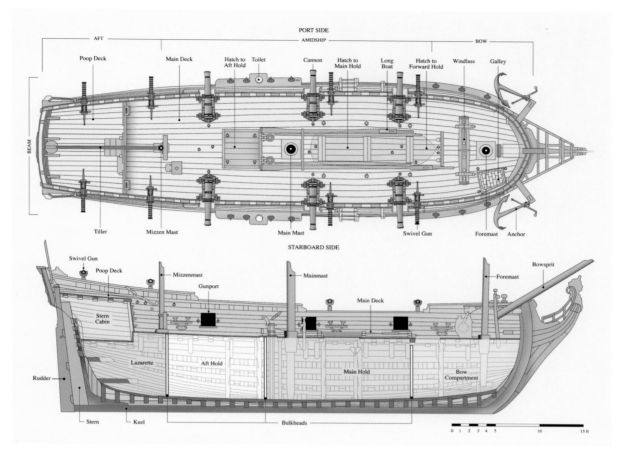

Views of *La Belle* based on archaeological remains and historical documents; after Boudriot, 2000.

the quoted passage above: the officers and royal pilots thought La Salle was headed for *Canada,* not the Gulf of Mexico. The crew roll of *l'Aimable* provides additional evidence that La Salle's original destination was Canada. It refers to the "roll of the officers, mariners and sailors who comprise the crew of the ship *l'Aimable* for the passage to the coast of *Canada*" [emphasis added].

Further evidence for a planned Canadian route comes from a letter La Salle wrote his mother shortly before setting sail for the New World:

Madame and most honored mother,
At last, having waited a long time for the favorable wind, and having had many difficulties to overcome, we are leaving with four ships and nearly four hundred men. Everyone is well, including little Colin and my nephew. We all have high hopes of a favorable outcome. We are not going by way of Canada but through the Gulf of Mexico. We fervently wish that the result of this voyage may
contribute to your repose and comfort. Assuredly, I shall spare no effort [to that end]. I beg you to preserve yourself for the love of us.[16]

While some have speculated that La Salle deliberately spread misinformation about the expedition's destination, the archival records indicate that this was not the case. As the letter to his mother suggests, he had previously informed her that he was going by way of Canada, as this is the direction he wanted to travel, but was now correcting her about his itinerary.

Recent work by Robert Weddle, project historian for the La Salle shipwreck investigation, helped unravel this part of the puzzle.[17] Letters and other documents La Salle wrote in the months leading up to his expedition show that he was indecisive about the best way to get to the mouth of the Mississippi River. A journey through the Caribbean and into the Gulf of Mexico would be the direct route, but it would be difficult. The explorer was uncertain that he could even find the Mis-

View of the hull from the stern end showing the bulkheads that separate the bow compartment, main hold, and aft hold.

Belle was assembled in two months and readied for the voyage.

FURTHER CLUES IN THE TIMBERS

When we dismantled *La Belle*'s hull three centuries later, we discovered distinctive marks that revealed still more about her construction. Saw, adze, chisel, gouge, and auger marks revealed the tools and techniques the shipwrights used to build *La Belle*. Timbers were fastened together with iron bolts or square spikes and with wooden treenails. Many of the bolts had metal wedges inserted at one end to lock them into place. The treenails were driven into pre-drilled holes, and the ends were sawed off. Then a wooden wedge was driven into the exposed end to secure it.

The interior and exterior surfaces of the frames that formed the ship's interior support were covered with planks running from bow to stern. These planks helped form the sides of the hull and added overall strength. The spaces between the exterior planks were caulked with oakum, a mixture of hemp (or some other fiber) and tar. We actually found twisted strands of oakum still preserved between some of planks.

While the hull was being cleaned and conserved, Taras Pevny, a graduate student in Texas A&M's nautical archaeology program, noticed several surmarks— small carved lines—cut into the frames.[18] As mentioned before, seventeenth-century shipbuilders relied on several critical measurements, such as those identified in the official order for *La Belle*'s construction. From these measurements, the master shipwright used a geometric system made up of a series of arcs that dictated the shape and size of the individual frames. The arcs would become progressively shorter and narrower from the widest point—the middle of the ship—to the bow and stern. The hull tapered in those two directions, giving the vessel its boat-like form and making it seaworthy.

Pevny observed that the shipwrights had put surmarks on every third frame. These would have been used to trace the curvature of the hull from stem to stern. The surmarks show that every third set of frames was cut first and put into place. Then, using these first frames as a guide, the other frames were cut and placed in between.

Additional analysis of the hull is being undertaken by Toni Carrell of Ships of Discovery in Corpus Christi. Carrell, the assistant project director of the excavation,

sissippi River by this southerly voyage. He would be sailing waters uncharted by French ships, and the geography of the coastline and even the location of the river's mouth were not well known. On the other hand, it was easy to sail to Canada, as many French ships did each year. From Canada, La Salle was sure he could find the mouth of the Mississippi simply by following his route of two years earlier. This itinerary would require a small, unassembled vessel that could be portaged at key points such as Niagara Falls along the St. Lawrence River and then transported overland to the Illinois River, where she could be assembled for the journey down the Mississippi.

Unfortunately for La Salle, Louis XIV was more interested in an expedition that traversed the Gulf of Mexico, then claimed by Spain as its sole dominion. Louis wanted to challenge Spain's exclusive right to the gulf, and since he was providing half or more of the expedition's funds, La Salle had to concede. The selection of the southerly route meant that La Salle had no need for an unassembled *barque longue*. In 1684 *La*

Overhead view of the mast step, pump locker, and bulkhead separating the main and aft cargo holds.

Letter *T* (for the French *tribord*, or starboard) on hull frame timber and roman numeral IIII (today's IV). The label indicates that this timber is on the starboard side and the frame is the fourth from the ship's main mast.

took on the task of analyzing and preparing a report on the hull.[19] One of her fascinating discoveries relates to the two dominant methods of shipbuilding in Europe at the time. Honoré Mallet, the master shipwright, was from Toulon in the southern region of France, where he learned Mediterranean shipbuilding methods, rather than those of shipwrights working in the port cities on the Atlantic coast of Europe.[20] Most French ships of the day were built by shipwrights trained along the Atlantic. Shortly before *La Belle* was constructed,

the secretary of the navy, Jean-Baptiste Colbert, was attempting to invigorate France's shipbuilding industry, and he sought to merge the two schools of ship design by bringing craftsmen trained in the Mediterranean techniques to Rochefort.

We know from descriptions of Atlantic and Mediterranean shipbuilding that both groups began a ship's design in the same way—for example, by determining the vessel's overall proportions and locating the midship frame in the central part of the vessel. But the two

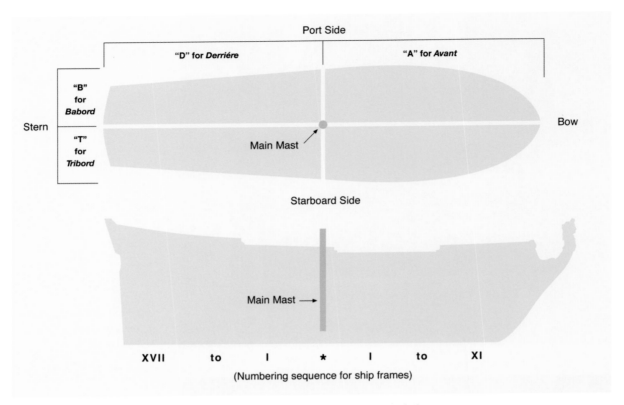

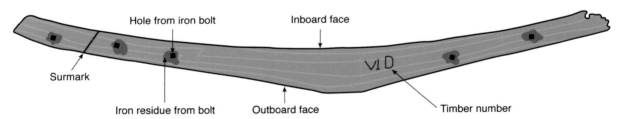

Major timbers of *La Belle* were numbered by the shipwright, using roman numerals for the frames from the main mast toward the bow and stern and alphabetic characters dividing the ship into quadrants. The presence of these numbers supports historical documents that show *La Belle* was built as a kit to be assembled in the New World. *Illustration by Roland Pantermuehl*

Frame labeled *VID,* the roman numeral VI followed by the letter *D* for *derrière,* or stern. The label indicates that this is the sixth timber from the main mast towards the stern. Note the surmark carved into the timber to aid the shipwright in assembling the ship. *Illustration by Roland Pantermuehl*

traditions diverged in how the frames fore and aft of the midship frame were formed. The evidence shows that both were employed to construct *La Belle.* Some of the frames that form the sides of the hull were tipped outward, which was a Mediterranean method. However, the timbers that form the bottom of the hull were progressively shortened and those that form the sides were increased in height, an Atlantic method. While several examples of the Atlantic style are known to ex-

ist, *La Belle* contains the first archaeological evidence of the Mediterranean method and clearly shows that the two styles had been merged at the port of Rochefort.

SCARCE TREES AND OLD SHIP TIMBERS

When Colbert took control of the French navy in 1661, he found it suffering from serious neglect, in part because building materials had become scare. By the early

Louis XIV's minister, Jean-Baptiste Colbert, who reorganized France's industry, commerce, and navy. *Illustration courtesy Musée national de la Marine*

1660s, the mismanaged forests of France had been overcut. Colbert imposed royal control over the forests and began to regulate logging, but the fact that only trees with certain shapes could be used exacerbated the problem.[21] Because ships' hulls are curved, trees that approximated the curvature of the frames were desirable, and, in fact, trees were sometimes trained as they grew to assume seaworthy shapes.

Carrell discovered that the French were dealing with deforestation in an additional way. She submitted very small samples of wood from twenty-six frame timbers to the Laboratoire d'Analyses et d'Expertises en Archéologie et Oeuvre d'Art in Bordeaux. Their dendrochronological analysis of the timbers showed that nearly all had been chopped down more than twenty years before *La Belle* was constructed.[22] This was sur-

Illustration of how trees of various shapes were selected for specific ship timbers. *Illustration by Roland Pantermuehl*

prising. But it was astonishing to learn that some of the timbers had probably been cut as early as 1460, more than two hundred years before *La Belle* was built.

Carrell concluded that the French were practicing systematic reuse of wood from old ships. Considering that ships of that time remained seaworthy for about twenty years, it is likely that several of the major timbers in *La Belle* had been recycled from other vessels.[23] Certain frames of great antiquity must have been recycled repeatedly. Before they made the long journey from France to the New World with La Salle in 1684, some timbers may have traveled the world's seas for decades as parts of other ships.

Most of *La Belle*'s timbers came from forests in the Charente River region of France, which is the middle part of the west coast, centered around Rochefort. The wood of four timbers could not be confidently placed within this region and may have been imported from another area of Europe.[24]

Seventy-three percent of the timbers were made of French white oak. Oak is generally preferred for shipbuilding because of its hardness and durability. All of *La Belle*'s frames, keel, keelson, deck beams, and planking were made of this oak. About 21 percent of the timbers were made of European pine; this wood was used in the construction of the bulkheads, which divided the ship below deck into compartments, and the ship's pump. European fir was used for three percent of the hull, mostly for selected support posts. Elm, spruce, and live oak were also identified. The presence of live oak was at first perplexing, since it is generally considered a North American species. There is no indication in the archival records that *La Belle* was repaired while in service along the Texas coast, and therefore the live oak is probably a Mediterranean species rather than a New World live oak.[25] Since only the bottom of the hull survived, we do not know what the decks and cabins were made of, but similar types of wood, especially oak, seem likely.

By using dendrochronological analysis, Carrell was also able to determine the age of the trees when they were harvested, though some had too few growth rings for an accurate assessment to be made. Sixteen of the twenty-six samples came from trees more than one hundred years old when cut and the rest from younger trees, with the youngest between sixty and sixty-nine years old.

LA BELLE'S ORIGINS: A STORY TOLD

Through rigorous study of the archaeological remains, from searches of the archives of France, and by construction of detailed scale models, the story of *La Belle*'s origins has come to light. *La Belle* was a beautiful vessel: a *barque longue* with three masts, a single deck, five compartments below deck, including a small stern cabin that provided accommodations for the ship's captain. She was intended to move goods across water, not to transport passengers. Her construction represented a merging of two different styles of seventeenth-century ship construction as part of a royal effort to modernize the shipbuilding practices of the French navy.

Pieces of the petite vessel, many of them recycled

from other ships, lay unassembled in the Rochefort shipyard until La Salle claimed them in 1684. At first he wanted the ship to remain in pieces so that it could be transported to Canada and assembled later. The major frame timbers were labeled with numbers to assist in their assembly. The political struggle between France and Spain ruined La Salle's plan, however, when the French king forced La Salle to sail through the Gulf of Mexico instead. This required that *La Belle* be assembled and sailed directly to the New World.

During her crossing of the Atlantic Ocean, *La Belle*'s cargo holds would have been stuffed with supplies for the colonial adventure, and any passengers would have been confined to the deck or below deck to share accommodations with the cargo. Only the captain and crew would have had accommodations, and these would have been modest at best.

Ultimately La Salle's fears about the southerly route to reach the Mississippi River were justified. He failed to find the mouth of the river, and as a consequence, tragedy befell his entire enterprise, including the loss of *La Belle.* La Salle's misfortune, however, was good luck for the twentieth-century archaeologists who recovered an exceptionally well-preserved shipwreck that yielded extraordinary insights into seventeenth-century shipbuilding.

Chapter Six

CARGO FOR A COLONY

La Belle turned out to be more than simply a well-preserved vessel: she contained a wonderful array of cargo, a unique time capsule.[1] These materials were similar to what most explorers took with them as they journeyed to the New World, but here—through a chance occurrence—they remained virtually untouched, waiting for us to uncover them. Essentially, the artifacts, numbering more than one million, represent a "kit" for building a colony in the seventeenth-century New World, and we had the rare opportunity to peer back in time to see what a colonial enterprise required.

Before we started our excavation, we had important clues about what we should find aboard *La Belle* from several historical documents. Most important is a statement La Salle drew up before leaving Fort St. Louis in October, 1685, to search for the Mississippi River. La Salle had the following materials loaded onto *La Belle*:

For that purpose they put on board La Belle *4,000 livres of dried meat and 800 livres of fat, besides the 800 livres of bacon, 2 livres of butter, 6 casks of wine, 4 of brandy,*

3 of vinegar, with the salt, oil and 108 hundredweight of bread or flour which were already on the vessel. All the boxes, clothing, papers, utensils, linen and plates and dishes belonging to the Sieur de La Salle and the monks, officers and private persons in his company were also put on board, and all the goods, over 2,000 livres in gold, arms, tools, cannon, 40 hundredweight of powder, nearly 50 hundredweight of lead, the petards, the forge and everything needed for [La Salle's] purpose.[2]

Henri Joutel, chronicler of the expedition, adds that some smoked buffalo meat and eight pigs were also loaded aboard the ship as provisions for the crew.[3] After *La Belle* wrecked in February, 1686, the survivors rescued some cargo:

[A] number of things were saved among them La Salle's clothes, specifically one scarlet dress coat and another blue coat with large gold braid, as well as some of his papers, dampened though they were. Chefdeville took care to dry them. They were careful to bring some barrels of meal ashore and a few casks of wine which were the most

Brass hawk bells from the main cargo hold.

necessary. *After this they tried to save some linen clothing belonging to La Salle, his brother, and Chefdeville. They also saved a few beads and other similar things.*

They went on board almost every day for this purpose, bringing what they could each time until a wind blew in from the sea that stirred up the waves and made the hull of the ship settle deep into the sand.[4]

And finally, when the Spanish discovered *La Belle* in April, 1687, they found some cargo on shore and took some of the ship's rigging and artillery:

We gathered up some cordage that still might be serviceable for us and embarked the 5 pieces (cannons) for ballast, two of them in our galley. We also took an anchor of up to 6 quintales and some 30 fathoms of 8-inch cable, half of which was divided into strands for yarn. On the beach were found the other gun carriage and the main yard, which was measured and found to be 16 cubits. Therefore I am saying that the ship's keel is 24 cubits. We brought this yard and that of the fore topsail for making oars, and from that of the foresail a boom was made for oars. Captain Pedro de Yriarte took that of the mizzen

also. There were found some large smith's bellows and some other very small ones of hand type, a large cooper's plane, some leaves torn from an arithmetic and artillery book in the French language with a piece of map, from which I conclude that she was a French ship.[5]

These historical documents tell us that, while some cargo was salvaged, much was not, probably due to the strong southerly winds that drove the hull deeply into the bed of Matagorda Bay.

Armed with this information, we began excavation of the ship's contents. We found cargo in the ship's holds, packed in wooden casks, or barrels, and in wooden boxes. Some larger items, such as cannons, cannon balls, and large grinding stones, were found individually, carefully stacked in between the casks and boxes.

Eighty-five barrels were recovered, made mostly of white oak staves, though some were of beech and willow. Split willow and chestnut branches formed the hoops of all but the largest casks, which had iron hoops. A wicker-like binding held the ends of the willow hoops together.

La Belle's cargo was stored in wooden barrels, as shown above, and in a few wooden boxes.

The casks stored five basic commodities: liquids such as water or wine in the largest casks; tars or resins for ship repair and waterproofing in medium-size casks; gunpowder in smaller casks; lead shot and birdshot in the smallest containers; and dry goods such as ship's tackle, iron tools, and trade goods in casks of varying sizes.

Ten wooden boxes, or chests, were recovered during the excavation. Although detailed wood identifications have not been completed, they all appear to be made of sawn white pine boards. One empty box was found off the bow of the ship and, based on its style, appears to be a chest that once held someone's personal items. Two boxes contained trade goods, another contained carpentry tools and other items, and four held muskets and swords. Another contained kettles, pewter plates, candlestick holders, and a ladle. The end of another box was found, but none of its contents were preserved. All but one of the barrels and boxes were found within the hull.

In the main hold, we excavated sixty-three casks and seven packing crates, which were still arranged exactly as they had been when loaded into La Belle more than three centuries ago—oriented to fit tightly together to prevent shifting while at sea.[6] Behind the main hold, the aft hold also contained cargo—rope coils, brass wire, twenty-two barrels, and two boxes. The barrels and boxes held gunpowder, bird shot, water, trade goods, and tar or resin—but unlike in the main hold, they were in a jumbled mess. Why was this cargo in such disarray when the adjoining hold con-

tained everything in precise arrangement? We had to excavate down farther to figure it out. When we reached the bottom of the aft hold we discovered that underneath the jumbled layer was another stratigraphic layer containing bricks from a cooking galley, butchered animal bones, empty wine bottles, eating utensils such as forks and spoons, and some pieces from board games.

While at sea, the aft hold would have been fully loaded with supplies, but at some point, probably while La Belle was anchored in Matagorda Bay waiting for La

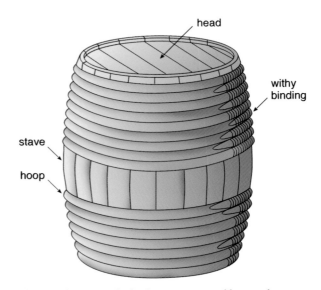

The barrels consisted of oak staves wrapped by wooden hoops bound by wicker-like binding, called *withies*. Illustration by Roland Pantermuehl

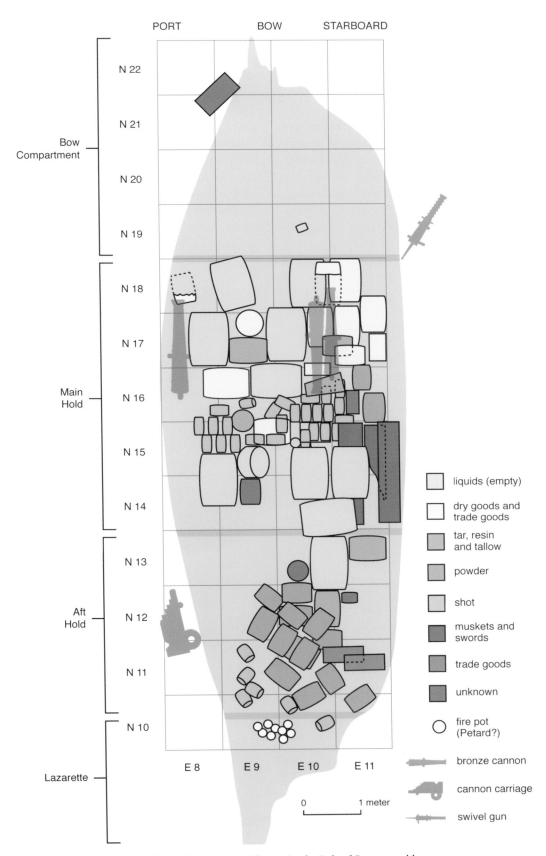

PORT   BOW   STARBOARD

N 22
N 21

Bow
Compartment

N 20

N 19

N 18

N 17

Main
Hold

N 16

N 15

N 14

N 13

Aft
Hold

N 12

N 11

N 10

Lazarette

E 8   E 9   E 10   E 11

liquids (empty)

dry goods and
trade goods

tar, resin
and tallow

powder

shot

muskets and
swords

trade goods

unknown

○ fire pot
(Petard?)

bronze cannon

cannon carriage

swivel gun

0   1 meter

Distribution of barrels and boxes in the wreck. *Illustration by Roland Pantermuehl*

Salle's return, the central portion of the aft hold was emptied to provide a place for the crew to go below deck and escape from the cold winter winds. Here they cooked and ate, drank wine, and even played board games, with the cargo neatly stacked around them. At some point, probably when *La Belle* was wrecked during the storm, the cargo around this central open area tumbled into the empty interior and was mixed by waves. At the same time, sailcloth and rigging stored in the hold became dislodged and were also mixed by the seawater, much as a washing machine churns clothing. Over time the destructive forces of the sea attacked the ship relentlessly. The bulkhead separating the aft hold from the lazarette, a small hold at the rear of the vessel, gave way. The lazarette held spare weaponry, including gunpowder and bird shot, which then spilled into the aft hold, adding to the chaos.

The top portion of the lazarette did not survive because it was not covered by Matagorda Bay sediments. The very bottom portion, however, was intact and contained nine firepots, incendiary devices for use against enemy ships, resting directly on the hull. Much like Molotov cocktails, these objects were small earthenware jars filled with a combustible liquid. Their wide mouths were plugged with a wooden stopper through which a fuse passed. Four of the firepots also contained grenades with separate fuses, and another contained a solid iron cannonball.[7]

Most of La Salle's cargo was not weaponry but trade goods purchased in France. The explorer and many of his men hoped to profit personally and handsomely from bartering with the native peoples. Louis XIV had granted La Salle the right to trade with the Indians for furs and hides. Beaver-skin hats were popular in France at the time, so cured beaver skins in particular would bring a good price.[8] In return the Indians would receive trinkets like glass beads, brass pins, bells, and rings.

CURRENCY FOR A TRADING COLONY

GLASS BEADS. Like most early explorers of the Americas, La Salle brought glass beads for trade with the native peoples, and beads were by far the most numerous trade items discovered in the cargo hold. La Salle learned of the Indians' attraction to the shiny, brightly colored objects during his expeditions in the Great

Firepot from the lazarette area that functioned much like a Molotov cocktail. A grenade (bottom left) with a wooden fuse was placed inside a ceramic jar filled with a flammable liquid and covered by a lid with a fuse (bottom right). *Photograph by Jim Bonar*

Glass beads found during the screening of mud in the wreck. *Photograph by Jim Bonar*

Lakes region, where he had often made contact with Shawnee, Illinois, Miami, and other native groups. The trade beads became part of necklaces and sacred ritual items and were often sewn onto clothing.

We found an estimated 790,000 glass beads on *La Belle.* The exact number is not known since they were so numerous and found in nearly every part of the ship. When Barto Arnold used the prop-wash deflector as a "blower" to remove sediments during testing of the wreck in 1995, a barrel was apparently blown apart, scattering beads and other goods across the wreck. Such use of a blower is controversial because it can cause damage, but the technique can also quickly uncover parts of a ship for better examination. At the time, Arnold was not sure what the shipwreck might hold, and he needed to assess it quickly. The blower enabled him to uncover artifacts that identified the ship as *La Belle.* It did damage the wreck, however, and in retrospect should not have been used as much as it was.

Most of the beads from *La Belle* are what archaeologists call *seed beads;* they are approximately the size of a small plant seed. Made with the drawn technique, they are in a variety of colors, with blue the most common, followed by white, black, green, and red. There were also about 2,500 larger beads, also fashioned using the drawn technique.

One of our most striking discoveries was a box in the aft hold containing 568,798 tiny glass seed beads. Bead boxes are described in historical documents, but to actually see one in an archaeological context was truly exciting. The contents of this single wooden box probably more than doubled the number of French

trade beads recovered from all North American archaeological sites. The box was made of white pine boards and measured 28 inches long, 11 inches wide, and 11 inches deep. The beads lay in rows, indicating that they had once been strung together. Further excavation showed that they were in fact strung by color, with all of the blue beads in one part of the box, white in another, and so on. The box was so well preserved that toward the bottom we even found some of the string holding the beads together. The ends of the strings were attached to a larger cord about $\frac{1}{5}$ inch in diameter. For easy access, each larger cord held beads of only one color. If La Salle wanted a selection of beads, he could take many strands at once by grabbing the cord that held them together. If he wanted only blue beads, he could remove the selected strands from the cord and carry just those with him.

Straw packing, still preserved, had been placed on the bottom of the box, the beads laid on top, and another layer of straw placed over the top of the beads. The lid was nailed shut. This suggests that the container, acquired in France, was never opened in the New World; the beads were probably reserved for the Mississippi River colony. Subsequent analysis indicated that they were likely made in Venice, which supports a historical French document of the period stating that *perles de Venise* (or Venetian "pearls") were acquired for use within France and for export to the colonies.[9] We know from Henri Joutel's journal that glass beads were traded to the Caddo Indians of East Texas: "I wanted . . . to make some present to them to thank them for their welcome. With this intention, I drew

*V*enice was the leading manufacturer of glass beads from the sixteenth through eighteenth centuries. The technique for making drawn glass beads is described in several historical documents. Suitable glass in the desired color was collected and heated into a molten state. A portion of the glass was then attached to the end of a hollow metal rod and air was blown into the center to form a cylindrical shape. Another glassmaker then attached another rod to the end of the molten glass opposite the first rod. The two glassmakers then quickly ran in opposite directions, stretching the glass into a very long, thin tube. Some of the tubes would reach one thousand feet or more in length. Once cooled and hardened, the tube would be cut into one-yard lengths and sent to other workers for further processing.

The tubes were then cut into tiny portions the size of seeds. To smooth the sharp cut edges, they were immersed in a mixture of ash and sand and agitated until the holes in the beads were filled. The beads were then placed in a large metal vessel, and more sand and ash were added. The metal vessel was heated and the beads were continually stirred until the heat smoothed the rough edges and gave the beads their spherical quality. The ash and sand mixture in the holes kept the beads from collapsing. The beads were cooled and washed to remove the sand from the holes, and finally, according to a nineteenth-century source, they were "strung by children upon separate threads, made up into bundles, and packed in casks for exportation."[1] The wooden bead box from *La Belle* was probably assembled in this way.

Notes

The primary sources for this feature are Roderick Sprague, "Glass Trade Beads: A Progress Report," *Historical Archaeology* 19, no. 2 (1985): 88; and Peter Francis, Jr., *The Glass Trade Beads of Europe, Their Manufacture, Their History, and Their Identification.*

1. Dionysius Lardner, *A Treatise on the Origin, Progressive Improvement, and Present State of the Manufacture of Porcelain and Glass.*

out . . . a few glass beads to give to the women, but we made them understand that it would be necessary to give us some provisions and that we would give them something else in exchange. They gave us a sign that they would do this."[10]

PINS AND NEEDLES. Nearly 15,600 small pins made from brass wire were found on *La Belle,* mostly in the main cargo hold. We recovered many from the soil encasing the cargo that were probably scattered when the blower damaged a barrel during testing in 1995. Several pins were found still housed in a partial barrel that was split longitudinally, representing about one-third of the original container. This portion of the barrel held items packed into small compartments, each containing a different kind of trade item. In one, several dozen brass pins were all aligned in the same direction, as if they had been pinned to a piece of cloth.

The manufacture of the brass pins in France was a labor-intensive activity. Workers cut brass wire into short lengths of about 1 to 1.5 inches. One end was filed to a point, and a shorter, thinner piece of wire was wrapped around the other end to make the head. The two pieces of wire at the head were anchored by a specialized machine that stamped the head of the pin. Because of the labor required, brass pins were relatively

Wooden box containing 568,798 glass trade beads from the aft cargo hold (10 cm scale).

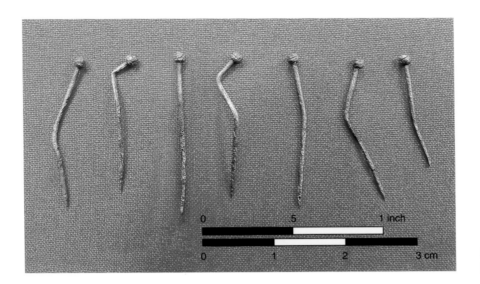

Brass pins used for trade with the Texas Indians.

expensive items in France and remained so until the early nineteenth century, when their manufacture became entirely mechanized.[11]

Several examples of iron needles, with eyes for threading, were also found. Joutel describes trading needles for animal hides: "One [of the Indians] had a finely dressed deer skin that was white as snow. I asked him by signs if he wanted to exchange it for a few needles. I showed him two and demonstrated the purpose they served. Threading each one, I showed him how to sew. Although the needles would not be of much use to them, he made signs to me to give him a few more. I gave him two more needles, and the skin provided a means for us to make shoes that would be much more comfortable than those we had made from freshly dressed bison hide. We had suffered sore feet from those shoes chafing us."[12] This account is of interest because it demonstrates that sewing needles were considered so desirable that only four constituted a good trade for a fully dressed deer hide.

BRASS BELLS. We recovered 1,345 brass bells, mostly from the main hold in an area adjacent to the bulkhead that separated the main hold from the bow. Evidently a barrel containing hundreds of bells had spilled into this part of the main cargo hold. Three different sizes of bells were found, and some were wired together in pairs.

In France the bells would have been used for falconry, or hawking. (The word *falcon* is a common name for hawks of the falcon family.) This ancient sport, popular in many countries, was probably introduced into Europe by the Romans. A hawk—usually a female because they were larger—was used to hunt smaller birds such as wild ducks, quail, and pigeons. The bells, tied to the leg of the hawk, allowed the owner to hear the bird as it pursued prey, even when it was out of sight.

The Indians, who lacked the technology to make metal objects, valued such items highly. They had no knowledge of falconry, of course, and instead used the bells to adorn their clothing. Bells were very important to native peoples; they have been found in graves as mortuary items to accompany the deceased on the journey to another world.

The bells from the shipwreck were of the variety known to archaeologists as *flushloop* and were probably manufactured in Holland from sheets of brass crafted into bowl-like hemispheres and joined to form a sphere. A small iron ball would have been placed inside to create sound. Holes were cut into the bottom and connected by a small slit so the sound would emanate easily, and the two halves were soldered together. A thin strip of sheet brass was bent into a loop and added to the top so that the bell could be easily fastened.[13] Most of the specimens from *La Belle* are still in beautiful condition, as brass preserves exceptionally well in seawater, though the iron clappers are rusted away. Several maker's marks, images identifying the place of manufacture, are stamped on them. The marks include a star, an *S*, a *Z*, and an *R*.

FINGER RINGS. We recovered 1,591 finger rings. Most are what archaeologists call *Jesuit rings*. The sample from *La Belle* is the largest collection of this type of ring ever found in the world. Their name derives from the

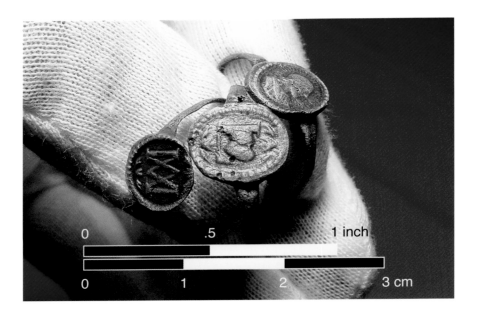

Jesuit finger rings from the main cargo hold.

religious symbols on the plaque as well as from the rings' geographic distribution. Most have been found in areas of North America where Jesuit missions were established. The majority of those from the shipwreck came from the main hold.

The most common symbols on the rings are the veneration of the Holy Name (IHS), with 612 rings exhibiting this design; the crucifixion scene (on 341 rings); the devotion of the Virgin Mary (on 115); and Mary Magdalene praying to a cross (on 107). The remainder bear a variety of designs, including the Virgin Mary, Christ, King Louis, St. Francis, other saints, angels, and an embossed *L* heart design.[14]

Although Jesuit missionaries undoubtedly gave them to native peoples, we believe they were not exclusively religious items. As a young Jesuit priest, La Salle had felt stifled by the order and over time developed an intense hatred for Jesuits. There were five or six priests with him on the expedition to Texas, including his brother, the Abbé Cavelier, but they were members of the Récollects, Franciscans, and Sulpicians. Joutel's account does not include any indication that only the priests distributed the rings or, indeed, that any religious significance at all was associated with them. On the contrary, he writes, "The [Indian] elders asked the women to bring us food provisions, as we had requested, and a little while later, several of them came, some bringing us corn, some meal and beans and similar things, and I gave them beads, *copper rings* [emphasis added], needles, and other trinkets in exchange."[15]

The inclusion of the rings with other "trinkets"

in Joutel's account, as well as their physical association with other trade items on the ship, suggests that the rings were used solely for trade with the Indians. La Salle, who had traded with Indians for many years around the Great Lakes, knew what kinds of goods they liked. Undoubtedly he was aware that these rings would be popular.

BOX OF TRADE GOODS. This container from the aft cargo hold exemplifies a means of shipment at one time quite common on vessels sailing to the New World, but today it is the only physical evidence we have of how trade goods were then packed. The box measures 28 inches in length, 9 inches in width, and 9 inches in depth. Made of white pine boards, it appears much like the wooden box containing the glass trade beads. In fact, when we first found it, we thought it was another case of beads, but instead it was filled with a broad assortment of brass pins, sewing needles, Jesuit rings, clasp knives, small mirrors, and wooden combs. The brass pins and Jesuit rings were well preserved and much like others found in other parts of the ship. The other artifacts were not as well preserved, and it was only through careful examination by Texas A&M staff that important details have been identified.[16]

The knives were all made of iron and identical to clasp knives found in one of the barrels. The mirrors were made of glass with a lead coating on one side. The glass is convex in cross section, indicating that it was cut from a large blown sphere of glass. The mirrors were stored in tin containers that measured about two

Wooden barrel, with many of the staves removed, containing iron axe heads. The axe blades are pointing inward.

inches in diameter and about ¾ inch in thickness, with lids slightly larger in diameter and about ⅜ inch deep. An estimated sixty containers of mirrors were present. The needles, with eyes for threading, were all made of iron that had largely rusted away, leaving encrustations that provided important clues about them. About one hundred were packaged together in a paper container. The wooden combs had teeth spaced relatively far apart on one side for the normal combing of hair; on the other, they were closely spaced for removing head lice, a common problem in the seventeenth century.

AXE HEADS. In the main cargo hold of *La Belle* we found three barrels filled with axe heads intended for trade with the Indians. They had no handles, which would have taken up cargo space and which could easily be fabricated later from local wood. The axes in one barrel were packed in a helical pattern, with the blades pointing to the interior and the eyes along the barrel's walls; this method allowed the maximum number to fit within a single container. The other two barrels contained axes loosely packed, as if the containers had been opened at some point, the axe heads removed and then hurriedly put back into the barrels. The Texas A&M laboratory counted 579 axe heads in the barrels, but since many were fragmentary and partially deteriorated, the actual number could have been slightly higher.[17]

The axes were made cheaply, in the style typical for trade with the Indians. The blades ranged in size from three to five inches. Several maker's marks were stamped into the faces of the axes, including the initials *DG*, fleurs-de-lys over the symbol ♀, asterisks, a star, a sunburst star and moon in a circle, and an impressed diamond. The marks identified the individual blacksmiths who had made the axe heads. Various sizes of axe heads and several maker's marks were found in each barrel, suggesting that they had been obtained from a number of different blacksmiths.[18]

Joutel's journal mentions axes on several occasions.[19] During preparations for departing from Fort St. Louis to seek help, "seven or eight dozen hatchets" were loaded onto the horses. While traveling through eastern Texas, the men traded these axes for additional horses. The Indians valued iron blades so greatly that one axe could be exchanged for a horse, which itself was a highly prized possession. The native stone axes, hafted to a wooden handle, were no match for the Europeans' iron blades.

KNIVES. Joutel mentioned knives as a trade commodity, and indeed, more than two hundred specimens were found on the ship. Some are known as *case knives* because they were packed in shipping cases for trade to North American Indians. They measured 9.6 inches in length, including the wooden handle. Each knife had been individually wrapped in paper and packaged in bundles of twelve.[20]

We also recovered clasp, or folding, knives that look much like today's folding knives, with the exception that the blades are narrower at the tang and wider near the point. These would have been very

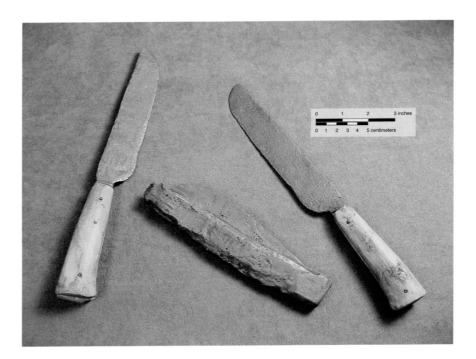

Case (left and right) and clasp (center) knives from the main cargo hold. The wooden handles are original; the blades are cast from molds in concretions.

handy for skinning deer and buffalo. The iron handles measured about six inches in length, and the blades were slightly shorter. These were packaged six to a bundle, with paper wrapped around the entire bundle rather than around individual knives.[21] Most of the knives came from a barrel in the main hold and a box in the aft hold.

Maker's marks, indicating the cutler that produced the knives, were found on some knives. At least one of the case knives has the letter *Y* stamped into the blade; due to deterioration of the blades, no marks were observed on the other case knives. Several of the clasp knives had a maker's mark consisting of a fleur-de-lys to the left of the name "HUGUES Y PERRINET" and an outlined heart to the right.[22]

VERMILION PIGMENT. We found one piece of vermilion in the main cargo hold. It would have been traded to the Indians, who used this red pigment made from ground cinnabar to decorate their bodies. It produced a much brighter red than their native red ochre.

WEAPONS AND AMMUNITION FOR DEFENSE

CANNONS. The ornately decorated cannon discovered during the 1995 testing gave us hope that more cannons would be recovered. Careful inspection of the area where the first cannon had been removed revealed an impression of another, clearly showing that *two* cannons had been lying next to each other on the port side and that one was missing. Don Keith from Ships of Discovery in Corpus Christi visited the site and took a cast of the impression, which revealed that the missing cannon was an exact duplicate of the first. The two cannons had been placed in parallel, with the muzzle of one pointing to the bow and the muzzle of the other pointing to the stern.

We never found the missing cannon. Speculation abounds about what happened to it. Local inhabitants say it was snagged by a shrimp boat in the 1930s and displayed in Port O'Connor for several years until it was donated for scrap during a World War II metal drive. Fortunately this account remains unverified; it may simply be part of the local lore that developed around La Salle's exploration of coastal Texas.

A more credible story is that in the 1960s a local shrimper named Robert Holcomb snared the cannon while trawling. According to his son Hank, the elder Holcomb tried to salvage the cannon but was only able to drag it for some distance and eventually had to release it. Holcomb's account suggests that the missing cannon is still in Matagorda Bay. Because it is made of bronze, a nonmagnetic metal, it cannot be detected with a magnetometer and perhaps will never be found.

Since two cannons had been on the port side of the hull, we theorized that another two might have been located on the starboard side. We created a map show-

Two more bronze cannons discovered in the main cargo hold.

ing the precise location, deep in the main cargo hold, where we thought the other cannons should be. When we had nearly emptied the main hold, our hope of finding them was fading. But on a wintry day in January, 1997, as archaeologist Aimee Green was excavating near the bottom of the cargo hold, she removed a concreted mass from between two wooden barrels. This exposed a shiny bronze spot, and Aimee quickly called for other archaeologists, who confirmed that she had in fact found the other two cannons. The cannons had evaded detection for so long because they were lying deep in the hold directly on rock ballast. They were located where our map projected them to be, but even deeper than expected. The cannons were well preserved, identical to the first cannon, and every bit as beautiful.

Just as the first two cannons had once been positioned, these lay adjacent and parallel to one another, with one cannon's muzzle pointing to the bow and the other to the stern. The orientation of the two guns, close together but pointing in opposite directions, minimized the space they occupied in the hold. Like the original cannon discovered in 1995, they have lifting handles shaped like leaping dolphins, and they are inscribed with a similar set of markings. On the midsection of each is a pair of crossed anchors with a scroll containing the words "LE COMTE DE VERMAN-DOIS." A crowned L with a large fleur-de-lys at its apex, representing Louis XIV, is inscribed on the cannons as well. The three cannons have very similar dimensions: a length of 5 feet 7 inches, a width at the vent hole of 11 inches, and a diameter of bore of 3.4 inches (in modern-day measurements).

All three of the guns also possessed some puzzling markings on their base rings near the breech. One was marked *741#* and *N° 4*, the second *746#* and *N° 84*, and

the third *744#* and *N° 85*. Before we found the second and third cannons we thought that the *N° 4* might refer to the caliber of the cannon (the size of ball it could shoot), since it was a four-pounder. But the other two cannons, also four-pounders, were marked with much higher numbers, 84 and 85 respectively, so our original hypothesis could not be correct. We also thought that perhaps the numbers 741, 746, and 744 referred to the weight of the guns, but the cannons actually weighed closer to eight hundred pounds.

Archaeological researcher John de Bry solved this mystery by delving back into the seventeenth-century materials at the Archives du Port de Rochefort. Here he found a document dated September 15, 1682, that contained an inventory of cannons removed from the warship *Faucon*. It listed four bronze four-pounders. The markings noted in the document perfectly match the markings on *La Belle*'s three cannons. The numbers 4, 84, and 85 refer to the sequence in which the bronze guns were cast and were used for identification. The other numbers refer to the weight of the cannons in *French* pounds. A French pound in the seventeenth century equaled 1.07 of today's English pound—this explained the discrepancy in the numbers.[23] The document also provided the numbers for the missing cannon: *745#* and *N° 3*. It is obvious that these four cannons were removed from the *Faucon* and loaded onto *La Belle* for the voyage to North America.

De Bry also found a document drafted in Versailles on March 23, 1684, that included a list of the supplies the king had provided La Salle. The king granted him four bronze cannons of four-pound caliber to be used by the new colony for rapid fire. This document demonstrated that the four bronze cannons were intended to guard the new settlement, not to be used on board the ship. The fact that the cannons were left in

24	2090	Idem	Idem	
151	2117	Idem	Idem	
4#	fonte			
n° 4	741	Latache	5 pied	
85	744	Idem	Idem	
3	745	Idem	Idem	
84	746	Idem	Idem	
8#	feet			
n° 20	2240	angoumois	8 pied	α
19	2200	Idem	Idem	

List of *La Belle*'s bronze cannons, which was discovered in the Archives du Port de Rochefort, France. The columns from left to right show the cannon's casting number, its weight in French pounds, the person responsible for the casting, and the length of the cannon in French feet.

the cargo hold and not used at Fort St. Louis argues convincingly that La Salle did not intend the site along Garcitas Creek to be a permanent settlement but rather a temporary fortification.

CANNON CARRIAGE. A wooden carriage for one of the iron deck cannons was found under the port side of the vessel. Oyster shells were attached to parts of the carriage, and teredo worms had tunneled into the wood. This indicates that the cannon had not always been buried in the bay sediments and must have been exposed in the seawater for some period of time.

Steve Hoyt, state marine archeologist for the Texas Historical Commission, is now analyzing the carriage, which consists of the bed that held the cannon; the transom, or rear part; brackets for securing the cannon's trunnions; and two of the four wheels. Judging from the lack of symmetry of certain features, such as the caps that secured the trunnions, the carriage appears to be of poor construction, probably built in haste.

How it ended up beneath the vessel, and why the other five carriages are not present, is a mystery. When the Spanish found the vessel, they recovered five cannons but made no mention of taking the wooden carriages.[24] Presumably the others fell off the ship, were not incorporated into the bay sediments, and thus have not survived.

VERSO. Another intriguing large gun on the shipwreck was a verso, or swivel gun, essentially a small cannon that would have been mounted on the ship's gunwale

by a yoke that swiveled vertically and horizontally. A long rod called a tiller extended from the rear to allow the gun to be quickly pivoted to fire against an enemy ship. The verso fired small iron balls, about two-thirds the diameter of the ones used in the bronze cannons. The gunpowder was kept in a separate cylindrical container, called the *breechblock,* which is shaped like a German beer stein with a handle for easy loading and unloading. Extra breechblocks would have been kept nearby to allow quick reloading of the gun. The breechblock was in place, and a small iron ball was in the chamber of the verso from *La Belle;* it was ready to be fired at a moment's notice. We know that *La Belle* originally had eight versos on board and the Spaniards salvaged some, but we found only one during excavation, off the starboard side of the vessel. An additional breechblock was found in the main cargo hold.

MUSKETS. We discovered evidence of smaller guns in the vessel, principally in the main hold. Four white pine boxes in the main cargo hold contained flintlock muskets. Three of the boxes were incomplete but one was nearly intact. At first we suspected that the muskets had never been used, but subsequent work at the Texas A&M lab and by project consultant and noted historical archaeologist Jay Blaine demonstrated that in one of the boxes several guns were loaded—one even contained a gunflint. Since they would not have been loaded for shipment across the Atlantic, it seems likely that the guns must have been hurriedly repacked at the Fort St. Louis settlement for use at the Mississippi River colony.[25] Another box, when opened by archaeologists,

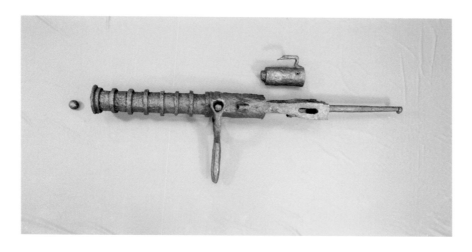

Conserved verso, or swivel gun, found outside the hull. This deck gun fell off the ship when it wrecked.

showed that the guns were in their original packing and had never been opened since leaving France.

At least four different types of muskets were represented, packed twenty to twenty-four to a crate. To save space in each box, half the muskets were oriented with muzzles to one end and half to the other. Some packaging material, probably straw, was found between the muskets. Although the metal barrels and lock mechanisms were concreted together, many of the wooden stocks were beautifully preserved. Some of the guns were decorated with a molded brass symbol of Louis XIV, a small face surrounding a radiating sun ray pattern. Several swords were packed inside the box that contained the loaded guns.

IRON SHOT. The shot used in the cannons and the verso was made of cast iron. The 312 examples fall into three

categories. Spherical balls of about three inches in diameter would have been used as shot for the cannons. The verso would have used a small iron ball measuring two inches in diameter. Bar shot, a variant of cannon balls, was basically two halves of a cannon ball with an iron rod 9.5 inches in length attached to the flat sides, forming something that looks like a dumbbell. These were inserted into a cannon barrel and fired at the sails of an enemy ship at close range. Their wobbling trajectory tore the sails and rigging, making it impossible for the crew to maneuver the vessel.

LEAD SHOT. Fully one-third of the barrels from the ship contained lead shot, which numbered nearly 300,000. We discovered shot inside barrels throughout the main and aft holds, as well as loose in the sediments covering the wreck. Some barrels contained larger balls that

Wooden box, 82 inches long, of flintlock muskets from the main cargo hold. The gun barrels are concreted together, but the wooden stocks are in good condition.

Cannon balls and bar shot (bottom) from the main cargo hold. *Photograph by Jim Bonar*

Small barrels containing lead shot for flint-lock muskets and cannons in the main cargo hold.

could be used individually in flintlock muskets, or in groups of a dozen or so packed in a burlap bag and used as cannon shot. We were puzzled at finding several different sizes mixed together in these barrels, because it would have been difficult to pick the right size of shot for a particular musket in an emergency. Six smaller barrels in the aft hold contained birdshot, very small BB-size balls that had been cast in small molds. They were probably originally stored in the lazarette. These balls would have been used to kill birds and

other small game, serving much the same purpose as a shotgun does today.

GUNFLINTS. *La Belle* contained 318 gunflints, most in the main hold but also some in the aft hold and immediately outside the ship. These were used to ignite a small amount of gunpowder in a small pan near the breech of the gun. The gunflint would be locked into the cock of the gun by a small clamp. When cocked and released, the flint would strike the *frizzen*, an *L*-shaped

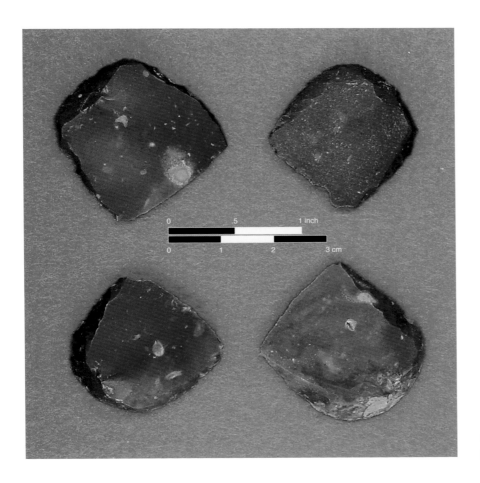

Gunflints were used to create a spark and ignite gunpowder in flintlock muskets.

metal arm, and create sparks to ignite gunpowder in the pan. The ignited gunpowder would burn through a small hole into the barrel of the gun and in turn ignite the gunpowder charge, thereby firing a small lead ball.

Most of the gunflints from *La Belle* were of the spall variety and made of a dark flint, very similar to the flint-rock ballast in the bottom of the ship's hull. The fact that similar stone was used for the ship's ballast indicates that the ballast not only helped steady *La Belle* while at sea, but could also be used to make more gunflints in the New World.

On one visit to France, we discovered that the flint probably came from the central Loire Valley. For more than three centuries, most French gunflints were made in this region, particularly in the villages of Meusnes and St. Aignan. The flint was mined in deep holes dug into river terraces and worked by local families. It was in essence a cottage industry: photos from the 1800s show husbands and wives in front of their homes making gunflints, sometimes with a bottle of wine at their sides. Special hammers and other iron tools were used to detach large flakes from the quarried flint, and the flakes were then fashioned into the characteristic wedge shape of a gunflint. A good worker could produce one thousand flakes per day, and in another day could finish five hundred gunflints.[26] The specimens from *La Belle* would have been packed in a wooden cask, though all were found loose in the soil in and around the wreck, probably after spilling from one or more deteriorated wooden containers.

GUNPOWDER. Fourteen of the ship's eighty-five barrels contained the gray, gooey remains of three-hundred-year-old gunpowder now mixed with saltwater. Its powerful odor of sulfur assaulted our noses, and we had to wear gloves to keep it from contaminating our skin. Gunpowder was one of the most important supplies for La Salle and his colonists, whether for hunting or self-defense. Quite simply, Europeans were helpless in the New World of the seventeenth century without gunpowder.

The gunpowder was poured from the barrels into powder flasks and wooden cartridges, both of which were found on *La Belle*. A single powder flask made of bronze was found off the starboard side of the ship. It has a measuring device at the opening for dispensing a precise amount of gunpowder into the barrel of a musket. Wooden cartridges, sometimes called *apostles,* were found in the aft cargo hold. They probably fell from the lazarette when it disintegrated. Each cartridge consisted of a long, narrow wood container with a wood top. A string, no longer preserved, would have run from the container through the top and onto a bandolier, or shoulder belt. The purpose of the string was to prevent loss of the cartridge and top. Each cartridge held a premeasured, single shot of gunpowder. To load a musket, one simply placed the gun barrel near the bandolier and emptied a cartridge into it.

POLE ARMS. This style of weapon dates from the Middle Ages, and the *La Belle* specimens fall into the halberd, spontoon, and partisan types. These instruments consist of long wooden poles with a metal blade attached to one end. The shapes of the blades could be complicated, with a central blade and smaller curved points radiating out toward the base. In seventeenth-century France, muskets with bayonets were replacing pole arms, which had become more ceremonial than functional. Some were ornately decorated to serve as show pieces. Since La Salle's men probably did not need ceremonial pole arms in the remote reaches of the New World, the specimens on *La Belle* were probably meant to be used as defensive weapons if an enemy ship got too close or to help position *La Belle* as she docked or approached another ship.

PROVISIONS FOR DAILY LIFE

CERAMIC CONTAINERS. The wreck contained relatively few ceramic dishes: thirty-one complete or nearly complete vessels, most of which were in the main and aft cargo hold.[27] Most are earthenware, made from generally coarse clays and not highly fired. The majority of the earthenware vessels came from the Saintonge region of western France, about seventy miles inland from the coast city of La Rochelle where the expedition was launched. More specifically, most were probably made in the family pottery workshops in and around the small village La Chapelle des Pots, which specialized in the production of bowls, jars, and plates partially covered with a distinctive green glaze. This glaze consisted of finely ground glass combined with copper

A concreted pole arm recovered from the wreck. *Photograph by Jim Bonar*

oxide and suspended in water. It was used to decorate the vessels as well as to make their interiors water resistant. These vessels would have been used for cooking, serving, and food storage.

Twelve of the vessels are stoneware, which is made from high-quality clay high-fired to form a wall impervious to liquid. The stoneware would have been used as pitchers and storage containers for liquids. A very small stoneware vial, measuring about 2.2 inches tall and 6.4 inches around, contained mercury that was still perfectly preserved. Today we consider mercury a deadly poison, but in the seventeenth century it was thought to be a cure for illnesses such as syphilis. Henri Joutel's journal reveals that during the expedition's stay at the Caribbean port Petit Goäve, some of the men contracted venereal disease. One man on board *La Belle* just before it sank suffered from syphilis so severely that he was unable to walk.

The remaining ceramic vessels from *La Belle* are all faïence, an earthenware ceramic glazed with a com-

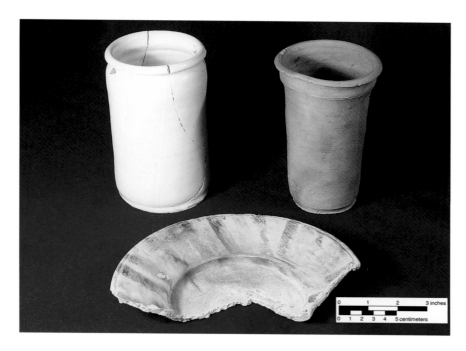

French ceramic jars and plate. The jar on the left is faïence, probably from La Rochelle; the jar on the right is Beauvaisis stoneware from the Normandy region; and the portion of a plate is from the Saintonge region.

pound containing lead and tin oxide. When fired, the glaze creates a bright white finish. Faïence dishes in France were often painted with blue decorations and were fashioned to imitate the expensive Chinese porcelains imported from the Far East. Locally produced faïence was less expensive, though still considered a luxury ware for fine dining. All the faïence vessels from *La Belle* are plain white jars. Several have the cylindrical shape of apothecary jars commonly used in Europe and probably contained medicines. Even though seawater and muddy sediments from Matagorda Bay had seeped in, many still held their original contents, a greasy substance that gave off unpleasant odors.

PEWTER TABLEWARE. One hundred and sixteen pewter containers were recovered. Bowls, porringers, cups, and other miscellaneous objects were among the items found, but the most common by far were plates. In fact, the 101 pewter plates from *La Belle* comprise the largest collection of its type from any excavated archaeological site in North America. There were four different sizes of plates: chargers of 19–22 inches in diameter, smaller dishes of 12–15 inches, still smaller plates of 7–11 inches, and a solitary saucer of 5 inches in diameter. Pewter plates were more expensive than ordinary earthenware, but on board a ship or ashore in a remote colony, they would surely have been more durable.[28]

We recovered the plates mainly in the main and aft

cargo holds. A stack of 22 plates was discovered in the main hold. Some isolated plates found off the starboard side had probably been used higher up in the vessel, perhaps in the stern cabin. As the upper structure of the ship deteriorated, these plates fell to the bottom of the bay.

Many of the pewter containers carry maker's marks, small impressions stamped into the metal that identify the maker as well as the quality of the pewter. The mark *IP* is the most common maker's identification on the pewter objects from *La Belle*. At that time in France, local guilds monitored the quality of the pewter by assessing the ratio of tin to lead. Since tin was more expensive, the plates containing the most tin were considered the highest in quality. Several from *La Belle* bear the mark *FIN*, meaning "fine," which indicated that the pewter was of high quality.

Some pewter items were also stamped with their owners' initials. The initials *L. G.* were stamped on the bottom of all the plates in a large stack. These plates may have belonged to the Sieur Le Gros, La Salle's wealthy financial record keeper, who died after suffering a rattlesnake bite. Hunting for shorebirds, Le Gros had taken off his shoes to retrieve a bird he had shot in a marsh. The snake bit him in the leg, the bite became infected, and his leg finally had to be amputated by the colony's doctor—who had never performed such a surgery before. Le Gros died a couple of days later. La Salle took control of his pos-

Pewter plates from the main cargo hold.

sessions, and they were loaded onto *La Belle* just before she sank.

One of the most unusual pewter specimens we recovered was a cup, or handleless beaker. The base bears the *IP* mark and an image of an oak tree, both signifying the maker of the object. Crudely scratched on the base is the name *Phily*. More scratches on the exterior wall of the cup initially seemed to be additional writing, but the form of the letters failed to make any sense. Once the cup was turned upside down, however, the lettering became recognizable as *Jean Phily*, un-

doubtedly the name of Jean Phily, a young man of twenty-nine years who was a pilot and shipmaster from La Rochelle. He signed a contract with La Salle on June 19, 1684, to join the expedition. In the late 1600s, all contracts of this type were notarized to make them official, and the notarized record of this action still exists today.[29]

Another small pewter bowl is marked on the bottom with the initials *C. D. L.* Could this article have belonged to La Salle? He was commonly known as Cavelier de La Salle, and these initials thus match the first

Ladle, candlestick holder, colander, and kettles from a wooden box in the main cargo hold.

three in that name. Although many of La Salle's personal possessions sank with *La Belle,* no artifacts have so far been positively linked with him.

WOODEN CHEST WITH COOKING EQUIPMENT. A set of cooking kettles and other brass objects for furnishing a dwelling was discovered in the main hold. The upper parts of the chest, including its lid, had deteriorated, thus exposing the contents. Three kettles, all with bail handles to permit their being suspended over a fire, were nested together in the chest. Kettles were common then; they are depicted in several French paintings from the same time period. Inside the upper kettle was a colander, its holes in a six-petal floral design. It was in such good condition that it might be mistaken for one you could purchase today. Also inside the chest were two finely made brass candlesticks and a ladle for serving liquids such as soups. The handle of another tool, perhaps a strainer or a ladle, was also found. Who was the owner of this chest and its contents? We found a latch marked *J. Saignioy* on the chest, but this name does not appear anywhere in the archival records. He was probably a previously unknown individual on board *La Belle.*

CANDLEWICK TRIMMER. A fragmentary candlewick trimmer, a device that would have been used to trim candlewicks, was found in the main hold. The snuffer consists of a scissors-like handle on one end and a lid and small pan on the ends of the blades. A lit candlewick could be trimmed with it and the smoldering wick fragment held safely in the pan until it was completely extinguished. Such an item was unnecessary for a New World colony and clearly reflects the attempt of an expedition member to bring a small part of civilized France to a wild and distant land.

GLASS BOTTLES. All of the fifteen broken bottles and the many pieces of bottle glass found in the main and aft holds are the remains of containers that once held wine or other distilled liquors such as brandy. Most are what archaeologists call *case bottles,* so named because their square bodies allowed them to be easily packed in wooden cases. During the manufacturing process the glass was blown into a square wooden mold to form an overall square shape.

We also found several pewter screw tops, some still attached to the bottle collar. These consisted of two parts: a piece of pewter with threads attached to the collar and a lid that could be screwed on to the collared neck. These screw tops could be opened and closed tightly for careful use and storage.

Another kind of bottle from *La Belle* has a bulbous shape and a flat bottom. It is called an *onion bottle* because of its rounded shape. This bottle would have had a stopper, probably a loose-fitting cork tied to the neck by a string.

GOURD CONTAINERS. Two whole and four partial gourd containers were found in the main and aft cargo

Onion bottle from the main cargo hold.

holds. These were ripened and dried fruit rinds—bottle gourds, tree gourds, and coconuts—that had been cut in half for use as cups or scoops. Bottle gourds are native to North America and could have been obtained along the Texas coast, but tree gourds come only from tropical areas such as the Caribbean, and were probably brought aboard as cargo during the ship's stay in Petit Goâve. The coconuts as well must have been obtained in Petit Goâve, since they are not native to Texas.[30]

EATING UTENSILS. Two complete forks and seventy complete or fragmentary spoons were found, mostly from the aft hold. The forks include three-tined brass and four-tined silver varieties. Five of the spoons were made of brass, four of pewter, and two of wood. One of the pewter spoons has a crowned *F* mark, indicating that it was made of less than 10 percent lead and therefore of high quality. Another spoon has the mark of a crowned pewterer's hammer, indicating common pewter with a content of more than 10 percent lead.[31]

BRUSHES. Wooden brushes, numbering five, were recovered from several locations in the ship. They fall into three different categories: round, oval, and rectangular. The round brush, the most complete, still has animal bristles in some of its handle holes. This style was typical for men's shaving brushes of the seventeenth century. The other brushes are fragmentary and would have been utilitarian types used for a multitude of chores.[32]

MEDICAL INSTRUMENTS. Two items recovered from the main cargo hold appear to be parts of medical instruments. The first is a hollow pewter rod measuring about two and a half inches in length. One end of the tube is closed and slightly bulbous; the other is open, belled, and flanged with a threaded interior. This object may have been a rod used to withdraw fluids or gases during surgery.

The other is a silver catheter, four and a half inches long. This tubular object consists of five thin-walled fragments with scroll-like handles at one end. The size of the artifact indicates that it would have been used on adult males.[33]

WRITING INSTRUMENTS. Writing instruments were recovered from the aft and main holds. Among them was a small knife used for sharpening quills, which came from the main hold. The knife consists of a wooden handle with six longitudinal facets, with only the stub of the iron blade still present.[34]

We marveled at the delicate manufacture of a small implement found in the aft hold. Used to hold pencils or brushes, it was a small brass tube with flared and closed-end caps that slipped onto the ends. If it did indeed hold pencils, this artifact would be an example of an early mechanical pencil. Also in the aft hold was a small piece of slate with a pointed end, which appears to be part of a pencil.

Another find in the aft hold was a small brass inkwell with a twelve-sided barrel. It has a lead liner and would have had a hinged lid, now missing.

WHISTLES. Two whistles made of bone came from the main hold. Both are very light and probably made from the leg bones of birds. They most likely would have been used to signal on land or sea.

MEASURING WEIGHTS. Three small bronze discs, to be used as measuring weights with a scale, were found in the aft hold. One disc has a fleur-de-lys on the bottom.

The scale's principal use would have been to weigh gold and silver coins.[35]

FURNITURE TACKS. Seventy-four small brass tacks were found mostly in the aft hold and represent metal decorations on leather-covered chests. Fifty-seven have plain heads, while seventeen have embossed dots on the heads. None of the whole boxes from La Belle had decorative tacks on them, and the placement of these tacks in the aft hold suggests that they may have been from chests in the stern cabin, perhaps belonging to the captain of the ship. When this area of the vessel deteriorated after the wreck, the chests rotted and the durable brass tacks simply drifted downward, settling among the cargo in the aft hold.

BRASS WIRE. Two large coils of brass wire were found in the aft cargo hold and were clearly supplies for the colony. They were almost perfectly preserved and, in fact, if they had not been found deep inside the hold, might have been mistaken for modern wire. The coils are about two feet in diameter and made up of thirty-two smaller coils of wire representing different diameters. Wire was a multipurpose material. It could be cut into small lengths to make pins, or used to bind together two objects, connect poles to construct fencing, or cut into smaller lengths to trade with local Indians. Such brass wire could be considered an analogue to today's duct tape, something that can be used in a multitude of ways.

GRINDING STONES. Several grinding stones were found, primarily in the main hold, including small abrasive stones used for sharpening knives and other hand tools. We also found large sandstone discs, rough preforms for later use. These would have been mounted in a wooden frame that would rotate the stone by pushing on a paddle attached to the wheel. The preform shape would have been finished during the construction of the wooden frame. Settlers could then use the device to sharpen axes, cleavers, and adzes easily and repeatedly.

IRON BAR STOCK. After nearly all the cargo had been removed from the bottom of the main hold, we discovered a large mass of concreted iron bars. Some of the iron from the bars had actually permeated into the floor planking (called ceiling) of the ship and had become heavily concreted, which made it extremely difficult to remove without damaging the interior ceiling. It took us many days to extricate it. The iron stock was

Crucibles for smelting ore, found hidden beneath a floor in the bow. *Photograph by Jim Bonar*

in three shapes: rectangular, square, and round or rod-shaped. We know from Joutel's journal that a blacksmith on the expedition made various items, including nails, for construction of colony buildings. This bar stock would have been worked into nails and other objects. One barrel contained thousands of square nails; these may be finished products from the blacksmith's work.

IRON CRUCIBLES. The ship contained six very heavy iron crucibles for melting lead and other metals, which La Salle could have used to assess ore for silver content had he succeeded in reaching the silver mines of northern New Spain. These items were found deep in the bow beneath a small wooden deck. The presence of the crucibles provides one more piece of evidence of La Salle's secret mission to reconnoiter and invade the mines.

CARPENTRY TOOLS. Immediately behind the main mast as one views the stern of the ship was a small closet that functioned as a locker for the pumps that removed water from the bilge. Carpentry tools and some items intended for the colony were stored here as well. Perhaps the most exciting was a nearly complete cooper's plane, which would have been used in manufacturing staves for barrels. The barrels holding the ship's cargo would have leaked eventually and required repair.

A partial broom was also found in the pump locker of the ship. It consists of several twigs bundled together with a cord and a pitch-like substance to better hold the twigs together. Since the ship's carpentry tools were stored in the pump locker, the broom may have been associated with carpentry activities.

A small wooden box from the main hold contained a number of carpentry tools. Meticulous work on the chest by Texas A&M graduate student Michael West uncovered the following partial or complete items: adzes, augers, boat hook, chape, chisels, cloth, dividers, drawknives, drumsticks, fork, gimlets, hatchets, lead calibration weight, lead shot, line weight, pieces of fur or hide, plumb bob, rope, saw, sickles, small chest locks, sounding weight, spear, square, and sword pieces. Several items in the box would have been used for activities other than carpentry. The drumsticks were for beating a drum, for example, the sounding weight for checking the depth of water, and the sword and lead shot for armament. The box likely was packed at the Fort St. Louis colony. La Salle had to do the carpentry on the main buildings at Fort St. Louis because his carpenters were insufficiently skilled, so perhaps La Salle himself used these tools. Joutel describes the building of this main structure, the settlement's principal fortification:

It was necessary to construct a large lodging. La Salle had a drawing of it. . . . Although logs were cut and squared, the ignorance of the carpenters was such that La Salle was forced to act as master builder and marked the pieces of timber for the building design he had in mind. . . . The

Coil of rope recovered from the aft cargo hold.

pieces were closed with dovetailed corners with a good peg so that they would be most unlikely to slip. . . . When the house was ready, it was divided into four rooms. One quarter was the Sieur La Salle's lodging; another that of the Récollect fathers; another was for several gentlemen; and the fourth served as a storehouse.[36]

COILS OF ROPE. Two bundles of rope, coiled to fit into as compact a space as possible, were found in the aft cargo hold. Since they show no signs of wear, they were probably never used and were supplies for the colony to be built at the mouth of the Mississippi River. The rope was manufactured in the Corderie Royale of Rochefort, the major rope works for the central coast of France in the late 1600s. These two bundles and the other rope from *La Belle* represent the only surviving examples of rope produced in the seventeenth century at the Corderie Royale.

PADLOCK. A small padlock for securing a chest or box was found in the aft hold. It is triangular in shape and has a brass back plate, partial sides, and an iron hasp. No key for the lock was found.

PERSONAL EFFECTS

RELIGIOUS ITEMS. An artifact found in the sediments of the main cargo hold attests to a crew member's religious devotion: a small crucifix made of wood and cast brass, measuring about 2.4 inches in length and

1.2 inches in width. At its center is a cast of the crucified Christ, above which a piece of brass represents a scroll for a title. Below the figure of Christ are a skull and crossbones. The cross was probably part of a rosary; we also found forty-three wood and bone rosary beads scattered in the ship, though not in direct association with the cross.

LEATHER SHOES. At least nine leather shoes were found from several different locations on *La Belle*. These were of the lower quality commonly worn by middle- and lower-class French people. All nine of the nearly complete shoes are large enough to have been worn by males. The most common style was square-toed with a short heel. A leather strap, or latchet, would have been buckled or laced in the front to secure the shoe on the foot. Less common stylistic variations had rounded toes and open sides. We are uncertain why so many shoes, relative to other personal items, were found on the ship. The shoes might have been slippery on the ship's wet deck and perhaps were being stored below for later use on land.[37]

SMOKING PIPES. Twenty-four fragments of clay smoking pipes were found, with most coming from the aft hold. They were made from kaolin clay and probably imported from Holland. With the exception of two pipe-bowl fragments, the specimens from *La Belle* are pipe stems, which on a complete pipe could be as long as twelve inches.

Crucifix from the main cargo hold.

BUTTONS AND WOVEN CLOTH. Twenty-four pewter and 329 wood buttons were found in the bow and the main and aft cargo holds. The pewter buttons were cast in wooden molds in two parts and then soldered together to create a round button. The wooden buttons were carved into a hemispherical shape, and some still possessed their crocheted coverings, showing how they would have been decorated and attached to garments.

The preservation of organic materials on *La Belle* was so outstanding that even pieces of clothing re-

Cloth, buttons, and button loops from clothing found in the main cargo hold.
Photograph by Jim Bonar

mained in portions of the wreck where conditions were exactly right. In the main cargo hold, we found fragments of fabric and several sewn buttonholes of what was probably a uniform, as well as a piece of silk that still bears a red coloration. La Salle had placed all his personal possessions in *La Belle*, including his clothing, just before the ship was lost; these might well be remnants of his garments.

SIGNETS. In the main and aft cargo holds, we discovered three small brass signets, used to stamp papers with a wax seal. Each signet has a distinctive design that would allow a personalized emblem to be stamped in wax on a piece of paper. One signet has a rope-and-frond motif surrounding the script initials *PWR*. Another bears an eagle with outstretched and down-turned wings on a shield with garlands on either side. The third signet has an oval design with the initials *AM*.

Also in the main and aft cargo holds, we found a small bar of sealing wax, about four inches long and one-half-inch thick. It would have been melted and dropped onto a piece of paper so that the signet could be pushed into the liquid to leave the seal's impression. In addition, forty-one fragments of wax letter or document seals had survived and were recovered, though the relatively less durable paper to which they had been affixed had degraded. Three of the seal fragments have identifiable markings: one is a person

in a boat with waves in the background, another has a crown with a line-and-dot design, and the third has a cluster of grapes.[38]

AGLETS. These items are small sheet brass tubes that were tied to the ends of cordage or shoelaces. They tapered slightly at one end and would have been used to keep the ends of cordage and laces from unraveling. Five of these artifacts were found in the main and aft holds of *La Belle*.

BUCKLES. From various parts of the ship we recovered fifteen complete or fragmentary buckles; one was made of pewter and the rest of brass. Eight of them, known as *baldric buckles,* consist of an oval frame with a longitudinal hinge bar. They were attached to military straps or bandoliers by weaving the ends through the buckle. Two other buckles are round and plain and would have been used on belts.[39] The remaining five buckles were decorated; all of these are small and would have been used mostly on clothing.

JEWELRY. In addition to the hundreds of Jesuit rings for trade to the Indians, two rings in the main and aft holds belonging to crew members were found. One nearly complete brass ring with glass settings was found in a wooden barrel. The central glass set, in a pale amethyst color, is present, but the side clusters are missing. The large central "stone" has a flat face with a beveled edge. Of the second ring we have only a pale aquamarine glass set that would have been attached to a metal ring. It is also possible that it was once part of a brooch. A small brass pin found outside the ship on the starboard side may also have been part of a brooch.

GAMING PIECES. Nine wooden artifacts from the aft hold are parts of board games. All but one are disks, and the six larger ones appear to be from the same game set. The disks would have been used to play backgammon and checkers, both popular in the late 1600s. The ninth gaming piece looks like a king from a chess set.

SHOE LAST. A carved wooden block roughly in the shape of a human foot, found in the bow, would have been used as a mold to make leather shoes. The letters *EDI* are carved on one side and the letters *LIC* on the other. One set of letters may be the owner's initials and the other an indication of shoe size. Most likely this last belonged to one of the crew and was used to make new shoes as needed.

SHIP'S EQUIPMENT

In addition to the many artifacts that were part of the ship's rigging and the fasteners for securing hull timbers (described in chapter 5), we recovered several other items that also relate to sailing and living aboard *La Belle*.

We found a relatively small number of artifacts related to navigation, including eleven pairs of brass dividers. The dividers fell into three types: five are straight compasses with straight legs, two are straight compasses with a large ring at the top for easy opening, and four are chart compasses with pronounced hemispherical bends midway along the legs. One set of dividers bears the stamped initials *TP*, presumably identifying the owner.[40] The dividers would have been used for measuring distances on maps, measuring scales, and dividing measurements into equal parts.

We discovered a unique navigational tool in the main cargo hold: a nocturnal, which was used at night to get a rough indication of time, perhaps to an accuracy of fifteen minutes. This nocturnal is one of the few ever found in a shipwreck. It is comprised of three circular disks of wood. Two of the disks are four inches in diameter. The other, which is six inches in diameter, is engraved with a calendar scale, compass degrees, and constellations. Just above the disks is a rotating pointer. By sighting the relative positions of the North Star and another constellation, such as Ursa Minor, and figuring in the time of year, a crew member could ascertain the approximate time of night. The nocturnal is made of English boxwood and, in fact, was made in England judging from the English words on its face. The calendar engraved into the wooden face would have been good for only about four years, which meant that the nocturnal would have to be replaced after that time.

On the back side of the nocturnal is a planisphere,

Navigational dividers for charting the ship's course while at sea. The examples on far left and right are straight compasses with ring at top; example second from left is a straight compass; and third from left is a chart compass.

Nocturnal instrument for calculating time at night while at sea.

which was used to calculate the constellations viewable in the sky at night. Once the time of night was calculated from the nocturnal side, the instrument could be flipped over to determine which constellations would be visible in the night sky at different times.[41]

We found two lead sounding weights that would have been tied to a rope to measure the depth of water. One is 14 inches and the other 9.5 inches in length. Both have a small indentation in the bottom where wax or tallow was inserted to collect a small amount of soil from the sea bottom.

We recovered other ship's equipment, including portions of three sunglass timers, aperture discs from a cross-staff used to measure the altitude of the sun, a brass gimbal that was part of the ship's compass, and a brass lantern called a *lampion* that still had its three oil-burning wicks present. A gimbal mechanism on the lampion allowed it to remain upright as *La Belle* rocked back and forth while at sea.[42]

CLOCK PARTS. Two items were found that are part of a clock mechanism used on *La Belle* to help keep track of time. Accurate timekeeping was especially important for navigation while at sea. One item is a sold brass wheel with sixty-four finely cut teeth around the edge; it is three-quarters of an inch in diameter. It was found outside the starboard side of the ship adjacent to the main hold. The clock part is a key, cast in brass. It has a rectangular projection with a recessed square hole to fit into a clock winder. The wheel measures slightly more than three-quarters of an inch and was found in the aft hold.[43]

SAIL MAKER'S NEEDLES. Five brass needles were found either in the aft cargo hold or immediately outside of it, having become dislodged from the ship when it wrecked and deteriorated. One end of each has a needle point and the other end splits into four prongs. They would have been used to patch and repair the sails.

PUZZLEMENTS

SILVER COIN. One question we are often asked is whether *La Belle* contained any coins or other objects of great monetary value. *La Belle* was not carrying large quantities of precious materials such as gold and silver

Lead sounding weight from the main cargo hold, used for determining the depth of water in shallow areas. *Photograph by Jim Bonar*

coins but instead was loaded with practical items that La Salle felt were important for the establishment of a colony. From Joutel's journal, we know that La Salle had loaded two thousand gold livres on board. Although the meaning of this is somewhat unclear, it is thought that the coins were still on *La Belle* when she sank. Yet none of these coins were recovered dur-

ing the excavation, and one must therefore conclude that they may well have been among the first items the surviving crew rescued. It is remarkable that in this remote part of the New World where gold coins were largely worthless, the crew evidently managed to retrieve every one of them.

Only a single coin, made of silver, was found dur-

IF ONLY A COIN COULD TALK

*T*he only coin we recovered from *La Belle* was Roman, dating to A.D. 69. This discovery was quite puzzling. Found in the main cargo hold in sediments excavated between barrels and other large artifacts, the coin is about an inch in diameter. It bears a portrait of the Roman emperor Otho Caesar. Born in A.D. 32, he became emperor in January of A.D. 69 after overthrowing the emperor Nero. After a crushing defeat in battle that same year, Otho committed suicide, ending his brief rule.[1]

The coin is a denarius, which was the major currency in first-century Rome and throughout the central and western Mediterranean. Around Otho's portrait are several letters and words;

the following can be made out: "IMP. OTHO CAESAR AVG TRP." The back of the coin is badly deteriorated but likely bears the image of Ceres, the goddess of agriculture. She stands holding two stalks of grain and a cornucopia.

How did this Roman coin end up on *La Belle?* Our best guess is that one of the crew took it from a Roman ruin in France and brought it along for good luck. Somehow the owner lost the coin, and it became incorporated into the bottom of the ship. Imagine the story this coin could tell about Roman antiquity, subsequent European history, and its journey to the New World.

Note

1. *Encyclopaedia Britannica,* CD deluxe version, 2001, under the heading "Otho."

Roman coin dating to A.D. 69 from the main cargo hold.

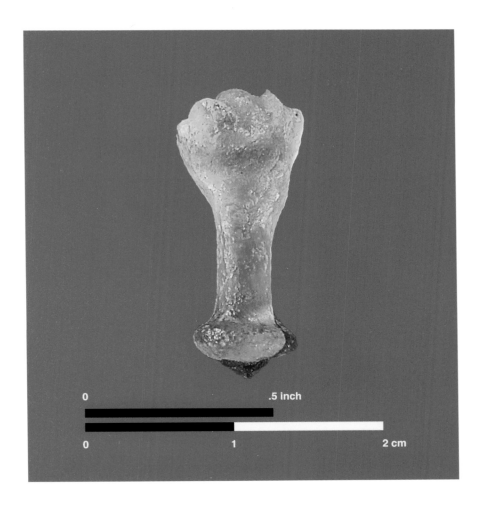

Glass *fica* would have been used to ward off evil.

ing the excavation, and it was too badly corroded to identify at first. About a year after it had been delivered to Texas A&M for conservation and had been sufficiently cleaned, this coin turned out not to be a French louis—a common coin of the time—but a Roman coin dating to A.D. 69.

FICA. A small glass *fica*, measuring three-quarters of an inch, was found in the main cargo hold. Ficas, which were thought to ward off the evil eye, are commonly found on Spanish colonial archaeological sites but not usually on French sites. The fica, a clenched fist with the thumb protruding between the index and middle figure, represents female genitalia, and is considered to be a symbol of insult. Ficas were used for at least two thousand years in European countries along the Mediterranean Sea, including Greece, Italy, and Spain—but not France. How this out-of-place charm ended up on *La Belle* is a mystery. We know that La Salle recruited men of different nationalities for his expedition, and

perhaps one of them from Spain or Italy brought the charm with him for protection.

FOSSIL. We found a stone fossil ammonite in the main hold, a find that surprised everyone. What was this doing on board *La Belle?* Ammonites were marine animals that existed millions of years ago. The soft-bodied creatures lived in spiral shells and floated in the water collecting food with their tentacles. The fossil was evidently picked up somewhere along the expedition as a curiosity piece.

INDIAN ARROW POINT. One of the most unexpected finds occurred during the fall of 1996, when a crew member excavated an Indian arrow point in the central part of the main cargo hold. Its distal, or pointed, end was broken off. It is made of black chert, stone not local to south Texas and probably imported into the area. On the basis of a typology of arrow points categorized by time periods and regions, the shape of this arrow

Partial arrow point found in the main cargo hold.

point was determined to be of the Cuney type.[44] Cuney points have been found elsewhere in south central Texas at several sites and date from the Late Prehistoric to Historic period (about A.D. 1200 to 1700). Why it was on *La Belle* is unclear. It seems unlikely that one of the crew would have carried the arrow point onto the ship, since the French had been fighting the local Karankawa Indians from the beginning, and an arrow point would only remind them of the capability of these people to inflict harm. Perhaps a more probable explanation is that an arrow was shot at the ship after it had run aground and been abandoned. Almost certainly the Karankawas would have been keenly interested as the ship lay stranded in Matagorda Bay and would have investigated it to determine whether the French were still on it, as well as to find items they

might want. Coastal Indians routinely scavenged shipwrecks and sometimes burned them to recover metal items such as nails.

PLANT REMAINS

The holds of *La Belle* contained a wide variety of plant remains, including portions of food stores and containers made from plant parts, as well as what archaeologists refer to as *incidental inclusions*—things that have accidentally become part of the wreck. All were analyzed by paleobotanist Phil Dering, who specializes in the study of plant remains from archaeological sites.[45] He found that the most abundant plant food remains were seeds and seed fragments from typical

Mediterranean olives that were pickled and loaded onto the ship in France. A single grape seed was among the remains, probably from the stores of wine, which are mentioned several times in the historical documents. Our recovery of one seed of a date palm indicates that dates were part of La Belle's provisions, although they were not specifically mentioned in the historical narratives. A few fragments of English walnuts were also found. Their thin shells suggest that they too were probably brought from La Rochelle, since New World walnuts have thicker shells than their European counterparts.

Plant foods native to North America were found as well. These included the remains of acorns, blackberries or dewberries, wild grapes, mulberries, persimmons, wild plums, wild cherries, pecans, sugarberries, and prickly pear. The acorns are somewhat puzzling because they require extensive treatment to remove the tannin to make them edible. Either they were obtained from the Indians in trade, or they are accidental inclusions in the vessel. All the other species are foods the colonists must have obtained along the Texas coast and loaded onto La Belle for consumption. The prickly pear, represented by a single seed, would have been from the consumption of the plant's ripe fruit, called the tuna. Joutel observes the following about that plant: "One must strip the fruit before eating it because, although the quills are quite small and almost imperceptible, without fail they make one sick once they lodge in the throat and on the roof of the mouth. One of our soldiers even died from having eaten the fig greedily without wiping it. All these quills caused tremendous inflammation of the throat and eventually suffocated him. These fruits do not have much taste; they are in all sizes, shapes, and colors." [46]

Woolly crotons and bur-clover were the two plant types that were accidentally introduced into the holds. The woolly croton is a low growing, herbaceous annual that is quite common in the open areas cleared by humans. The bur-clover from La Belle is clearly an Old World species that found its way into the ship's stores in France. Today this plant is ubiquitous in the eastern half of Texas—La Salle and his colonists may very well have been the first to introduce it. [47]

WHAT DOES THE CARGO TELL US?

The evidence shows that the cargo we recovered matches fairly well with the cargo historical documents tell us was loaded onto La Belle, minus the items later removed by the ship's survivors and by the Spaniards who discovered her. The historical documents state that casks of dried meat, fat, bacon, salt, bread flour, and butter were loaded. The survivors were not able to rescue all the food barrels but did manage to get "some barrels of meal." [48] During excavation we found several casks of dry goods, and while their contents were not readily recognizable, their shape and size indicate that they were stored foods. One barrel we opened contained a white glutinous mass, much like you would get from mixing flour with water. This was likely one of the flour barrels the survivors could not reach.

The historical records also indicate that ten casks of wine, brandy, oil, or water were loaded onto the vessel. Our excavation recovered twelve barrels that would have contained liquids, although none still had their original contents. We can tell from the presence of a bung hole on one of the side staves that these barrels held liquids. The bung hole would have held a stopper that could be removed to pour the liquid out.

The archaeological evidence fits well with the historical documents recording that boxes of utensils, plates, dishes, papers, and clothing were loaded, some belonging to La Salle. We found a stack of pewter plates that had been in a box, and we also recovered a set of nested kettles and a colander inside another box. Pieces of clothing and many buttons were recovered from uniforms and other garments that would originally have been packed into chests.

Numerous examples of iron tools, arms, cannons, gunpowder, and lead shot were also found, supporting La Salle's statement about what was loaded on La Belle. The mention of petards in his statement is a little unclear but probably refers to the nine firepots we discovered in the ship's lazarette. The items missing from La Salle's list are the ubiquitous trade goods, found over much of the wreck. These items were obviously loaded onto the vessel, as the survivors rescued "a few beads and other similar things." [49] These items may not have been important enough to deserve special mention, or more likely, La Salle did not want to highlight in his official statement (which would eventually make its way to the king) the quantity of trade goods he possessed. The trade goods were the property of La Salle and his men, to be used as barter with the Indians for furs and hides. They represented the personal profit that he and his men hoped to gain from the expedition, and he may have thought it impolitic to show how heavily laden the king's vessel was with these items.

The only items mentioned in the historical records we did not find were the forge and other items related to blacksmithing.[50] The Spanish found a large smith's bellows and smaller ones on shore, evidently rescued by the survivors as part of their general salvage of the ship's cargo. The forge must also have been removed from the ship and was simply not reported or had been taken by the Karankawa Indians before the Spanish found the shoreline camp.

Overall, the artifacts from *La Belle* give us an unparalleled view of what a seventeenth-century explorer needed to establish a colony in the New World. Nowhere else have these types of North American colonial artifacts been found so beautifully preserved and in such great numbers.

Large quantities of gunpowder and lead shot were found aboard. Without these items the colonists' guns would be useless: they could neither defend themselves nor hunt for food. Above all else in the seventeenth-century wilderness, these commodities were critical for success. The bronze cannons, so deeply concealed in the hull of *La Belle,* would have been magnificent showpieces to demonstrate the grandeur of France in the remote wilderness of the New World and to guard against attacks by Spaniards, pirates, or hostile Indians.

Other supplies simply made life at the colony more livable. The dishes and utensils allowed food to be eaten with civility and brought back pleasant memories of dining in France. Tobacco pipes helped to pass the time over an evening fire. The candlestick holders and ship's lantern would have been useful for nighttime illumination. The wine was for communion and other religious sacraments, as well as to celebrate the good days and dull the mind on the bad days. Medicines, in their small ceramic containers, were important curatives for sickness and injury.

The cargo also reveals much about La Salle's intentions leading up to the voyage. Some have argued that this expedition was more military than commercial in nature, but the artifacts indicate that nothing could be further from the truth. The most abundant items from the vessel are overwhelmingly trade goods—beads, pins, rings, bells, and the like for barter with the Indians. In the minds of La Salle and his men, *La Belle* was primarily an entrepreneurial venture. The king had provided supplies for the colony, but La Salle and his men had to purchase their own trade goods to profit from the settlement. Aside from the crucibles that hint of La Salle's hidden plan to explore a takeover of the silver mines of northern New Spain, the contents of *La Belle* point to establishing a colony for large-scale trade with the North American Indians.

Chapter Seven

SKELETONS IN THE SHIP

Late in October of 1996, we discovered that *La Belle* contained far more than cargo. While working deep in the bow of the ship, we found a human skeleton, lying face down with its arms and legs curled up. We later discovered parts of another human skeleton, this time in the rear part of the ship.

It is one thing to find objects the colonists brought with them from Europe but quite another to recover the actual remains of the people themselves. Finding the bones made us feel a very personal connection with La Salle's colonists and appreciate their misfortune even more. We removed the bones carefully and treated them with great respect, since these were not just artifacts but the physical remains of human beings.

We referred to the remains as Individual One and Individual Two. We found Individual One, consisting of a right fibula (lower leg bone), a metatarsal (foot bone), two foot phalanges (toe bones), and two hand phalanges (finger bones) alongside cargo in the rear portion of the ship. No other parts of the skeleton were recovered. However, even these few bones, especially the fibula, provide important clues about Individual One's life. Professor Gentry Steele of Texas A&M Uni-

versity, who studied all the human remains, determined that the epiphyses, or joint ends, of Individual One's fibula, were completely fused.[1] At birth the epiphyses are separate and slowly fuse with the long bone during childhood. The fused epiphyses, therefore, indicated that Individual One had reached adulthood. The bone had not been broken or injured and did not exhibit degenerative problems such as arthritis.

This evidence—or lack of it—suggests that Individual One was still fairly young when he died, probably between twenty and forty years old, since nearly all adults develop detectible abnormalities in the long bones as they age. Given the length of the fibula, Individual One probably stood about 5 feet 11 inches. This was rather tall for Europeans of that time, so Individual One was probably male.

One might reasonably ask: Where are the other bones from Individual One? How did these isolated bones end up in the aft cargo hold? For possible answers we can return to Henri Joutel's journal. Writing at Fort St. Louis, Joutel based his account on stories told by the shipwreck's survivors who had made their way back to the colony. "After [the ship] had remained

Skeleton found on coil of anchor rope in the bow of the ship. *Photograph by Robert Clark*

in that same place for some time and the water supply had begun to run low, [the captain] decided to send the shallop ashore with four or five casks to fill them with water. [The men failed to return and it] . . . was thought that they must have perished. . . . The loss of . . . [these men] . . . forebode a deadly end for the survivors. Meanwhile, they stayed a few more days in the same place waiting to learn something. During this time, several people among them died from a lack of water."[2]

Dying of thirst on a ship so near land may seem almost unbelievable today. One might reasonably assume that after *La Belle*'s longboat was lost people would simply swim to shore to get water, rather than endure an agonizing death by dehydration. But Joutel's journal is unmistakable: people did not swim ashore, and they did die of thirst. It is surprising but true that most sailors of the seventeenth century could not swim at all—in fact, Europeans in general lacked the ability, and swimming was not the recreational sport it is today. Furthermore, the crew was well aware that the Karankawa Indians inhabited the area and were constantly on the lookout for opportunities to kill the colonists. To those huddled on board *La Belle*, it seemed that the only hope of salvation was to wait patiently for La Salle to return and rescue them. Sadly, he was hundreds of miles away futilely seeking his great river.

Although it cannot be determined with certainty, the isolated bones from Individual One probably belonged to a member of *La Belle*'s crew who died of thirst. We can hypothesize that his corpse was situated on the poop deck at the stern of the ship or perhaps in the stern cabin just below the rear deck. After *La Belle* was wrecked, her upper structure was broken apart by waves and rotted away. As the ship disintegrated around the corpse, fish and other predators such as sea crabs would have scavenged Individual One's flesh. The few bones left from this poor soul fell into the hold, preserving his sad story.

In the case of Individual Two, where more of the skeleton survived, much more is known. We found the skeleton while painstakingly excavating the anchor rope, which the sailors had neatly coiled and stored in the bow for future use. The excavation was a slow and tedious job because the rope was intertwined and so fragile that only short segments of three to four feet could be removed at a time. Altogether, we recovered more than nine hundred feet of it. As we reached the middle of the coil, we saw a few bones protruding, and as more rope was exposed, so too were more bones, until eventually the complete skeleton was uncovered. We also found a long, narrow platform, perhaps a bunk for the ship's crew, in the bow of the ship just above the anchor rope. Probably two or more of these

Water cask found near Individual Two in the bow.

platforms were attached to the sides of the bow as a place for some of the crew to sleep. Others would have slept in hammocks suspended from the deck above. This part of *La Belle* would have served a dual purpose: as storage for rope not being used and as a berth for some of her crew.

Lying next to the skeleton was a small cask that could have contained water. We will never know for sure, but Joutel's journal coupled with the archaeological evidence suggests that Individual Two died of thirst after all the water in the cask was gone. The archaeological evidence portrays a miserable sailor desperately clinging to life, probably lying on one of the wooden bunks overlooking the anchor rope in the bottom of the bow. It is likely that he died before the ship sank. After the wreck his body was dislodged from the bunk and dropped to the bottom of the bow, settling directly on the coiled anchor rope, with his empty water cask falling next to him.

INTRODUCING MR. BARANGE

Our excavations gradually uncovered other artifacts near the remains of Individual Two. First we dis-

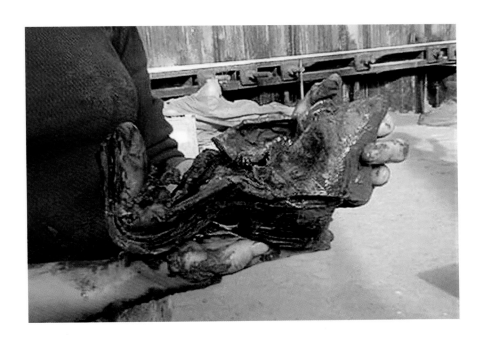

Leather shoe found in the bow near the remains of Individual Two. *Photograph by Bill Pierson*

Open leather wallet with two wooden combs exposed. The left comb has fine teeth for removing head lice, and the right comb has normally spaced teeth for grooming hair.

covered a leather wallet, which opened to reveal two wooden combs, one for the hair and another with fine teeth for removing head lice. A leather shoe was found next. Finally we uncovered a remarkable artifact near the skeleton: a small pewter cup, or wine taster, for consuming liquid. The handle was marked with the touch mark of a master pewter maker, Pierre Préveaux of France, and the side was stamped with *C. Barange,* the name of the cup's owner. The evidence strongly suggests that Individual Two was C. Barange.

Gentry Steele's examination showed that Individual Two, or Mr. Barange, was male, since the pelvis lacked female characteristics.[3] The overall robust size of the bone structure was also consistent with male gender. Barange was probably in his mid-30s to early 40s when he died. He was between 5 feet 4 inches and 5 feet 6 inches tall, shorter than Individual One, but of a more average height for a French man of the late 1600s.

Even though the evidence pointed to a European ancestry for Individual Two, we knew that La Salle did bring local Indians on his ships from time to time, and it was prudent to verify the racial origin of the skeleton. To do this, Steele compared the remains with those described in published studies of European, American Indian, and even African skeletons. Subtle but nonetheless distinctive morphological characteristics can be used to identify racial origin. The results of Steele's analysis clearly showed that Barange's measurements fall neatly in the center of those of Europeans of the pe-

riod and at the periphery, or beyond, the measurements of American Indians and Africans.[4]

Barange's nose had been broken at some time, probably from a blow to the left side of his face. The injury was consistent with what one would expect from a fight with a right-handed adversary. His lower back showed considerable damage, perhaps from heavy lifting, aggravated by a pinched nerve, which would have made one leg shorter than the other. This condition would have caused Barange to walk with an asymmetrical gait.[5] He had also badly sprained his right ankle, tearing the ligaments that held his lower long bones together.

His jaws and teeth revealed even more. He had very bad, abscessed cavities that caused the loss of the upper right first and second molars, the upper left third molar, and the upper left premolar. We know this even though those teeth were missing because it was clear that Barange's jaws had deteriorated as a result of infected, abscessed teeth. The teeth that remained also showed significant decay. To compensate, Barange had been forced to use only his front teeth to chew food, which was evident from the severe wear on those teeth. Furthermore, the upper canines and incisors were canted in a manner that suggested they were used as tools, perhaps to grip objects such as cordage.

Inside his skull, astonishingly, almost the entire brain was preserved. Scientists at Texas A&M removed the brain tissue by pouring ethanol and water into the

At top, pewter wine-taster cup found in the bow near the skeleton of Individual Two. Below, close-up that shows the name *C. Barange* stamped onto the side. C. Barange may be Individual Two's name. *Photograph by Bill Pierson*

skull, causing the tissue to float out freely in a consistency much like soggy turkey dressing.[6] This method allowed all of the brain tissue to be obtained for storage and analysis. The scientists then cleaned the skeleton and found small pieces of tendons still clinging to some of the bones, as well as tiny bits of a knit sweater adhering to the tendons.

The excellent state of skeletal preservation and the existence of brain tissue offered an opportunity to analyze Barange's DNA and attempt to link him to modern-day relatives. Barange is a common family name of Basque origin in southern France and northern Spain, and several families with the name still live in and around the La Rochelle area of France. We hoped to find an association between Individual Two and those Barange family members.

To extract DNA from the skeleton, Wayne Smith of Texas A&M removed very small samples of bone from the right fibula. These were processed by Gentra Systems, a Minnesota-based DNA-analysis company. The scientists performed their work meticulously but were unable to isolate DNA that was convincingly that of Barange, probably because the bone fragments had been contaminated with DNA from other organisms while buried in Matagorda Bay. We then asked Andrew Merriwether of the University of Michigan, a pioneer in the extraction and analysis of ancient DNA, to see whether any genetic material could be isolated. This time, two teeth were selected for DNA extraction—the hard enamel of the tooth often protects the pulp inside from contamination. Each tooth was split in two, allowing samples to be taken from the interior. Six sam-

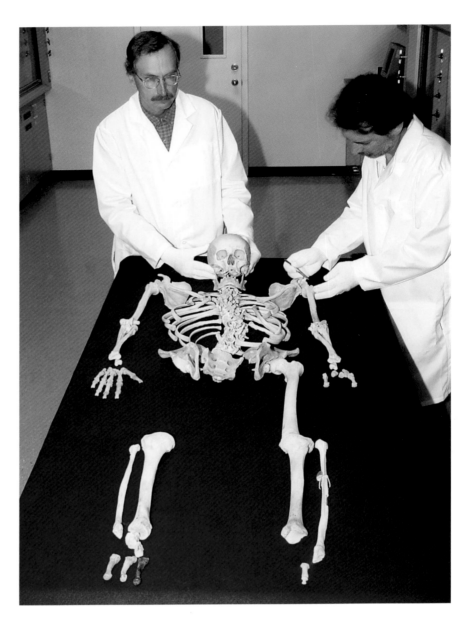

Individual Two laid out for examination by senior author James Bruseth and archaeologist Jeff Durst. *Photograph by Bill Pierson*

ples were prepared from the two teeth and submitted for DNA extraction, as was a bone sample from a rib segment. Despite all efforts, however, this work also failed to find an adequate DNA sample. Much DNA was found, but none was human; rather, tests identified the remains of bacteria and marine organisms that had inhabited the skeleton over the past three centuries. Regrettably, we were not able to genetically link Barange with any modern-day relatives.

But we could still get a pretty good idea of what he looked like. By means of computed tomography (CT), we were able to obtain a scan of Barange's skull.[7] CT scans have become commonplace in medicine as a means of obtaining images of internal body organs.

The images were stored on a computer disk, and a series of three-dimensional graphical slices were digitally made through them. Cyberform International, a company specializing in CT imaging, then transformed the computer slices into a three-dimensional model of the skull by means of stereolithography, a technique in which a laser supplies ultraviolet radiation to transform a liquid photo-polymer into a solid resin. In medicine, stereolithography is used to develop perfect casts of internal body parts to give surgeons an idea of what they will encounter during surgery. In the present instance, the result was a perfect replica of Barange's skull, without subjecting it to casting. Although casting is commonly used to duplicate skeletal remains, the

*D*NA analysis is the study of the variation in the chemical substance responsible for our biological inheritance. DNA is present in every cell of the human body, and each individual's DNA sequence is unique. Although the vast majority of genes are common to all members of the human species, over time small changes have naturally occurred that make each individual slightly different. Mutations might occur during the natural cell-replication process when a specific nucleotide is changed, and they can also be caused by environmental factors, as when one is exposed to certain chemicals or types of radiation. Once a mutation occurs, and provided that it is not fatal, it can be passed down to future generations. Scientists have developed techniques to isolate DNA from human tissues and fluids, and they can compare DNA sequences to determine whether two individuals are directly related.

Old DNA, such as that extracted from material in archaeological sites, can become fragmented and chemically altered. Scientists must extract many fragments of the same DNA segment and compare them before they can confidently conclude that they have found usable DNA. Mitochondrial DNA is often used for this purpose. Mitochondria are small bacteria-like bodies found in every cell of the body. Each cell contains hundreds, if not thousands, of them. Mitochondrial DNA generates energy for cell maintenance and growth. A good example of the use of mitochondrial DNA in archaeology was a study of the remains of a Bronze Age man found in the Alps between Italy and Austria. Nicknamed "Oetzi," the man died in a snowstorm about five thousand years ago. Duplicate fragments provided sufficient segments of his DNA for comparison with that of populations now living in the area. Oetzi's mitochondrial DNA was remarkably similar to that of modern inhabitants of this region of Europe and convincingly shows that his descendants could be living in the same area today.

molding process can leave a residue and if not done very carefully can actually damage the bone surface. Barange's skull was still in good shape after more than three centuries of burial at the bottom of Matagorda Bay, and we wanted to make sure it stayed that way for many more centuries.

Professor Dennis Lee of the University of Michigan School of Medicine offered to create a facial reconstruction of Barange's face. Lee, who is highly experienced in helping police identify homicide victims by reconstructing their faces, studied the dimensions of the replica cranium and determined that standardized

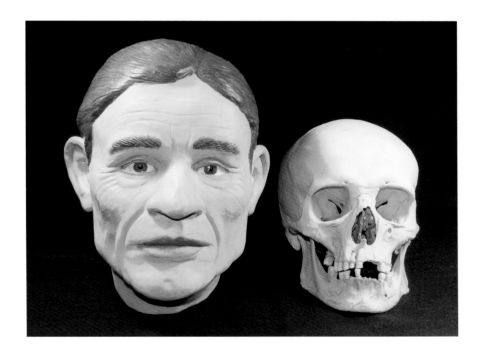

Reconstruction of the face of Individual Two by Dennis Lee of the University of Michigan School of Medicine. On the right is a replica of his skull. *Photograph by Bill Pierson*

tissue-depth measurements would be appropriate to model a seventeenth-century European male. He carefully applied modeling clay to the replica to recreate muscle tissues over the entire face, and then applied a thin layer of clay over that to simulate skin. The facial reconstruction that resulted is likely to be very accurate. We do not, of course, know the color of Barange's eyes or hair, but all other aspects of the reconstruction are good enough so that his family and friends would recognize him.

On February 3, 2004, we buried Barange in the Texas State Cemetery, the final resting place for in-dividuals who have made significant contributions to the state. Stephen F. Austin is buried there, along with eleven governors, legislators, judges, and other notable citizens. Almost 400 people attended the ceremony. Tributes were delivered by Texas State Cemetery committee chairman Scott Sayers, Texas Historical Commission chairman John Nau III, Texas Secretary of State Geoffrey Connor, French Ambassador to the United States Jean-David Levitte, and James Bruseth. The Reverend Albert LaForet of St. Mary's Cathedral in Austin presided over the religious portion of the ceremony.

Monument in the Texas State Cemetery in honor of the sailor whose skeletal remains were recovered from the shipwreck of *La Belle. Photograph by Bill Pierson*

Some have asked why Barange was buried in Texas instead of his French homeland. Shortly after completion of the excavation, we consulted with French government officials about where the remains should be interred when the scientific studies were complete. Their response: He had come to the New World to seek a new life and therefore should be buried here. We then decided that the long-forgotten sailor, as one of Texas' earliest European colonists, deserved an honored place among the distinguished residents of the Lone Star State.

ANIMAL BONES IN *LA BELLE*

The discovery of the human remains in *La Belle* provided exciting information about two of the French colonists, but these were not the only skeletons recovered: hundreds of animal bones were also found. These remains fell into three groups: unintended guests on the ship, animals that had been eaten by people on board, and fish that had died in the remains of *La Belle* after she sank.

A total of 824 animal bones were recovered from the shipwreck excavation. They were examined by Susan deFrance, who specializes in the study of animal bones from archaeological sites. She determined that the 824 bones were from a minimum of 59 individual animals. DeFrance's work provides a fascinating glimpse into the diet of the people on board *La Belle*.[8]

The most common animal bones, however, were not from meat the colonists ate but rather from the black rat, or "ship rat." Ninety-five skeletal elements from this creature were found from at least nine individual animals. The rats were uninvited stowaways that had come on board *La Belle* in France, most likely in the Rochefort shipyards. Once rats invaded a vessel, it was almost impossible to eradicate them. The ship's cargo of barrels and boxes had created numerous tunnels and cavities where the rodents could hide and evade capture. And of course the rats were not just residents on the ship; they were also breeding. During excavation of one of the large boxes of flintlock muskets deep within the cargo hold, we found straw that had cushioned the muskets during shipping. A black rat had used the straw to make a nest there, an almost perfect place to raise her brood of infant rats. Only when *La Belle* had been completely unloaded would the nest have been uncovered.

Henri Joutel stated that La Salle brought with him from France pigs, at least one cow, a pair of goats, chickens (both hens and a rooster), and dogs. The colonists took no horses across the ocean because they required too much space on board and would not be that useful in the dense vegetation and overgrown trails along the Mississippi River.[9] Pigs were the most common animals eaten by people on *La Belle*. The pigs La Salle brought did well at the Fort St. Louis colony, as Joutel notes: "Our pigs were multiplying, the sows each having had a litter. Since the hunting was plentiful, the pigs benefited from it for they also ate meat."[10]

Joutel further tells us that La Salle loaded eight young pigs from the settlement onto *La Belle* in anticipation of raising them at the Mississippi River settlement. They were five or six weeks old and easy to raise.[11] While these pigs were on board *La Belle* as she lay anchored in Matagorda Bay waiting for La Salle's return, the crew ran out of water to give them. They eventually killed and ate all of the pigs.

The archaeological evidence from *La Belle* corroborates Joutel's statements in many ways. Fifty-four pig bones were found on the ship, representing at least five individual animals. Archaeologists estimate the minimum number of animals present by counting the number of a single skeletal element—the number of right hind upper leg bones, for example. Obviously an animal has only one of these bones, so the number of those bones will determine the minimum number of animals present. It is important to remember, however, that this number is only a minimum, since some right hind upper leg bones from other pigs might not have been preserved through time. Thus, the archaeological evidence indicating a minimum of five pigs could equally support Joutel's count of eight.

The age breakdown of the pigs also supports Joutel's statement that immature animals were brought on board. DeFrance noted that of the 55 remains, most, or 49, were from immature pigs. The archaeological record indicates that, in addition to the young pigs on *La Belle*, older pigs were also present, or at least that dried meat from older pigs was part of the ship's food stores. The most common pig bones we found were ribs, vertebrae, and hind limbs—the portions that would have been the most desirable cuts for consumption.

We also found four skeletal elements from at least two goats or sheep (one fragment of a mandible and three femurs). It is very difficult to distinguish between the remains of these two species because many of their bones are similar, a problem that is compounded when only a small sample of bones survives.

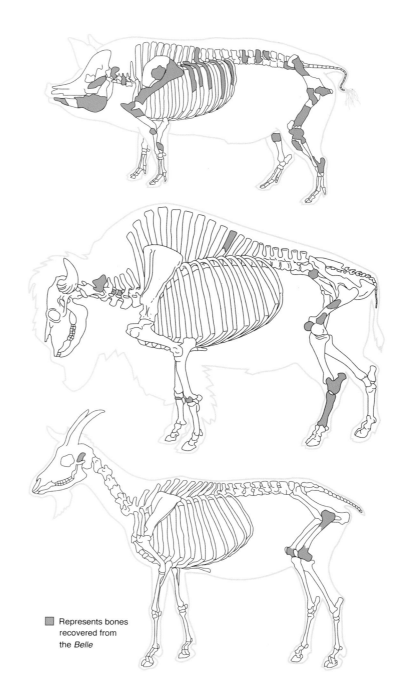

Bones of pig (top), buffalo (middle), and goat (bottom) found on *La Belle.* The bones found indicate that entire pigs were on the ship, while only selected portions of buffalo and goat were present. *Illustration by Roland Pantermuehl*

☐ Represents bones recovered from the *Belle*

Joutel stated that La Salle brought both sheep and goats for his colony.[12] Since Joutel makes no mention that live sheep or goats were loaded onto *La Belle,* the bones are probably from smoked meat that was brought on board as a food reserve.

Twenty-one bison bones were recovered from *La Belle,* mainly hind legs and portions of vertebrae. The colonists spent much time hunting bison, which were plentiful in the prairies around the settlement at cer-

tain times of the year. The animals were usually butchered where they were killed, and portions of the carcasses were brought to a *boucan,* or smoking station, that the colonists had established farther up Garcitas Creek from Fort St. Louis. Smoking cured the meat so it could be stored for later use. The process of butchering an animal in the field and smoking the meat at a *boucan* would have resulted in very few bones on board *La Belle.* Bison bones were indeed relatively rare

Buffalo were once numerous along the southern Texas coast and were a favored food of La Salle and his colonists.

on the ship, and most of the bones present were from cuts of meat that would have been most desirable and would have remained with the meat during the smoking process.

Another native animal found on *La Belle* was the white-tailed deer; the remains of at least four adult males were present. Perplexingly, though, only the antlers were found, three of which were still attached to portions of the cranium. Most of the antlers have four- or five-point racks. No other parts of deer skeletons were found, indicating that venison was not a significant food among the people on the ship. The antlers were probably stored on *La Belle* for future use at the Mississippi River colony, where they could be made into knife handles or other tools.

The remains of birds from at least five species were found on the ship, represented by 14 bone elements. The remains show that local ducks and geese were commonly hunted, which supports Joutel's statement that waterfowl were abundant and were one of the colonists' preferred foods. In addition to geese, one bone each was found from a turkey, a plover, and a tern.

We recovered 31 turtle fragments; those that could be identified were from the western box turtle, a terrestrial species. Remains of turtles were found throughout the ship and indicate that turtles were hunted on land and loaded onto *La Belle*. It is uncertain whether the turtles were captured alive and kept on the ship or were immediately prepared in some fashion. Joutel commented that the turtles often had eggs inside them, which they used to thicken sauces.[13]

The bones of at least 13 species of fish were recovered, all but one native to the Gulf Coast. This exception was the Atlantic cod, a salt-cured staple of transatlantic voyages. Remains of this fish were found in several contexts within the ship. The cod was almost certainly obtained in Rochefort or La Rochelle as part of the expedition's provisions. Joutel noted that the "seamen eat almost solely salted fish" during the journey across the Atlantic Ocean.[14]

Other fish species from the wreck include sea catfish, hardhead catfish, gulf toadfish, killifish, jack, Atlantic bumper, grunt, red snapper, drum, mullet, flounder, and puffer fish. Although many of these were undoubtedly leavings from the ship's mess, others were probably not sources of food. Sometimes fish simply die near a shipwreck and become part of the archaeological deposits. Archaeologists can often tell from the context whether this has occurred. DeFrance identified the skeleton of a possible killifish in the matrix of Cask 25, a small barrel in the central part of the ship. The remains were part of a concretion inside the barrel, a solidified mass of the fish skeleton and marine sediments. The concretion was removed carefully, the cask and the fish skeleton were identified, and the context of each relative to the other confirmed that the fish was part of *La Belle*'s provisions—most probably a fish caught and prepared at sea. Other remains that almost surely represent incidental inclusions in the wreck are the tail spines and crushing plates of stingrays.

DeFrance identified two types of cuts to the bones made during butchery.[15] One type, made with a metal

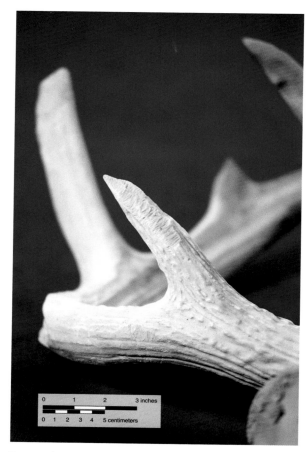

Deer antler gnawed by ship rats. This artifact was found in the aft cargo hold.

the swivel gun we found parts of cockroaches, including wings and legs. Since cockroaches are land-based insects, their presence indicates that they probably boarded the ship in La Rochelle or Rochefort. As with black rats, once cockroaches inhabited a ship it would have been nearly impossible to exterminate them. Moreover, the modern concept of cleanliness would not have been a concern to the crew of *La Belle*, and the cockroaches were probably tolerated as part of life at sea.

THE CREW'S DIET

Despite the cockroaches and rats, it appears from the archaeological evidence that the diet of the people on board was varied and, in fact, rather good. Bison and pigs were prepared and eaten, as were aquatic fowl and a variety of fish. Joutel, however, paints a markedly different picture.

The lack of water . . . forebode a deadly end for the survivors. . . . They had eight pigs from the settlement that were put aboard and they ate them, not having water to give them. They [the colonists] began to fade one after another as they saw that their hopes for news were in vain. Also they realized that the longer they waited, the weaker their condition became to save themselves.

They had cooked some flour with seawater; but that did not agree with them at all. They could not even eat it. They still had some wine and some brandy and even a case of Spanish wine that the Abbé Cavelier had put aboard. He had abstained from this in order to say mass on his return because none was left at the settlement. The ship's master took possession of the wine and filled his gullet well indeed. According to Chefdeville's report, he hardly spent a day that he was not drunk.[16]

How can we account for the apparent contradiction between the archaeological record and Joutel's statements? La Salle thought it would take him no more than two weeks to find the Mississippi, so *La Belle* was provisioned for only a couple of weeks to a month. Meanwhile, the ship was to stay anchored in Matagorda Bay until his return. But La Salle was gone for more than two months, and the ship's provisions were wholly inadequate for this longer period. To make matters worse, the loss of the only longboat meant that provisions could not be replenished.

If we take into account both the archaeological

knife blade, demonstrates that the colonists were cutting into the bones as they carved meat into suitable pieces for cooking. The other type, likely made by a metal cleaver or ax, were hacks—larger and deeper cuts into the bone—which we saw most often on the bones of larger animals such as bison and pigs. These marks likely occurred when the colonists were butchering the animals for food preparation or transport, as when bison were killed away from Fort St. Louis.

Many of the bones of pigs, sheep or goat, deer, bison, birds, turtle, and fish showed evidence of gnawing. The culprit was the ubiquitous black rat, which scavenged the carcasses for meat as well as calcium in the bones. We even found rat gnaw marks on one rat bone; even dead rats were not spared by other rats.

INSECT REMAINS

The shipwreck was so well preserved that we were able to detect even tiny insect remains. Inside the barrel of

Today the Matagorda Bay area, dominated by farms and ranches, looks markedly different from the way it did when the French occupied Fort St. Louis. According to the colonists, most notably Henri Joutel, the land was predominantly a prairie that extended as far as the eye could see. Small groves of trees, mostly oaks, dotted the landscape. Joutel likened it to the French Caux region where there were "small country estates and mottes of trees."[1] During many months of the year, large herds of buffalo grazed on the lush prairie grasses. The French hunted the buffalo and considered this game their "daily bread," often smoking the meat to preserve it.[2]

The land was rich with other game animals. Deer were plentiful, and the wide variety of birds included "turkey, Canada geese, other geese, swans, cranes, ducks, teals, coots, plovers, jack-snipes, sandpipers, white and brown curlews, and grouse of two kinds, one large and one small (which is better)."[3] The grouse, described as similar to pheasants, were probably prairie chickens, now endangered.[4] The rivers and lakes contained a wide array of fish; the French colonists caught catfish, trout, and a fish with a long snout that was probably gar. Joutel describes a fascination with one very unusual creature: "I noticed a certain animal that is shaped like a rat, but larger, like a medium-sized cat. It has the appearance and color of a rat except it has a longer snout. Beneath one side of its abdomen is a sort of sack in which it carries its young. This seemed to me to be quite extraordinary. We killed several which we ate. They are quite good when fat and taste like a suckling pig."[5] Undoubtedly, Joutel was referring to the New World opossum, which has no parallel in Europe.

Notes

1. William C. Foster, ed., *Joutel Journal*, p. 123.
2. Ibid., p. 126.
3. Ibid.
4. Ibid., Foster's footnote 34.
5. Ibid., p. 170.

Wild birds abound today on Matagorda Bay as they did more than three hundred years ago.

record and Joutel's report, it becomes apparent that those on board were at first well provisioned, but with time the food and water ran out. Joutel explains that the crew was unable to go ashore and hunt for game or collect water. Faced with the prospect of attempting to swim ashore only to face the hostile Karankawa Indians, many crew members chose to remain on board *La Belle* in hopes that La Salle would soon reappear. The human remains we recovered are sad testimony to their fateful decision.

Chapter Eight
LA BELLE'S LEGACY

La Belle has opened a window into the past, revealing an unprecedented view of French colonists attempting to build a settlement in the New World. The archaeological evidence tells an often poignant, sometimes tragic, but always compelling story of their struggle. The underlying force was the overwhelming ambition of Robert Cavelier, Sieur de La Salle, to exploit the interior of North America for French expansion and personal gain. La Salle's arrogance, and the harsh realities of an uncharted land, led to the dismal failure of the enterprise and the death of nearly all who depended upon him.

The tiny *barque longue* was La Salle's last lifeline for help, as he planned to sail her to the Caribbean island Saint Dominique to seek new supplies for his fledgling colony. The loss of *La Belle* was the proverbial last straw: the tiny settlement was then doomed, and with it, La Salle's grand dream. That single event, the sinking of a ship, ruined France's scheme to colonize the Gulf Coast and opened the way for Spain to assert its dominion.

LESSONS FROM *LA BELLE*

With the failure of his last expedition, La Salle left a wide and deep mark on history, though not the one he would have wished—and he also left a ship. Our discovery, excavation, and extensive analysis of *La Belle* have told us a great deal, especially about the events leading up to the expedition.

At first we were puzzled by the carefully formed roman numerals on the hull timbers. Further research revealed that *La Belle* had been fabricated as a kit to be assembled; the numbers were essential to putting her together later in a distant land, in keeping with La Salle's original plan. La Salle's desire was not to conduct a bold naval expedition into the Spanish Sea but to find his river and exploit the land's riches by way of Canada. Louis XIV's scheme to challenge Spain's claim to the Gulf of Mexico, however, ultimately won the day.

La Belle's hull also added to our understanding of European shipbuilding in the seventeenth century. The forests of France had been so mismanaged that suitable trees for shipbuilding were scarce, and many of *La*

*D*uring the years we worked on *La Belle,* several people contacted us to say that they were descendants of La Salle's colonists. Their stories seemed surprisingly plausible. One of the best documented claims came from Mida Griego West of Albuquerque, who said she was descended from two survivors of La Salle's expedition. She sent us a family tree to back up her claim, which showed that her mother was the daughter of David Gurulé and Petra Archibeque.[1]

West's lineage extends back to Jacques Grollet from La Rochelle, France, and Jean L'Archevêque from Bayonne, France, which is near the Pyrénées. The two men were lured by the excitement of La Salle's expedition and his promises of wealth. Their dreams faded, however, as La Salle's hopes for his colony dimmed, and the two became disenchanted with the expedition. Young L'Archevêque participated in the murder of La Salle by leading the explorer into an ambush where he was shot in the head. L'Archevêque knew that he could not return to France, where he would certainly be executed. He decided to stay with the Caddo Indians of eastern Texas. Grollet had defected about a year earlier and was already living with the Caddos when he was reunited with L'Archevêque.

Both men later gave themselves up to Spaniards who were searching for Fort St. Louis. They were taken to Mexico City, interrogated, and then sent to Spain for imprisonment. Authorities there could not return L'Archevêque and Grollet to France because they feared that the two Frenchmen's familiarity with the geography and peoples of the northern frontier of New Spain could help France reoccupy the region. L'Archevêque and Grollet were exiled to New Spain, condemned, ironically, to work in the silver mines that La Salle had once coveted.

A few years later, in 1692, L'Archevêque and Grollet convinced their captors to let them participate in the resettlement of northern New Mexico after the Spaniards retreated during the Pueblo Revolt of 1680. They settled near today's Albuquerque and Santa Fe and changed their names to the more Hispanic-sounding Juan Archibeque and Santiago Gurulé. The men married and fathered several children, leaving a legacy of prominent New Mexican descendants, one of whom is Mida West.

Note

1. Much of the information about Jean L'Archevêque and Jacques Grollet comes from Kathleen K. Gilmore, "Treachery and Tragedy in the Texas Wilderness: The Adventures of Jean L'Archeveque in Texas (a Member of La Salle's Colony)," *Bulletin of the Texas Archeological Society* 69 (1998): 35–46.

Mida Griego West of Albuquerque is descended from two of the survivors from the La Salle expedition.

Belle's frame timbers were made from recycled wood. Evidence shows that some were cut two hundred years earlier, tangible testimony to the forest crisis that made the king's attempts to modernize and expand the royal navy so difficult. As part of those efforts, France was importing ideas from remote reaches of the kingdom, and here again *La Belle* furnishes material evidence, in this instance for the merging of Mediterranean and Atlantic styles of shipbuilding.

The more than one million artifacts offer a rare glimpse of the supplies needed for building a stronghold in the North American wilderness. The most common artifacts from *La Belle* were not the kinds one would expect, such as dishes or cooking vessels, but rather goods for bartering. The ultimate success of La Salle's enterprise depended on establishing trade with native peoples. European money was useless for barter in the New World; the currency du jour was beads, brass pins, finger rings, knives, and iron hatchets. These were the Indians' equivalent of silver and gold coins, so the cargo holds of *La Belle* were full of such items. They were essential to obtain furs and hides, which could be transported back to France for a handsome profit.

The next most common items were arms, particularly flintlock muskets and ammunition. We excavated barrel after barrel of gunpowder, and many others were later found to contain lead shot. These artifacts demonstrate the supreme importance of hunting and self-defense.

After trade goods and arms, the most common artifacts were those necessary for daily life. There were carpentry tools for building houses, kettles and pots for cooking, dishes and utensils for dining, and alcoholic spirits for drinking and the Catholic mass. There were medicines from France to cure ailments, though most of them would have been folk remedies with little value from a modern medical standpoint. Some colonists brought fine accoutrements, such as brass signets

for sealing official correspondence, candlestick holders, and fine pewter plates.

CONSERVING THE CARGO

All these artifacts, which reveal so much about the expedition, have been transported to the nationally recognized Conservation Research Laboratory at Texas A&M University to be preserved for exhibition and study. The lab's staff, under the direction of Professor Donny Hamilton, conducts cutting-edge research into new methods of conservation. The day-to-day operations of the lab are under the direction of Jim Jobling, who keeps all the mechanical systems working and purchases supplies for the lab's conservation projects. Jobling has also encouraged hundreds of individuals and organizations to make contributions of services, equipment, and supplies, without which *La Belle*'s conservation could not be completed.

The conservation of artifacts from shipwrecks has become a highly specialized field, with its own college curriculum for the training of conservators. The goals of artifact conservation are to make objects chemically stable and prepare them for exhibition and study. Although many of *La Belle*'s artifacts appear to be well preserved, they are in fact very fragile and can easily be

Senior author James Bruseth collecting samples of sediments from apothecary jars.

LA SALLE ARTIFACTS IN THE TEXAS STATE HISTORY MUSEUM

In Austin's Bob Bullock Texas State History Museum, the La Salle expedition is one of the featured exhibits on the first floor. This is particularly fitting because Bullock secured the initial legislative funding to begin the excavation of *La Belle*.

The exhibit is divided into three parts, each telling a different part of the La Salle saga in Texas. At the front, a large display case houses artifacts that document France's attempt to take its place in the Spanish-controlled part of the New World. Several of the items were used aboard *La Belle*. There are navigational dividers and a lantern that may well be the one the captain used in his failed attempt to provide a beacon for the sailors who had gone ashore to get water. Other objects in the display case were intended for defense of the ship; these include a firepot, cannon balls, lead shot for bullets, a bronze cannon, halberds, and a sword handle. A crucifix affirms the Christian impe-

tus for all French expeditions to the New World. Glass beads, finger rings, and brass hawk bells underscore the motivation of La Salle and his men to profit personally from trade with the American Indians.

The second display case contains objects intended for the colony. The variety of these artifacts illustrates the range of materials thought important to a seventeenth-century colony: brass cooking pots, candlestick holders, and axe heads. There is a millstone, used for sharpening edged tools, as well as a powder flask for flintlock muskets. There are small apothecary jars that held medicines for treating diseases, such as those the colonists might have acquired at stops in the Caribbean. The cooper's plane was used to make barrels for storage, and writing implements, such as a pen and an inkwell, were important for documenting the needs and accomplishments of the colony.

The last part of the exhibit dramatizes the many failures of the expedition; it includes a replica of the skeleton of the sailor who died on board the ship while she lay at anchor in Matagorda Bay, waiting for La Salle's return. Around him are a small cup stamped with the name *C. Barange,* a water cask, a wallet with two combs, and leather shoe fragments. The artifacts were found near the skeleton and were likely his personal possessions. This exhibit is a poignant example of the many challenges the expedition faced, all of which led up to the death of La Salle himself.

On the carpet below the displays, but overlooked by most visitors, is an outline of the hull of *La Belle.* Once its restoration has been completed, the hull will be placed in this part of the museum, serving as a reminder of how one small ship changed Texas history forever.

Vats of water containing artifacts waiting for conservation at Texas A&M University.

damaged if they do not receive the proper treatment. The wooden objects, for example, look much as they did three centuries ago, but significant quantities of cellulose and lignin in the wood have disintegrated and been replaced by water. The water has thus become the primary agent in maintaining the objects' original shapes. If these artifacts dry out, the cell walls of the wood will collapse, causing considerable shrinking and warping. Some wood, depending upon the degree of deterioration of the original matrix, will simply turn into piles of dust. Salt in the seawater can cause the disintegration of other objects, such as bottle glass and even metal.

The conservators must first remove the water and chlorides (salts) from wooden artifacts and replace them with a substance that keeps the cells from collapsing. Polyethylene glycol (PEG), which is basically a water-soluble synthetic wax (a short-chain polymer), has traditionally been the chemical of choice. Wooden artifacts treated with PEG can be dried and displayed in the open air with adequate controls for humidity, temperature, and ultraviolet light.[1] The hull of *La Belle* is being treated with PEG in a process that will take seven to ten years.

An alternative treatment for organic materials has been developed at Texas A&M by Professor C. Wayne Smith and the Dow Corning Corporation. It involves the use of silicone oil—a long-chain polymer (a long molecule formed around silicone)—to permeate wooden objects.

The procedure begins with a series of chemical dehydration baths that replace the water in the cells of organic materials with organic solvents. The object is then submersed in silicone oil with a cross-linker solution added to it; the cross-linker establishes chemical links between the molecular chains in the polymers and makes the silicone oil bond tightly with the object. An exchange of the acetone with the treatment solution then occurs on a cellular level. Once the exchange has been made, the artifact is removed from the solution, and the excess is allowed to drain. The cells in the organic material retain only enough polymer to coat or adhere to the cell walls. After all the surface polymer has been removed and the artifact is aesthetically pleasing and as close as possible to its original state, it is then exposed to a catalyzing agent that completes the cross linking of the molecular chains in the silicone oil.[2]

The result is an artifact remarkably natural in color, and the texture of its surface is nearly that of its original state. Several artifacts from *La Belle*, including

a variety of wood objects such as knife handles, barrel staves, and combs, have been treated with this technique. It works equally well for other materials such as glass bottles and beads, basketry, textiles, paper, leather, and rope. Rope treated in this process is pliable, can be handled, and in some instances can even be unwound to allow study of the rope-making process.

Although silicone-oil treatment results in remarkably good-looking artifacts, the process is controversial because it is not reversible. Since the long-term effectiveness of many conservation treatments is not fully known, some conservators prefer to use reversible techniques that do no harm to the object and can be removed at a later date. This way an object can be retreated with a future alternative technique that might hold more promise. Silicone oil was selected for several *La Belle* artifacts after studies showed that it could preserve objects for at least 250 years and that the objects could be repeatedly retreated with more oil for an indefinite period. Most importantly, the finished artifacts looked more lifelike than objects stabilized with other treatments such as PEG, which can take on an unnaturally dark tone.

Iron objects from the shipwreck present one of the greatest conservation challenges. When ferrous metals are submerged in seawater, basically a galvanic cell is created in which two metals, or two parts of the same metal, become an electrochemical cell. The metal with the more negative reduction electrode potential loses electrons, and the other metal gains electrons. Over time, this causes the iron object to corrode. Sulfate-reducing bacteria that live in seawater cause further damage; their life cycle stimulates electrochemical corrosion. Given these factors, it is no wonder that iron is one of the first metals to disappear from shipwreck sites.

Fortunately, many iron objects become encrusted long before they completely disappear, and often what is left are nearly perfect molds of the original artifacts. Encrustations can form around tiny artifacts the size of a dime as well as huge conglomerations of objects that weigh a hundred pounds or more.

By examining the interiors of such encrustations, conservators can identify the original artifacts. They start with X rays to see whether any of the original metal has survived and to get a general idea of the original object's shape.[3] In some cases the metal (iron, copper, brass, or bronze) is almost pristine and is conserved by electrolytic reduction. This process can convert some of the nonferrous corrosion products back to a metallic state and stabilize iron artifacts by remov-

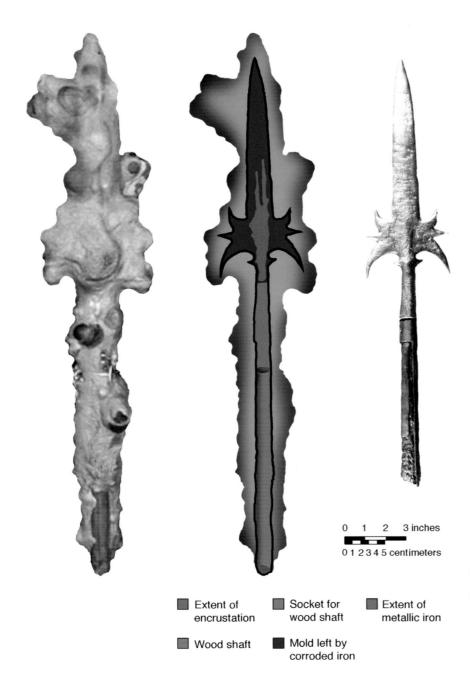

Extent of encrustation

Socket for wood shaft

Extent of metallic iron

Wood shaft

Mold left by corroded iron

0 1 2 3 inches
0 1 2 3 4 5 centimeters

Example of how the void inside a concretion can be cleaned to reveal the mold of a pole arm. On the left is the original concretion, in the middle is a diagram of the interior of the concretion showing the preserved materials and voids left by rusted iron, and on the right is the reconstructed pole arm. *Illustration by Roland Pantermuehl*

ing most, if not all, the chlorides. In the process, the superficial encrustation and adhering products are softened and slough off.

Sometimes the X rays reveal that little or no metal remains and that there is only a void left in the encrustation. In such a case, the encrustation is opened, either by inscribing a line around it and hitting the line with a hammer or by making a hole in a segment of the encrustation to expose a portion of the interior void. Any residue is cleaned out and the void is filled with an

epoxy resin. The remaining surface of the encrustation is then removed, revealing a cast of the original object.

Helen Dewolf, the chief conservator of *La Belle* artifacts, is an expert in this method of replicating corroded iron artifacts. She and student workers at the Texas A&M laboratory have cast hundreds of iron objects, mostly knives, tools, and fasteners from *La Belle*. Dewolf has been able to cast subtle maker's marks and other identifying inscriptions from knife blades and axe heads. She was even able to cast a tiny void left

Helen Dewolf of Texas A&M's Conservation Research Laboratory is the chief conservator of the artifacts.

by the paper that once covered iron case knives in one of the wooden barrels. In fact, some of the completely corroded artifacts in the encrustations from *La Belle* are providing one of the most complete sets of ship's rigging of any shipwreck in North America.

To reassemble *La Belle*'s hull timbers, a concrete vat 60 feet long, 20 feet wide, and 12 feet deep, with a capacity of over 100,000 gallons, was built to provide a container large enough for the timbers to be reconstructed inside. A large platform that covered the entire bottom of the chamber allowed the timbers to be raised and lowered. The platform was raised during the day so that conservators could have better access as they put the hull back together. Sprinklers sprayed water over the wood to keep it from drying out during those periods of exposure to the air. At the end of the workday, or whenever necessary, the platform was lowered to the bottom of the vat to submerge the wood, ensuring that between reassembly periods the timbers were always in water and could not deteriorate. James Stasny, president and owner of Dynacon, Inc., designed and fabricated the vat's steel elevator platform and winching system as a donation to the project. Four remote-controlled electric winches were placed along the two long sides of the platform, each with a lifting capacity of more than ten tons. The frame of the platform was designed so that there was almost no deflection when it was lifted or lowered, so as not to cause stress to the wooden hull. The open grid of the frame was covered with twelve hundred square feet of nonskid fiberglass grating, which formed a strong working floor to support the reassembled hull. The fiberglass grating also allowed the conservators to safely stand on the platform while they worked. This material is ideal: it is easy to work with and install, strong yet lightweight, chemically inert, and corrosion-resistant.

PUTTING IT ALL BACK TOGETHER

The task of reassembling *La Belle* fell to Peter Fix and a team of archaeologists at Texas A&M. For Fix this was the challenge of a lifetime, and he spent countless hours planning and designing the best method to reconstruct *La Belle*. It would not be easy. While 40 percent of the bottom portion of the hull was found intact, many of the timbers had deteriorated, especially those close to the top of the sediments covering the wreck. We think that over the three centuries during which *La Belle* lay buried in the bay, portions of the upper surviving structure were periodically uncovered and exposed directly to seawater. This exposure changed the preservation environment from anaerobic to aerobic. In the aerobic environment, oxygen-loving bacteria could once again destroy the wood. The exposed timbers could even be attacked by the notorious teredo worm, which bores through the timber. Teredo worms were already eating at the hull planking when *La Belle* was still sailing in warm ocean and bay waters. During the excavation, we could see extensive areas of damage

A large concrete vat constructed at Texas A&M University is used to hold the reassembled hull.

from these ubiquitous sea worms. The timbers, especially the hull planks, were very fragile and were very difficult to put back into place.

Fix also had to take into account the need for the assembled *La Belle* to be aesthetically pleasing so that it would make a good museum exhibit in the Bob Bullock State History Museum in Austin, her final resting place. The museum designed its atrium exhibits to accommodate the hull, and when it arrives it must look like a ship. It cannot have rows of braces and supports along the sides that would obscure the viewer's sight. The ideal solution would be a largely invisible bracing system. Unfortunately, the wood is so degraded and fragile that it needs substantial support.

These considerations were discussed at great length by Fix and Hamilton, the archaeological team working on the hull, and archaeologists from the Texas Historical Commission. The solution was to place the keel of *La Belle* on a long, form-fitted fiberglass support that would sit atop a steel beam. The support, which pro-

vided added stability, was molded to fit the underside of the keel. The steel beam was the backbone of support for the keel and ultimately for the entire ship.

The frames, or ribs, of the ship were attached perpendicular to and directly on the keel and were covered at the contact point with the keel by another long timber, the keelson. Normally, the sandwiching of frames between the keel and the keelson tightly locks them together and provides a sturdy support for the upper structure of a hull. However, *La Belle*'s wood was not strong enough, and the degraded wood of the keel, frames, and keelson required an independent support system to prevent compression and collapse.

Fix and his team hit upon an ingenious solution. They put fiberglass bolts through the keel, using the holes originally drilled into it when it was assembled in 1684. These bolts, which extend through the keel, have a narrow shoulder at the top surface of the keel. A laminated support was placed on the shoulder above the keel, which in turn held the frames onto the bolts. The

Peter Fix of Texas A&M University's Conservation Research Laboratory makes fiberglass and carbon fiber supports for hull timbers.

result was that the frames were not sitting directly on the keel, but were held up by the laminated support and the bolt, and all of the weight was transferred to the steel beam supporting the entire hull. The keelson was attached over the frames in the same manner.

The next problem was how to support the weight of the frames that arc out and upward, forming the curvature of the hull. One obvious solution would have been to construct numerous support posts, or stanchions, positioned at several points under each frame. But that would have required dozens, if not hundreds, of posts, creating a very conspicuous support structure.

Instead, Fix developed a series of rigid, narrow, laminated supports to hold each frame individually. Each timber would rest on a molded platform that followed the outward and upward curvature of the wood. The frame would lie directly on the platform and would not have to support its weight or the weight of the planking that would eventually be put back on the ship. However, the supporting platform needed to be thin enough to be visually unobtrusive, hidden between the frames and the outer hull planking, so as not to mar the visual perception of the ship. Fix began to experiment with different materials to find one that was strong and thin enough. He finally decided to use a combination of carbon fiber and fiberglass. Separate platform supports were custom made to follow the individual curvatures of each frame.

This construction turned out to be very successful. The fiberglass bolts through the keel easily supported the frames, and the frame platform supports cradled the ship's frames well. The reconstruction team fitted *La Belle*'s timbers back into place, and slowly the hull reappeared. The visual impact of the supporting structure was minimized, almost to the point that it will be difficult for visitors to the museum to figure out how the ship is held together. More importantly, the badly deteriorated keel does not have to support the entire weight of the hull and thus will not be crushed or deformed over time. The keel is designed to be the backbone of the vessel, but it is not meant to take the weight of the vessel on dry land. Under normal conditions, the weight of a vessel is evenly supported by the water around the floating hull. The exhibit will certainly testify to the hard work, dedication, and ingenuity of the many who devoted years of work to putting *La Belle* back together.

PUBLIC AWARENESS

Before the shipwreck was discovered, excavated, and reassembled, most Texans knew only that the French flag was among those that fly over the Six Flags Over Texas amusement park. *La Belle* changed that. Through intense media attention, millions of Texans learned that the first European colony in Texas had been French, not Spanish.[4]

From the start, we wanted the public to be aware of the project. The Texas Legislature had allocated substantial public funds to us, and therefore we considered ourselves accountable to the state's citizens. Even

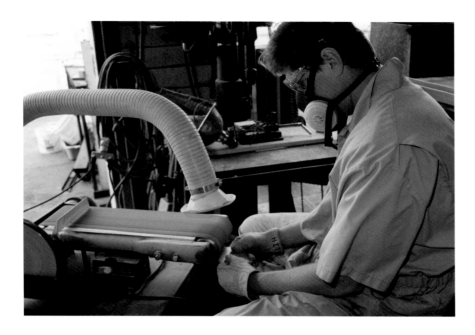

Peter Hitchcock of Texas A&M University's Conservation Research Laboratory manufactures parts for supporting the hull.

more important, we wanted the public to have the opportunity to share our excitement and sense of discovery. Previously, archaeologists had largely worked out of public view. Many archaeologists did not wish to be on display before the public, but others were simply unaware of the value of allowing lay people to watch excavations. Today "public archaeology" is a very important part of most major archaeological projects. Archaeologists now realize that the greater the public interest, the greater the opportunities and funding for future archaeological excavations.

To implement the public-archaeology component of the shipwreck project, the Texas Historical Commission established a Marketing Communications Division staffed with public relations professionals. Their top priority was to promote the shipwreck excavation. Regular press releases whetted the interest of the print and television media. To accommodate growing curiosity about the project, each week senior team members and a staff member from the Marketing Communication Division guided a group of media personnel on a tour of the cofferdam. Over the more than seven months of the excavation, well over one hundred media representatives visited, resulting in coverage by CNN, *The Today Show,* and newspapers across the country. Articles also appeared in *National Geographic Magazine, Smithsonian,* and the German *Geo.* Coverage was so extensive that the *Houston Chronicle* listed the excavation as one of the top ten Texas news stories of 1996, which was quite unusual for an archaeological project.

The project was also the subject of several documentary films shown to audiences worldwide. The Texas Historical Commission, Documentary Arts, Inc., of Dallas, and La Sept ARTE of Europe collaborated to produce *The Shipwreck of* La Belle, which was shown in twenty-two countries, mostly in Europe. The PBS program *NOVA,* in cooperation with Documentary Arts, Inc., and the Texas Historical Commission, produced another documentary, *Voyage of Doom,* for U.S. and Canadian audiences. That film is now in international distribution. Other documentary films about the project have been produced in Texas and the United Kingdom.

In addition, we allowed members of the public to visit the excavation. Thanks to a generous donation from Sandi Hyett and several others from the project's host city, Palacios, a public dock was built on one side of the cofferdam that was large enough for a sizable tour vessel to tie up. We set aside a portion of the cofferdam wall for visitors, who could look into the excavation pit and see La Salle's ship emerging from the mud. More than twenty-five thousand people from around the United States and many other countries visited the cofferdam.

The excavation offered an unparalleled opportunity for young people to learn about archaeology, shipwrecks, and Texas' early French history. We hired Pam Wheat-Stranahan as an archaeological educator to work with teachers and students. She developed a teacher lesson guide to accompany a traveling exhibit we had created about the excavation and La Salle's ex-

More than twenty-five thousand visitors traveled to the cofferdam during the seven months of excavation. *Photo by Stephen Myers*

pedition. From this she developed an Internet newsletter, *Journeys,* with sixty pages of lesson plans and resource materials for classroom educators. She then visited Texas Education Service Centers in Victoria, Corpus Christi, Midland, Austin, and San Antonio to instruct educators in how to use the lesson plans and other resources. This multiplied the reach to young people many-fold when teachers returned to their classrooms and shared the material with their students.

Wheat-Stranahan also wrote several articles that appeared in print publications for classroom teachers. In the fall of 1997, the back-to-school issue of *Insight, Newsletter of the Educational Services, Texas State Historical Association,* volume 1, featured the shipwreck in an article entitled "La Salle in Texas." This publication was distributed to three thousand teachers and others across the state. Another article, "New Evidence for the La Salle Expedition," which expanded the ideas for classroom application, was published in *Touchstone,* volume 17 (1998). And finally, the *La Belle* project was the cover story in the winter, 1997–98, issue of *The Classroom Teacher,* the magazine of the Texas Classroom Teachers Association.

Wheat-Stranahan's work educated thousands of young Texans about the excavation. She also wove into her work a number of ethical issues in archaeology, such as the importance of preserving the archaeological record and the necessity of proper excavation methods that incorporate modern scientific techniques.

Beyond working with educators and students, we allowed selected volunteers to actually participate in the excavation. All the sediments from inside and around the shipwreck had to be screened through fine mesh to recover small artifacts such as beads and pins, a task that could be done by nonarchaeologists under professional supervision. Roberta Ripke of the Communities Foundation of Texas, Palacios Area Fund, coordinated this process, spending hundreds of hours locating and scheduling volunteers to help out. Over the seven months of excavation, hundreds of volunteers were able to spend a day or more working on the shipwreck. For many, this was the experience of a lifetime. One couple scheduled their day of archaeology to coincide with their wedding anniversary; they said that it was by far the most interesting anniversary they had ever spent. A woman who scheduled her visit for her fiftieth birthday thought it the greatest gift she could have given herself. All the volunteers endured long days stooped over screens looking for tiny objects, not to mention the sometimes harrowing boat rides during inclement weather. Their contributions allowed precious financial resources to be used for other necessities.

After the excavations were finished, the public-awareness campaign continued. Both the Texas Historical Commission and Texas A&M's Conservation Research Laboratory placed numerous web pages on the Internet. Web cameras were installed so that the world could view the reassembly of the hull and other conservation projects such as the opening of one of *La Belle*'s cargo chests.

After the excavation, a coalition of museums in counties surrounding Matagorda Bay developed an innovative and far-reaching plan to exhibit the artifacts. They formed what is known as the La Salle Odyssey,

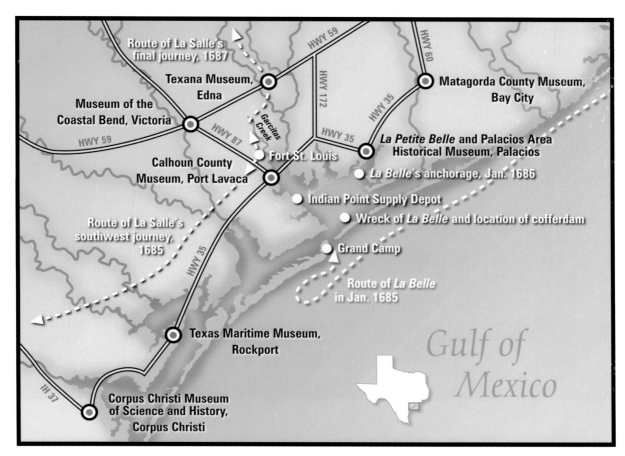

A network of seven museums along the central Texas coast, known as the La Salle Odyssey, exhibits artifacts and information related to La Salle's expedition to Texas. Each museum tells part of the story, which encourages visits to all seven to learn the entire history. *Illustration by Roland Pantermuehl*

an integrated series of exhibits that link museums in Matagorda, Jackson, Victoria, Calhoun, Aransas, and Nueces counties. Each museum in this "cultural-heritage trail" will tell a part of the story of the La Salle expedition, and visitors will be encouraged to visit the others to understand the entire story.

Exhibits at the Calhoun County Museum in Port Lavaca set the stage for the French colonization of the Texas Gulf Coast and explore the political situation that led to Louis XIV's decision to send the expedition through the Gulf of Mexico. The Texana Museum in Edna explores the native Karankawa Indians and their interactions with La Salle and his colonists. The Corpus Christi Museum of Science and History interprets the making of an expedition and the effect of La Salle's arrival on the peoples of southern Texas. This museum, which helped conserve some of the artifacts discovered in 1995, also showcases the science behind artifact conservation and hull reassembly. Rockport's Texas Mar-

itime Museum shows what life aboard *La Belle* was like and explores navigation in the seventeenth century. The Museum of the Coastal Bend in Victoria tells the story of Fort St. Louis. The Matagorda County Museum in Bay City has a major exhibition on the excavation inside the cofferdam. And Palacios—headquarters for the recovery project—is home to both an exhibit on the archaeological project and a fully functional half-scale replica of *La Belle*, christened *La Petite Belle*, that will sail from port to port, carrying with her information about the original ship.

Visitors to any part of the La Salle Odyssey will be encouraged to visit all the museums, stay a night in some of the local communities, and dine at area restaurants. The exciting history revealed in *La Belle* will therefore become a contributor to the local economies. In June, 2001, the Texas Legislature appropriated $300,000 for development of the exhibits; this is one-quarter of the amount necessary, but it was the

Statue of La Salle looking over Matagorda Bay at Indianola, Texas. *Photograph by Robert Clark*

critical seed money to start the project. The seven museums worked hard to raise the remaining funds and have made the La Salle Odyssey a reality.

A LASTING LEGACY

The discovery, excavation, and interpretation of the shipwreck provide a conclusion to a story that began with the bold dream of a driven explorer seeking fame and fortune in an unexplored continent. The conclusion is written in artifacts, analysis, and interpretation and finally brings to an end the sad story of La Salle's New World colony. As noted in the first chapter of this book, author Robert Weddle has written, "For want of an anchor the ship was lost; for want of a ship the colony was lost." The discovery and excavation of *La Belle* begs the addition of another phrase, "For want of a ship, *Texas changed forever.*" With the failure of France's effort to colonize an uncharted land, Spain seized the moment to fill the void, sent missionaries and soldiers to build missions and presidios in Texas, and indelibly imprinted Hispanic culture on the Lone Star State. *La Belle* is a great historical icon: a sunken ship that accidentally charted a grand new direction for the state's history. Millions of Americans now understand France's contributions to the Lone Star State's beginnings. What could be a better legacy for La Salle's diminutive, beautiful ship?

Notes

CHAPTER 1. Into a Watery Grave

1. Pierre Margry, ed., *Découvertes et établissement des Français dans l'ouest et dans le sud de l'Amérique septentrionale (1614–1754)*, vol. 2, pp. 539–40.
2. Robert S. Weddle correctly notes in *The Wreck of the Belle, the Ruin of La Salle*, pp. 196–213, that La Salle's colony was not a "fort" in the sense of a European stronghold, but rather a post built to house a fledgling colony. In this book we use the name Fort St. Louis because of its common association with the site.
3. Much of this chapter is based on *The La Salle Expedition to Texas: The Journal of Henri Joutel, 1684–1687*, ed. William C. Foster, trans. Johanna S. Warren; cited hereafter as Foster, *Joutel Journal*.
4. Weddle, *Wreck of the* Belle, pp. 6–12.
5. Robert S. Weddle, *Wilderness Manhunt: The Spanish Search for La Salle*, pp. 7–12.
6. Foster, *Joutel Journal*, p. 57.
7. Weddle, *Wilderness Manhunt*, p. 9.
8. Ibid., pp. 10–12.
9. Ibid., pp. 12–13.
10. Juan Enríquez Barroto, "The Enríquez Barroto Diary: Voyage of the Piraguas," in Robert S. Weddle, Mary Christine Morkovsky, and Patricia Galloway, eds., *La Salle, the Mississippi, and the Gulf: Three Primary Documents*, p. 171; cited hereafter as Weddle, et al., *La Salle*.
11. Ibid., pp. 171–72.
12. Juan Ysidro de Pardiñas Villar de Francos, "Declarations of Jumano and Cíbolo Indian Captains in April, 1689," in Charles Wilson Hackett, ed., *Historical Documents Relating to New Mexico, Nueva Vizcaya, and Approaches Thereto, to 1773*, vol. 2, pp. 263–81; the volume is cited hereafter as Hackett, *Historical Documents*.
13. Weddle, *Wilderness Manhunt*, pp. 159–73.
14. The pages from *La Belle*'s log and the ship picture were eventually archived in Seville, Spain, and were not appreciated for their historical importance until some two and a half centuries later when discovered by American researcher William Edward Dunn (see *Spanish and French Rivalry in the Gulf Region of the United States, 1678–1702, the Beginnings of Texas and Pensacola*, p. 99).
15. Foster, *Joutel Journal*, p. 137.
16. Nancy Parrot Hickerson, *The Jumanos: Hunters and Traders of the South Plains*, pp. xxii–xxiv. See also Nancy Adele Kenmotsu, "Seeking Friends, Avoiding Enemies: The Jumano Response to Spanish Colonization, A.D. 1580–1750," *Bulletin of the Texas Archeological Society* 72 (2001): 23–43.
17. Pardiñas, "Declaration of a Heathen Called Muygisofac," in Hackett, *Historical Documents*, pp. 277–78.
18. In fact, these were the remnants of the party that had murdered La Salle.
19. Pardiñas, "Declaration of a Heathen Called Muygisofac," in Hackett, *Historical Documents*, p. 279.
20. The gap reflects the time period from early October to late November when *La Belle* was in port at Petit Goäve. No log entries were made during that period.
21. The translation is by J. F. Jameson, "Fragments of the Log of the *Belle*," in Hackett, *Historical Documents*, pp. 474–81.

CHAPTER 2. La Salle's Grand Dream

The chapter 2 epigraph is from Anka Muhlstein, *La Salle: Explorer of the North American Frontier*, p. 157.

1. Francis Parkman, *La Salle and the Discovery of the Great West*, pp. 5–8.
2. Muhlstein, *La Salle*, p. 5.
3. Parkman, *La Salle*, p. 73.
4. Ibid., p. 237.

5. Muhlstein, *La Salle*, p. 81.

6. Robert S. Weddle, *The French Thorn: Rival Explorers in the Spanish Sea, 1682–1762*, p. 8.

7. Ibid., p. 26.

8. Muhlstein, *La Salle*, p. 86.

9. Parkman, *La Salle*, p. 246.

10. Weddle, *Wreck of the Belle*, pp. 87–98.

11. Parkman, *La Salle*, pp. 246–47.

12. Weddle, *Wilderness Manhunt*, p. 15.

13. Ibid., p. 19.

14. Margry, *Découvertes et établissement*, vol. 2, pp. 377, 382.

15. Weddle, *Wreck of the* Belle, pp. 121–25.

16. Parkman, *La Salle*, p. 253.

17. Ibid., pp. 223–25.

18. Foster, *Joutel Journal*, pp. 59–66.

19. Cavelier de La Salle to M. de Beaujeu, in Margry, *Découvertes et établissement*, vol. 2, pp. 528–29.

20. Weddle, *French Thorn*, p. 21.

21. Foster, *Joutel Journal*, p. 76.

22. Ibid., p. 85.

23. Ibid., pp. 87–88.

24. Ibid., pp. 88–90.

25. Ibid., p. 90.

26. Ibid., pp. 90–95, 95n31.

27. Ibid., pp. 97–131.

28. Ibid., pp. 112–31.

29. Ibid., pp. 151, 191–202.

30. Ibid., p. 199.

CHAPTER 3. A Monumental Discovery

1. Kathleen K. Gilmore, *The Keeran Site: The Probable Site of La Salle's Fort St. Louis in Texas,* Office of the State Archeologist Report 24, Texas Historical Commission.

2. During the 1970s, the search for the La Salle shipwrecks was undertaken by the Texas Antiquities Committee, a separate state agency administered by the Texas Historical Commission. In the mid-1990s, the Texas Antiquities Committee became part of the Texas Historical Commission.

3. H. Dickson Hoese, "On the Correct Landfall of La Salle in Texas, 1685," *Louisiana History* 19, no. 1 (1978): 5–32.

4. Jack Jackson, Robert S. Weddle, and Winston De Ville, *Mapping Texas and the Gulf Coast: The Contributions of Saint Denis, Oliván, and Le Maire*, p. 15; Jack Jackson, *Shooting the Sun: Cartographic Results of Military Activities in Texas, 1689–1829*, p. 34.

5. Robert A. Morton, "Appendix I: Approximate Inlet and Shoreline Positions in 1685, Matagorda Bay Area, Texas," in J. Barto Arnold III, *A Matagorda Bay Magnetometer Survey and Site Test Excavation Project.*

6. U.S. Army Corps of Engineers, *Annual Report, Chief of Engineers, Improvement of Rivers and Harbors,* House Ex.

Doc. 1, pt. 2, 46th Cong., 2d sess., vol. 2, pt. 1, App. K-11, 1879, pp. 921–27.

7. Arnold, *Matagorda Bay Magnetometer Survey.*

8. Ibid.

9. The marine archaeologists successfully located and mapped the submerged remains of the city courthouse, an imposing structure measuring sixty-two feet long by forty-seven feet wide, which was built in 1857 but destroyed only a few years later in the 1886 hurricane.

10. Jeffrey P. Brain, *On the Tunica Trail*, Louisiana Archaeological Survey and Antiquities Commission Anthropological Study, no. 1.

11. See, e.g., Jeffrey P. Brain, *Tunica Treasure.*

12. Ibid., pp. 34–35.

13. Olivier Bernier, *Louis XIV: A Royal Life*, pp. 107–45.

14. François Bluche, *Louis XIV*, pp. 392–94.

CHAPTER 4. Excavation inside a Cofferdam

1. David Roberts, "In Texas, a Ship Is Found and a Grand Dream Recalled," *Smithsonian Magazine*, Apr., 1997.

2. John D. Broadwater, "Shipwreck in a Swimming Pool: An Assessment of the Methodology and Technology Utilized on the Yorktown Shipwreck Archaeological Project," *Historical Archaeology* 26, no. 4 (1992): 36–46.

3. George Bass, ed., *A History of Seafaring Based on Underwater Archaeology.*

4. Lisa Moore LaRoe's story appeared as "La Salle's Last Voyage," in *National Geographic Magazine,* May, 1997, vol. 191, no. 5, pp. 72–83.

5. Peter Waddell, "The Disassembly of a 16th-Century Galleon," *International Journal of Nautical Archaeology* 15, no. 2 (1986): 137–48.

CHAPTER 5. The Beautiful Vessel

1. Toni L. Carrell, "*La Belle* Hull Analysis: An Overview of Results," on file at Texas Historical Commission.

2. Catharine L. Inbody, "*La Belle,* Rigging in the Days of the Spritsail Topmast" (paper presented at the Society for Historical Archaeology Conference on Historical and Underwater Archaeology, Providence, Rhode Island, Jan., 2003).

3. J. C. Lemineur, "Restitution Volumétrique de la Coque," in Jean Boudriot, ed., *Cavelier de La Salle, L'Expédition de 1684*, La Belle (cited hereafter as Boudriot, *Cavelier de La Salle*), p. 133.

4. Archives du Port de Rochefort, Service Historique de la Marine, "Construction Papers of *La Belle*," 1 L3 19, f 88v and f 89r, 1685; document located by John de Bry in 1998 and translated in de Bry, "Fleshing out the Cultural History of *La Belle* and the La Salle Expedition (1684–1687):

Archival Research in French Repositories," on file at Texas Historical Commission.

5. Masson eventually became Rochefort's master shipwright and received a gold medal from the king for outstanding service when he retired in the early eighteenth century (Boudriot, *La Belle,* p. 41).

6. Weddle, *The Wreck of the* Belle, p. 5.

7. Jean Boudriot, *The History of the French Frigate, 1650–1850.*

8. Boudriot, *Cavelier de La Salle,* p. 35.

9. A slightly different model that incorporates more of the archaeological evidence from *La Belle* has been built by Texas A&M graduate student Glenn Grieco; see Glenn P. Grieco, "Modeling *La Belle:* A Reconstruction of a Seventeenth-Century Light Frigate," master's thesis.

10. Bernard Allaire, "The Official Correspondence Concerning *La Belle* and the Expedition of Cavelier de la Salle to the Mississippi, 1684–1688," on file at Texas Historical Commission; cited hereafter as Allaire, "Official Correspondence."

11. "Orders from the King to Demuin (concerning a *barque* in bundle named *La Belle*)," Archives Nationales de France, Marine, B2-42, Apr., 1680. This document was translated by Bernard Allaire in "*La Belle* and the 'Bundle Technique,'" on file at Texas Historical Commission. Note that the name *La Belle* is coincidental and does not refer to La Salle's ship of the same name.

12. Weddle, *The Wreck of the* Belle, p. 47.

13. "Dépêches du ministre de la Marine," Archives Nationales de France, Marine, B 2, folio 210.

14. Toni Carrell, who is studying the hull remains, suggested (e-mail to James Bruseth, February 6, 2004) that the unassembled *barque longue* was ultimately not used by La Salle; instead another, older *barque* was extensively refurbished for the transatlantic journey. However, the archival evidence does not support this theory. An older *barque,* presumably the one Carrell thought La Salle took, was in fact still in Rochefort a year after the expedition set sail (Bibliothèque Nationale de France, NAF 21331, vol. 26, Correspondence of Pierre Arnoul, Intendant in Rochefort, General Correspondence, year 1685, f. 330–33, "Arnoul to Seignelay," July 17, 1685). The confusion stems from archival documents that indicate officials first suggested that an unassembled *barque longue* be specially constructed for La Salle. Later a decision was made to instead assemble for the expedition an *existing* ship that lay in pieces in Rochefort (Bernard Allaire, *Birth of a Bark*).

15. Allaire, "Official Correspondence."

16. Weddle, *Wreck of the* Belle, p. 128.

17. Ibid., pp. 99–100.

18. Taras P. Pevny, "Considerations for the Reassembly and Display of *La Belle,*" on file at Texas Historical Commission.

19. Carrell, "Hull Analysis."

20. Eric Rieth, *Le Maître-Gabarit: La Tablette et le Trébuchet: Essai Sur la Conception Non-graphique des Carènes du Moyen Âge au XX Siècle.*

21. Carrell, "Hull Analysis."

22. Dendrochronology is the use of tree rings to determine the age of wood samples. Each year trees grow new rings and they increase in circumference. The width of the ring varies each year depending largely on rainfall, with wide rings in most years and narrow rings during droughts. A scientist performing a dendrochronological analysis determines the age of a sample of wood by matching the pattern of wide and narrow rings against a master collection of wood samples with known ages, such as radiocarbon-dated specimens or wood from old buildings.

23. The timbers from *La Belle* exhibit remarkably little direct evidence of reuse, such as the presence of old fastener holes. While it might be argued that this suggests that the wood had never been used before, it seems illogical to assume that wood for *La Belle* would have been stored for two centuries waiting for a *barque longue* to be built. Moreover, the archival evidence supports the frequent disassembly of older ships and reuse of the salvageable wood (Bernard Allaire, "The Birth of a Bark," on file at Texas Historical Commission). Old timbers were likely selected for reuse to minimize the presence of old fastener holes.

24. Carrell, "Hull Analysis."

25. Amy Mitchell, "Wood Species Used in Timbers of the *Belle* Shipwreck," on file at Texas Historical Commission.

CHAPTER 6. Cargo for a Colony

1. The artifacts presented in this chapter represent the major and more interesting categories of items found on *La Belle.* An estimated 95 percent of recovered artifacts are discussed. Not every object is included because many are fragmentary barrel staves, concretions, or unidentified or fragmentary artifacts, and more artifacts continue to be discovered as additional concretions are examined during the conservation process. A technical report in preparation will list all the artifacts from the wreck.

2. La Salle, "Process Verbal," Apr. 18, 1684, in Margry, *Découvertes et établissement,* vol. 3, p. 541.

3. Foster, *Joutel Journal,* pp. 120, 136.

4. Ibid., p. 137.

5. "The Enríquez Barroto Diary: Voyage of the Piraguas," in Weddle, et al., *La Salle,* p. 172.

6. The description of the barrels is based on the extensive analysis by Brad Loewen, "The Casks from *La Belle* and the Rochefort Arsenal, ca. 1684," on file at Texas Historical Commission.

7. The firepot containing the cannon ball would not have

exploded as would a grenade. Whoever made it in France would have known this, but put the solid ball inside anyway.

8. Muhlstein, *La Salle*, pp. 27–28.

9. Timothy K. Perttula and Michael D. Glascock, "Glass Beads from the 1686 *La Belle* Shipwreck, Matagorda Bay, Texas," on file at Texas Historical Commission; and John de Bry and Jean Boudriot, "Discovering *La Belle,*" *Maritime Life and Traditions* 10 (2001): 35.

10. Foster, *Joutel Journal,* p. 208.

11. Brain, *Tunica Treasure,* p. 189.

12. Foster, *Joutel Journal,* p. 184.

13. Brain, *Tunica Treasure,* pp. 197–201.

14. Robert A. Birmingham and Carol I. Mason, "'Jesuit Rings' from the *Belle,*" on file at Texas Historical Commission.

15. Foster, *Joutel Journal,* p. 209.

16. The details about the artifacts in the box are known due to the meticulous work of Helen Dewolf at Texas A&M University's Conservation Research Laboratory. Dewolf is in charge of the conservation of *La Belle* artifacts and has had much experience working with encrusted artifacts from marine sites.

17. Mark A. Feulner, "An Analysis of Iron Trade Goods Recovered from La Salle's *Belle,*" master's thesis, pp. 12–13.

18. Ibid., pp. 16–21.

19. Foster, *Joutel Journal,* pp. 151, 180, 209.

20. Feulner, "Analysis of Iron Trade Goods," pp. 36–38.

21. Ibid., pp. 38–41.

22. Ibid, pp. 26–27.

23. Donald H. Keith, Worth Carlin, and John de Bry, "A Bronze Cannon from *La Belle,* 1686: Its Construction, Conservation, and Display," *The International Journal of Nautical Archaeology* 26, no. 2 (1997): 144–58; and de Bry and Boudriot, "Discovering *La Belle.*"

24. "The Enríquez Barroto Diary: Voyage of the Piraguas," in Weddle, et al., *La Salle,* pp. 172–73.

25. Much information also comes from John Hamilton, conservator working on *La Belle* artifacts.

26. T. M. Hamilton, *Colonial Frontier Guns,* p. 38.

27. Much of the description of vessels from *La Belle* comes from Kathleen K. Gilmore and Nancy G. Reese, "Ceramic Containers from *La Belle,*" on file at Texas Historical Commission.

28. Bonnie L. Gums, Gregory A. Waselkov, and Helen Dewolf, "Domestic Artifacts from *La Belle,*" on file at Texas Historical Commission; hereafter cited as Gums, et al., "Domestic Artifacts from *La Belle.*"

29. Credit for unraveling the story of the pewter cups goes to Jim Jobling and others at the Texas A&M Conservation Research Laboratory. The name Jean Phily was found by Bernard Allaire and reported in "Documents concernant l'expédition de Cavelier de La Salle de 1684 dans les archives notariales de La Rochelle et de Rochefort aux Archives départmentales de Charente-Maritime, France," on file at Texas Historical Commission.

30. All information about the gourd containers is from J. Phil Dering, "Plant Remains from the *Belle,*" on file at Texas Historical Commission.

31. Gums, et al., "Domestic Artifacts from *La Belle.*"

32. Ibid.

33. Ibid.

34. Ibid.

35. Ibid.

36. Foster, *Joutel Journal,* pp. 102–105.

37. Information about the leather shoes comes from Anthony Randolph's excellent report, "An Analysis of the *Belle* Footwear Assemblage," on file at Texas Historical Commission.

38. Gums, et al., "Domestic Artifacts from *La Belle.*"

39. Ibid.

40. Gregory D. Cook and Lois A. Swanick, "To Discover the River Mississippi: Navigational Artifacts from *La Belle* in the Context of La Salle's Final Voyage," on file at Texas Historical Commission.

41. Ibid. Much of the work on understanding the nocturnal was done by graduate student Lois Swanick and Professor Don Carona of the Texas A&M University Department of Physics.

42. Ibid.

43. Gums, et al., "Domestic Artifacts from *La Belle.*" There is a slight possibility that the clock key is actually part of a spigot.

44. Ellen Sue Turner and Thomas R. Hester, *A Field Guide to Stone Artifacts of Texas Indians,* Texas Monthly Field Guide Series, Texas Monthly Press, p. 171.

45. Dering, "Plant Remains from the *Belle.*"

46. Foster, *Joutel Journal,* p. 124.

47. Dering, "Plant Remains from the *Belle.*"

48. Foster, *Joutel Journal,* p. 137.

49. Ibid.

50. La Salle, "Process Verbal," April 18, 1684, in Margry, *Découvertes et éstaablissement,* vol. 3, p. 541.

CHAPTER 7. Skeletons in the Ship

1. D. Gentry Steele, "Skeletal Remains from the 1686 Wreck of La Salle's Ship *La Belle,*" on file at Texas Historical Commission.

2. Foster, *Joutel Journal,* pp. 135–36.

3. The pelvises of females are broad and shallow in comparison with those of males, and they have a rounded and capacious birth canal.

4. Steele, "Skeletal Remains from the 1686 Wreck."

5. Ibid.

6. C. Wayne Smith, Ellen M. Heath, D. Andrew Merriwether, and David Reed, "Excavation, Facial Recon-

struction, and DNA Analysis of Skeletal Remains from La Salle's Vessel, *La Belle,*" on file at Texas Historical Commission.

7. Scottish Rite Hospital in Dallas graciously agreed to perform the CT scan.

8. Susan D. deFrance, "The La Salle Shipwreck Project: Faunal Remains from the Shipwreck of the *Belle,*" on file at Texas Historical Commission.

9. Once La Salle reached Texas, he found that the terrain was not as dense as that of the Mississippi River area, and he eventually traded for horses with the Caddo Indians of eastern Texas.

10. Foster, *Joutel Journal,* p. 122.

11. Ibid., p. 112.

12. Ibid., pp. 73, 112.

13. Ibid., p. 128.

14. Ibid., p. 51

15. deFrance, "The La Salle Shipwreck Project."

16. Foster, *Joutel Journal,* p. 136.

CHAPTER 8. *La Belle's* Legacy

1. Donny L. Hamilton, "Methods of Conserving Underwater Archaeological Material Culture. Conservation Files: ANTH 605, Conservation of Cultural Resources I," online laboratory manual.

2. C. Wayne Smith, "Beating the Ocean," *Discovering Archaeology* (Jan./Feb., 2001), pp. 61–65.

3. Equipment and supplies to X-ray *La Belle* artifacts were generously donated by Fuji NDT Systems.

4. Some have argued that Spain had settlements in the El Paso and Presidio areas of Texas when La Salle settled along the coast. While this is true, the El Paso settlement was at the time on the southern side of the Rio Grande and thus not in Texas, and the Presidio settlement was not a colony but a mission and presidio complex, with a small number of priests and a few soldiers.

Bibliography

Published Sources

Arnold, J. Barto, III. *A Matagorda Bay Magnetometer Survey and Site Test Excavation Project.* Texas Antiquities Committee Publication 9. Austin: Texas Antiquities Committee, 1982.

Bass, George, ed. *A History of Seafaring Based on Underwater Archaeology.* London: Thames and Hudson, 1972.

Bernier, Olivier. *Louis XIV: A Royal Life.* New York: Doubleday, 1987.

Bluche, François. *Louis XIV.* Paris: Fayard, 1986.

Boudriot, Jean, ed. *Cavelier de La Salle, L'Expédition de 1684, La Belle.* Rotherfield, Eng.: Jean Boudriot Publications, 2000.

Boudriot, Jean, with Hubert Berti, collaborator. *The History of the French Frigate, 1650–1850.* Trans. David H. Roberts. Rotherfield, Eng.: Jean Boudriot Publications, 1993.

Brain, Jeffrey P. *On the Tunica Trail.* Baton Rouge: Louisiana Archaeological Survey and Antiquities Commission Anthropological Study, no. 1, 1977.

———. *Tunica Treasure.* Cambridge: Published jointly by the Peabody Museum of Archaeology and Ethnology, Harvard University, and the Peabody Museum of Salem, 1979.

Broadwater, John D. "Shipwreck in a Swimming Pool: An Assessment of the Methodology and Technology Utilized on the Yorktown Shipwreck Archaeological Project." *Historical Archaeology* 26, no. 4 (1992): 36–46.

de Bry, John, and Jean Boudriot. "Discovering *La Belle.*" *Maritime Life and Traditions* 10 (2001): 28–41.

Dunn, William Edward. *Spanish and French Rivalry in the Gulf Region of the United States, 1678–1702, the Beginnings of Texas and Pensacola.* Austin: University of Texas Bulletin, no. 1705, 1917.

Enríquez Barroto, Juan. "The Enríquez Barroto Diary: Voyage of the Piraguas." In *La Salle, the Mississippi, and the Gulf: Three Primary Documents,* trans. Robert S. Weddle, ed. by Robert S. Weddle, Mary Christine Morkovsky, and Patricia Galloway. College Station: Texas A&M University Press, 1987.

Foster, William C., ed. *The La Salle Expedition to Texas: The Journal of Henri Joutel, 1684–1687.* Trans. Johanna S. Warren. Austin: Texas State Historical Association, 1998.

Francis, Peter, Jr. *The Glass Trade Beads of Europe, Their Manufacture, Their History, and Their Identification.* The World of Beads Monograph Series 8. New York: Lapis Route Books, 1988.

Gilmore, Kathleen K. *The Keeran Site: The Probable Site of La Salle's Fort St. Louis in Texas.* Austin: Texas Historical Commission, Office of the State Archeologist Report 24, 1973.

———. "Treachery and Tragedy in the Texas Wilderness: The Adventures of Jean L'Archeveque in Texas (a Member of La Salle's Colony)." *Bulletin of the Texas Archeological Society* 69 (1998): 35–46.

Hackett, Charles Wilson, ed. *Historical Documents Relating to New Mexico, Nueva Vizcaya, and Approaches Thereto, to 1773.* Vol. 2. Washington, D.C.: The Carnegie Institution of Washington, 1926.

Hamilton, Donny L. "Methods of Conserving Underwater Archaeological Material Culture. Conservation Files: ANTH 605, Conservation of Cultural Resources I." On-line laboratory manual. Nautical Archaeology Program, Texas A&M University, World Wide Web, http://nautarch.tamu.edu/class/ANTH605. 1998 (cited February 19, 2003).

Hamilton, T. M. *Colonial Frontier Guns.* Union City, Tenn.: Pioneer Press, 1987.

Hickerson, Nancy Parrott. *The Jumanos: Hunters and Traders of the South Plains.* Austin: University of Texas Press, 1994.

Hoese, H. Dickson. "On the Correct Landfall of La Salle in Texas, 1685." *Louisiana History* 19, no. 1 (1978): 5–32.

Jackson, Jack. *Shooting the Sun: Cartographic Results of Mili-*

tary Activities in Texas, 1689–1829. Lubbock: The Book Club of Texas, 1998.

Jackson, Jack, Robert S. Weddle, and Winston De Ville. *Mapping Texas and the Gulf Coast: The Contributions of Saint Denis, Oliván, and Le Maire.* College Station: Texas A&M University Press, 1990.

Keith, Donald H., Worth Carlin, and John de Bry. "A Bronze Cannon from *La Belle,* 1686: Its Construction, Conservation, and Display." *The International Journal of Nautical Archaeology* 26, no. 2 (1997): 144–58.

Kenmotsu, Nancy Adele. "Seeking Friends, Avoiding Enemies: The Jumano Response to Spanish Colonization, A.D. 1580–1750." *Bulletin of the Texas Archeological Society* 72 (2001): 23–43.

Lardner, Dionysius. *A Treatise on the Origin, Progressive Improvement, and Present State of the Manufacture of Porcelain and Glass.* 1834. Reprint, Park Ridge, New Jersey: Noyes Press, 1972.

LaRoe, Lisa Moore. "La Salle's Last Voyage." *National Geographic Magazine,* vol. 191, no. 5 (May, 1997), pp. 72–83.

Lemineur, J. C. "Restitution Volumétrique de la Coque." In *Cavelier de La Salle, L'Expédition de 1684,* La Belle, ed. Jean Boudriot. Rotherfield, Eng.: Jean Boudriot Publications, 2000.

Margry, Pierre, ed. *Découvertes et établissement des Français dans l'ouest et dans le sud de l'Amérique septentrionale (1614–1754).* 6 vols. Paris: D. Jouaust, 1876–86.

Marx, Jenifer G. "Brethren of the Coast." In *Pirates: Terror on the High Seas, from the Caribbean to the South China Sea,* ed. David Cordingly, pp. 36–57. Atlanta: Turner Publishing, 1996.

Morton, Robert A. "Appendix I: Approximate Inlet and Shoreline Positions in 1685, Matagorda Bay Area, Texas." In *A Matagorda Bay Magnetometer Survey and Site Test Excavation Project,* by J. Barto Arnold III. Texas Antiquities Committee Publication 9. Austin: Texas Antiquities Committee, 1982.

Muhlstein, Anka. *La Salle: Explorer of the North American Frontier,* translated from the French by Willard Wood. New York: Arcade, 1994.

Newcomb, W. W., Jr. *The Indians of Texas from Prehistoric to Modern Times.* Austin: University of Texas Press, 1961.

Parkman, Francis. *La Salle and the Discovery of the Great West.* 1889. Reprint, New York: New American Library, 1963.

Ricklis, Robert A. *The Karankawa Indians of Texas: An Ecological Study of Cultural Tradition and Change.* Austin: University of Texas Press, 1996.

Rieth, Eric. *Le Maître-Gabarit: La Tablette et le Trébuchet: Essai Sur la Conception Non-graphique des Carènes du Moyen Âge au XX Siècle.* Paris: Comité des Travaux Historiques et Scientifiques, 1996.

Roberts, David. "In Texas, a Ship is Found and a Grand Dream Recalled." *Smithsonian Magazine,* April, 1997.

Smith, C. Wayne. "Beating the Ocean." *Discovering Archaeology* (January/February, 2001), pp. 61–65.

Sprague, Roderick. "Glass Trade Beads: A Progress Report." *Historical Archaeology* 19, no. 2 (1985): 87–105.

Turner, Ellen Sue, and Thomas R. Hester. *A Field Guide to Stone Artifacts of Texas Indians.* Austin: Texas Monthly Field Guide Series, Texas Monthly Press, 1985.

U.S. Army Corps of Engineers. *Annual Report, Chief of Engineers, Improvement of Rivers and Harbors.* Washington, D.C.: House Ex. Doc. 1, pt. 2, 46th Cong., 2d sess., vol. 2, pt. 1, App. K-11 (1879), pp. 921–27.

Waddell, Peter. "The Disassembly of a 16th-Century Galleon." *International Journal of Nautical Archaeology* 15, no. 2 (1986): 137–48.

Weddle, Robert S. *The French Thorn: Rival Explorers in the Spanish Sea: 1682–1762.* College Station: Texas A&M University Press, 1991.

———. *Wilderness Manhunt: The Spanish Search for La Salle.* Austin: University of Texas Press, 1973. Reprint, College Station: Texas A&M University Press, 1991.

———. *The Wreck of the* Belle, *the Ruin of La Salle.* College Station: Texas A&M University Press, 2001.

Weddle, Robert S., Mary Christine Morkovsky, and Patricia Galloway, eds. *La Salle, the Mississippi, and the Gulf: Three Primary Documents.* Trans. Ann Linda Bell and Robert S. Weddle. College Station: Texas A&M University Press, 1987.

Unpublished Sources

Allaire, Bernard. "The Birth of a Bark." Austin: Manuscript on file at Texas Historical Commission, 2002.

———. "Documents concernant l'expédition de Cavelier de La Salle de 1684 dans les archives notariales de La Rochelle et de Rochefort aux Archives départementales de Charente-Maritime, France." Austin: Manuscript on file at Texas Historical Commission, 2001.

———. "*La Belle* and the 'Bundle Technique.'" Austin: Manuscript on file at Texas Historical Commission, 2001.

———. "The Official Correspondence Concerning *La Belle* and the Expedition of Cavelier de la Salle to the Mississippi, 1684–1688." Austin: Manuscript on file at Texas Historical Commission, 2000.

Archives du Port de Rochefort, Service Historique de la Marine. "Construction Papers of *La Belle.*" 1 L3 19, f 88v and f 89r, 1685.

Archives Nationales de France. "Dépêches du ministre de la Marine." Marine, B2, folio 210.

———. "Orders from the King to Demuin (concerning a *barque* in bundle named *La Belle*)." Marine, B2-42, April, 1680.

Bibliothèque Nationale de France, NAF 21331, vol. 26, Correspondence of Pierre Arnoul, Intendant in Rochefort,

General Correspondence, year 1685, f. 330–33, "Arnoul to Seignelay," July 17, 1685.

Birmingham, Robert A., and Carol I. Mason. "'Jesuit Rings' from the *Belle*." Austin: Manuscript on file at Texas Historical Commission, 2002.

Carrell, Toni L. "*La Belle* Hull Analysis: An Overview of Results." Austin: Manuscript on file at Texas Historical Commission, 2002.

Cook, Gregory D., and Lois A. Swanick. "To Discover the River Mississippi: Navigational Artifacts from *La Belle* in the Context of La Salle's Final Voyage." Austin: Manuscript on file at Texas Historical Commission, 2003.

de Bry, John. "Fleshing Out the Cultural History of *La Belle* and the La Salle Expedition (1684–1687): Archival Research in French Repositories." Austin: Manuscript on file at Texas Historical Commission, 2003.

deFrance, Susan D. "The La Salle Shipwreck Project: Faunal Remains from the Shipwreck of the *Belle*." Austin: Manuscript on file at Texas Historical Commission, 2000.

Dering, J. Phil. "Plant Remains from the *Belle*." Austin: Manuscript on file at Texas Historical Commission, 2003.

Feulner, Mark A. "An Analysis of Iron Trade Goods Recovered from La Salle's *Belle*." Master's thesis, Texas A&M University, 2002.

Gilmore, Kathleen K., and Nancy G. Reese. "Ceramic Containers from *La Belle*." Austin: Manuscript on file at Texas Historical Commission, 2001.

Grieco, Glenn P. "Modeling *La Belle*: A Reconstruction of a Seventeenth-Century Light Frigate." Master's thesis, Texas A&M University, 2003.

Gums, Bonnie L., Gregory A. Waselkov, and Helen Dewolf. "Domestic Artifacts from *La Belle*." Austin: Manuscript on file at Texas Historical Commission, 2003.

Inbody, Catharine L. "*La Belle*, Rigging in the Days of the Spritsail Topmast." Paper presented at the Society for Historical Archaeology Conference on Historical and Underwater Archaeology, Providence, Rhode Island, January, 2003.

Loewen, Brad. "The Casks from *La Belle* and the Rochefort Arsenal, ca. 1684." Austin: Manuscript on file at Texas Historical Commission, 1999.

Mitchell, Amy. "Wood Species Used in Timbers of the *Belle* Shipwreck." Austin: Manuscript on file at Texas Historical Commission, 1998.

Perttula, Timothy K., and Michael D. Glascock. "Glass Beads from the 1686 *La Belle* Shipwreck, Matagorda Bay, Texas." Austin: Manuscript on file at Texas Historical Commission.

Pevny, Taras P. "Considerations for the Reassembly and Display of *La Belle*." Austin: Manuscript on file at Texas Historical Commission, 1999.

Randolph, Anthony. "An Analysis of the *Belle* Footwear Assemblage." Austin: Manuscript on file at Texas Historical Commission, 2003.

Smith, C. Wayne, Ellen M. Heath, D. Andrew Merriwether, and David Reed. "Excavation, Facial Reconstruction, and DNA Analysis of Skeletal Remains from La Salle's Vessel, *La Belle*." Austin: Manuscript on file at Texas Historical Commission, 2003.

Steele, D. Gentry. "Skeletal Remains from the 1686 Wreck of La Salle's Ship *La Belle*." Austin: Manuscript on file at Texas Historical Commission, 2003.

Wilbanks, Ralph L., Wes Hall, and Gary E. McKee. "Search for *L'Aimable*." Austin: Texas Historical Commission, NUMA Priority Data, Antiquities Permit no. 1852.

Acknowledgments

On a hot July afternoon in 1995, marine archaeologists from the Texas Historical Commission discovered a cannon buried in a shipwreck in Matagorda Bay, Texas. The cannon was raised a few days later, and its identification confirmed that La Salle's lost ship, *La Belle,* had finally been found. This discovery transformed a small-scale archaeological marine survey into one of the most exciting and complex shipwreck recoveries ever attempted in North America. Hundreds of individuals, corporations, foundations, and other organizations contributed to the ultimate success of the La Salle Shipwreck Project in innumerable ways. This acknowledgment honors many who were involved but does not include everyone who made valuable contributions. For those I cannot mention due to limited space, I offer my heartfelt thanks for your financial support, hard work, and donated resources.

La Belle's discovery generated concerns about protecting the ship and securing the necessary funds to recover her. The leadership and support of Texas Historical Commission chair John Liston Nau III, the other commissioners, and Texas Historical Commission executive director Curtis Tunnell were invaluable. While everyone realized that the cost of the project would be high, John, the other commissioners, and Curtis were absolutely committed to launching a major recovery effort employing the highest standards of scientific archaeology.

Buoyed by the agency's wholehearted support, we faced the daunting task of deciding where to begin. First, funding had to be secured for planning the project. I called John Crain, vice president of the Dallas-based Summerlee Foundation, for guidance. In his usual kind and knowledgeable manner, he advised me about sources of funds but suggested that the State of Texas should lead the initiative through its own contribution. With this in mind, John Nau and Curtis Tunnell began to seek legislative support while I approached the private philanthropic community.

John and Curtis first contacted Texas Lieutenant Governor Bob Bullock, who immediately became a great proponent of the project and enlisted the support of then-Governor George W. Bush, Speaker of the House Pete Laney, and other legislators. Through their efforts, $1.75 million in state-appropriated funds were set aside for the shipwreck project.

Meanwhile, at John Crain's suggestion, I contacted Houston Endowment grant officer Ann Hamilton. She instantly realized the importance of the discovery and suggested that I submit an emergency grant application, and only a short time after we turned in the proposal, the board of directors of Houston Endowment awarded us a $30,000 grant. This initial funding was crucial, because it enabled us to begin planning the excavation and to hire someone to monitor the wreck site. Another generous donation of $265,000 from the late Dennis O'Connor of Victoria allowed us to begin constructing the cofferdam.

The late Anice Read, deputy director of the Texas Historical Commission, was an invaluable guide in my fundraising efforts. Anice had been diagnosed with cancer just before *La Belle* was discovered, but this did not deter her. She would often fly to Houston to receive a chemotherapy treatment, and then immediately afterward pick me up at the airport in her rental car to make calls on potential donors in the Houston area. I can think of no one with this kind of dedication and fortitude but the incredible Anice Read.

Several others offered fundraising advice and help, including Edwin Allday, Jane Barnhill, J. P. Bryan, Shirley Caldwell, Bill Caruth, the late George Christian, Harold Courson, Roy Cullen, David Jackson, Mark McLaughlin, Dini Partners, Venable Proctor, Julian Read, and Pierre Schlumberger. My most sincere appreciation for your assistance.

Grants soon followed from a number of sources: the Federal Highway Administration and the Texas Department of Transportation, Intermodal Surface Transportation Efficiency Act, Enhancement Program; Houston Endowment, Inc.; the Meadows Foundation; Mobil Exploration and Producing US, Inc.; the Cullen Foundation; the Fondren Foundation; the Summerlee Foundation; Shell Oil Company Foundation; the Hillcrest Foundation; Blue Bell Creameries, L.P.; Diamond M Foundation, Inc.; the Melbern G. and Susanne M. Glasscock Foundation; Carolyn Bennett Jackson; the Kathryn O'Connor Foundation; the Trull Foundation; and Bill's Fund of the Communities Foundation of Texas.

During this fundraising campaign, a nonprofit corporation, the Friends of the Texas Historical Commission, was formed to help arrange financial backing for the project. Friends executive director Linda Lee, along with past board president Harriet Lattimer, current president Killis Almond, and the other board members, worked diligently with me to secure private monies. The organization also assisted with collecting and disbursing grant funds. Without the wonderful help of the Friends of the Texas Historical Commission, the excavation would not have been possible.

Additional grants and gifts came from numerous other donors: Jane and John Barnhill; the Brown Foundation, Inc.; Sandi Burmeister and Don Hyett; Clifton and Shirley Caldwell; the late George Christian; the Clements Foundation; the Communities Foundation of Texas; former Texas Historical Commission commissioner and long-time supporter of Texas archaeology Harold Courson; the Harriet M. Cunningham Charitable Foundation, Inc.; the Jean and Price Daniel Foundation, Inc.; the James R. Dougherty, Jr., Foundation; the Ella F. Fondren Foundation; Friends of the Corpus Christi Museum; R. B. and Kathleen Gilmore; Global Marine Drilling Company; Frank W. Gorman, Jr.; the Greater Houston Community Foundation/Chris and Don Sanders Charitable Fund; the Gulf Coast Medical Foundation; the Hobby Family Foundation; Dana and Myriam McGinnis; Mr. and Mrs. Robert E. McKee III; the Robert E. and Evelyn McKee Foundation; National Geographic Society; Neiman Marcus; the Potts and Sibley Foundation; the Propeller Club of the United States; Wayne Ralph; Julian Read; the Summerfield G. Roberts Foundation; San Antonio Conservation Society; the O. B. and Ethyl Sawyer Trust; the Social Studies Center for Educator Development; Jill and Stephen Souter; Paul P. Steed; the Strake Foundation; the Roy and Christine Sturgis Charitable and Educational Trust; and the Texas Classroom Teachers Association. Literally hundreds of others also contributed money to pay for the excavation of *La Belle*. I am deeply grateful for these generous contributions.

Donations of in-kind services or products supported the excavation and analysis as well. Among those who contributed were Areté Image Software; Autodesk, Inc.; Cellular One of Austin; Center for Historical Archaeology; Compaq Computer Corporation; Coroplast, Inc.; the Corpus Christi Museum of Science and History; Cyberform International; Dickies Work Clothes; Digital Vision, Inc.; Documentary Arts, Inc.; Don's Diving Service; EOS Systems; Epson American, Inc.; G&W Engineers; GTE Mobilnet; Houston Lighting and Power Company; Kingfisher Marine Services, Inc.; Mike Lagasse; L. A. Landry and Associates, Inc.; Marine Sonic Technology, Inc.; ORE International; Read-Poland Associates; Ships of Discovery; Silver Eagle Distributors, Inc.; Shadow Sloan; Sokkia Measuring Systems; South Texas Nuclear Project Operating Company; Sterilite Corporation; Rick Stryker; Texas A&M Galveston's Scientific Diving Program; Texas A&M Galveston's Small Boat Operations; Trimble Navigational, Ltd.; United Scaffolding America; Vinson and Elkins, LLP; and Jack Ward.

Many individuals and organizations from Palacios and other parts of Texas made valuable contributions to the project: the City of Palacios, Big Tu of Captain Tom's, Sandi Burmeister, Johnny Burton, C and B Photo/Video, Colleen Claybourn, Everett Cordray, Jim and Veda Dale, Ronnie Gallager, Robbie Gregory, Wayne Gronquist, Andy Hall, Judge Howard Hartzog, Harvey's Welding, Christi Herrera, Jack Hollister, Lain Hollister, Don Hyett, Don Keith, Leonard Lamar, Inga Larson, the Luther Hotel, Matagorda County Navigation District Number One, Tricia Matthew, Laddie Matusek, Terry Mosier, Randy and Lucy Muns, Gladys Murphy, Palacios Sporting Goods, Warren Pierce, Pier Drive Inn, Gary Poage, Wayne Pool, Dale Porter, Porter's Ace Hardware, Roberta Ripke, Jack Roca, Larry Sanders, Vic and Genie Strickland, Texas Parks and Wildlife Department, and J. and Lorraine Wilson.

My sincere thanks go to the wonderful crew that labored so long and hard under such difficult conditions. Toni Carrell, Joe Cozzi, and Mike Davis were the assistant project directors. Other crew members included David Ball, Noreen Carrell, Stefan Claesson, Greg Cook, Gary Franklin, Toni Franklin, Aimee Green, Layne Hedrick, Peter Hitchcock, David Johnson, Paul Jordan, Sara Keyes, Mason McDaniel, Chuck Meide, Sarah Milstead, Amy Mitchell, Taras Pevny, Brett Phaneuf, Kris Taylor, Henry Thomason, and Karen Tier.

A great many people generously volunteered their time to the field project. Each day four to six volunteers were selected to work with the professional crew to screen artifacts, build vats to hold artifacts, or undertake a myriad other tasks. Their efforts allowed the professional crew to make more rapid progress and save precious financial resources for other necessities. The incredible work of all the volunteers is greatly appreciated, but the following individuals deserve particular mention: Judd Austin, Colleen Claybourn, Karen and Mike Fulghum, R. C. Harmon, Lain Hollister, Paul Jordan, Doug Knowell, John Luce, Gary McKee, John and Shelly Preston, Ona B. Reed, Judge Loy Sneary, Karen Tier, and J. and Lorraine Wilson.

Special thanks go to Roberta Ripke, our volunteer coordinator. What started out as the occasional task of scheduling volunteers grew into a nearly full-time job as requests to work on the wreck poured in from across the country. Without Roberta's tireless efforts, we could not possibly have used so many volunteers so efficiently.

After *La Belle* had been recovered and the field project

ended, much of the work focused on conservation of the hull and artifacts by the Conservation Research Laboratory at Texas A&M University. The skilled and knowledgeable laboratory staff expertly guided the preservation of *La Belle* and her artifacts. This group, under the able leadership of Dr. Donny Hamilton, conservator Dr. Helen Dewolf, and project manager Jim Jobling, includes Cory Arçak, Erkut Arçak, Jason Barrett, Amy Borgens, Ben Cichowski, Michael Clifford, Stuart Collins, Jon Faucher, Mark Feulner, Glenn Grieco, John Hamilton, Sara Hoskins, Stephanie Judjahn-Creasy, Jeff Kampfl, Adam Kane, Ben Liu, Brian Mason, Troy Nowak, Anthony Randolph, Carrie Sowden, Lois Swanick, Jon Swanson, Dan Walker, and Michael West.

Special acknowledgment goes to Peter Hitchcock, Taras Pevny, and above all, Peter Fix, who orchestrated the reconstruction of *La Belle*'s hull and designed and implemented the innovative support system that allowed it to be conserved as an integral unit and installed in its final resting place in the Bob Bullock Texas State History Museum. Faculty from the Texas A&M Department of Anthropology and the Nautical Archaeology Program have also greatly helped the project and include Kevin Crisman, Fred Hocker, C. Wayne Smith, D. Gentry Steele, and Richard J. Steffy. A number of volunteers helped with the reconstruction of *La Belle;* they include Joe Cozzi, Charlotte Donald, Marianne Franklin, Catharine Inbody Corder, Colin McIntyre, and Micky Presley. Their unselfish work was a great help during the reconstruction and preservation of these unique remains.

More than 250 organizations and individuals donated materials and in-kind services to help conserve *La Belle*'s hull and artifacts. These include Ameron International; Applied Industrial Technology; Baldor Electric, Inc.; Browning-Ferris, Inc.; C. F. Jordan, Inc.; Chaparral Steel; Chicago Pneumatic; Chromalox; Davis Iron Works; Dow Chemical Company; Dow Corning Corporation; Dynacon, Inc.; Fibergrate Composite Structures, Inc.; Fuji NDT Systems; Gulf Coast X-Ray, Inc.; Harmsco Industrial Filters; Hexcel Schwebel; Hub City, Inc.; Huntsman Chemicals; Professor Dennis Lee; Mallinckrodt-Baker, Inc.; Nida-Core Corporation; Northrop-Grumman; Occidental Chemical Company; Perstorp Xytec; Remetek Corporation; Scottish Rite Hospital for Children; Strongwell Corporation; Texas A&M University; Trinity Industries; and Vetrotex CertainTeed. The support of these people, and many, many others, contributed a major part to the success of the conservation work, and we are indebted to them.

Special thanks go to the remarkable Bill Pierson, equipment manager for the project. Bill had an amazing ability to keep the complex mechanical systems of the cofferdam, boat, and headquarters operating despite long hours, adverse weather, and my unending requests for more help.

This book could not have been completed without the wonderful talents of editor Molly Gardner and graphic designer Roland Pantermuehl, both of the Texas Historical Commission. Molly's endless hours of proofing manuscripts, her masterful reworking of sentences, and her detail in the compilation of the bibliography transformed a rough manuscript into a finished book. Roland's great artistry and creativity lent beauty and vitality to many of the figures. My sincere thanks to both of you for your expertise and support. Independent artist Charles Shaw drew the wonderful watercolor illustrations that appear in this book. His artistic work helps bring to life the story of La Salle's colonial enterprise in Texas.

Additional important editorial assistance was received from several other persons: Helen Dewolf, Jeff Durst, Donny Hamilton, Steve Hoyt, Jack Jackson, Jim Jobling, and an anonymous reviewer.

The excavation of *La Belle* gained worldwide media attention. This was due to the talent of Renee Peterson Trudeau, then head of the Marketing Communications Division of the Texas Historical Commission. Others who worked hard to publicize the project were Debbi Head, Donnell Ocher, Darci Sinclair, and Nancy Nesbitt. Graphic support was provided by Roni Morales and Lin Altman. Jim Bonar took pictures of many of the artifacts from *La Belle.* Alan Govenar and Bob Tullier of Documentary Arts, Inc., worked diligently to make two wonderful documentary films about *La Belle,* which have been shown internationally.

Larry Oaks, executive director of the Texas Historical Commission and my boss, provided support and encouragement over the years I labored on this book.

Many individuals at the Texas Historical Commission and the Friends of the Texas Historical Commission helped in various ways. Lillie Thompson, my administrative assistant, helped keep my state bureaucratic duties going while I toiled in the field. Penny Black and Lynn Ward handled accounting matters. Peggy Claiborne and Pat Galvin of the Friends provided invaluable assistance. Commission attoney Joe Thrash of the Texas Attorney General's Office provided legal advice on all aspects of the project.

Interest and support for the project came from State Senator Bill Ratliff and his wife, Susie. They both visited the excavation and offered advice that was greatly appreciated.

Laurens Fish III of Weed-Corley-Fish Funeral Home and Clark Hoffman of Dietz Memorial Company provided the services and monument for the burial of the skeletal remains recovered from the bow of *La Belle* into the Texas State Cemetery in Austin.

Citizens and officials of France have been very supportive of the project. Jean Boudriot freely provided information about shipbuilding techniques and supplied images for this book. Admiral Georges Prud'homme, former director of the Musée national de la Marine in Paris, and Jean-Marcel Humbert, assistant director of the Musée, provided guidance and advice on research related to *La Belle.* Houston Consul Général Denis Simonneau; Joël Savary, Houston Attaché Culturel; and Christine Mossier, former Houston

Attaché Culturel, provided advice and support for the interment of Individual Two in the Texas State Cemetery and helped coordinate exchange with scholars in France. To all these individuals, my sincerest appreciation.

Publication of this book was underwritten by the generosity of the O'Connor-Hewitt Foundation, Harold Courson, the Trull Foundation, the Fondren Foundation, the Summerlee Foundation, and the Summerfield G. Roberts Foundation. This support has enabled a much wider audience to obtain copies of the book.

The generosity, commitment, and dedication of all these supporters were essential to the success of the project. Together, we recovered the archaeological record of a doomed dream and a lost colony. *La Belle* would change our understanding of Texas history when she sank into a watery grave and was reborn three centuries later. I hope all who supported this project will accept my heartfelt thanks and join me in celebrating the remarkable rescue of the tiny ship that opened a large window into our past.

JAMES E. BRUSETH

Index

Page numbers in *italic* type refer to illustrations; those in **bold** refer to maps

navigational problems for La Salle, 22–23, 75–76, 126
Navío Quebrado, 9
needles, 88–89, 91, 109
New France (eastern Canada), 16–17, 20, 73, 74–76
New Spain. *See* Spanish authorities in New World
Nika (Shawnee Indian hunter), 31
nocturnals, 108–109
Nuestra Señora de Loreto y la Bahía, Presidio de, 28
Nuestra Señora de Regla, 7
Nueva Vizcaya, Mexico, 9–10, 19. *See also* silver mines
NUMA (National Underwater Marine Agency), 45

oak for timbers, 80
oakum caulking, 76
O'Connor, Dennis, 49
olives, 113
onion bottles, 101, *102*
opossum, first encounter with, 127

packing of cargo, 84, 87, 90, 95
padlocks, 105
Palacios Area Historical Museum, 139
Palacios as headquarters of excavation, 56–57, 59
Pardiñas, Juan Ysidro de (Villar de Francos), 9–10
Pass Cavallo, *7*, 25–26, 35
PEG (polyethylene glycol) conservation material, 132
pencil holder, 103
pendant blocks, 64
Perinnet, Chevalier de (Barthélemy d'Aralle), 66
personal effects, 91, 105–108, *117, 118, 119*
personal profit motive of La Salle, 86, 113, 114, 128, 130
Petite Belle, La, 139
Petit Goàve (Haiti), 7, **9,** *10,* 102
Pevny, Taras, 76
pewter artifacts, 99–101, 102, 106, 118
Phily, Jean, 100
pigment as trade good, 92
pigs, 123
pine for timbers, 80
pins, 88–89
pipes, smoking, 105
pirates in Caribbean, 7–8, 11
planisphere, 108–109
planking timbers, 76, 135
plant life of Texas coast, 127
plant remains on *La Belle,* 112–13
plates, pewter, 99–100
pole arms, 98
polyethylene glycol (PEG) conservation material, 132
poop deck, location of, 69
pothunters and Tunica Indian grave artifacts, 41
pottery, 41–42, 98–99

powder flasks, 97–98
prairie chickens, 127
preservation level of *La Belle,* 54–55, 56, *57*
prickly pear, 113
private vs. public funding for excavation, 48–49
profit motive of La Salle, 86, 113, 114, 128, 130
prop-wash deflector, 40, 87
provenience of artifacts, 55
public awareness and publicity, 42, 45, 136–40
public vs. private funding for excavation, 48–49
pulley and block mechanisms, 64
pump locker, *77*

racial origin of skeletons, identification methods, 118
rats, black (ship), 123, 126
reconstruction of human head from skull, 121–22
recycling of old ship timbers, 79–80, 143n 23
red pigment, 92
religious items, 90, 105, *106,* 111
Renaudot, Eusèbe, 19
Retana, Gen. Juan de, 12
reuse of old ship timbers, 79–80, 143n 23
ribs (framing timbers), 71–73, 76–80, 136
Richaud, Capt. Elie, 3
rigging elements, 64–65, *67,* 68, 134
rings, finger, 89–90, 107–108
Rio Grande, reports of French exploration on, 11
Ripke, Roberta, 59, 138
Rivas, Capt. Martín de, 8
River of Canoes, 31
Rochefort, France, *24,* 66, *68,* 105
Roman coin, 109–11
ropes, 65, 105, 116
rosary beads, 105
Rouen, France, 16

sails, 63, 68, 109
Saint-François, Le, 20, 21
Saint-Mars, François Colbert de, 66
Saintonge region, France, 98
San Francisco de Conchos, Presidio de, **9**
scientific archaeology vs. treasure hunting, 47–48
sealing wax, 107
security issues for excavation, 41, 47–48, 49, 50, 56
seed beads, 87
seeds and seed fragments, 112–13
sheep/goats, 123–24
shipbuilding techniques, 77–78, 128–29. *See also* structure of *La Belle*
ship's equipment, 108–109, *110*
shoes, 105, 107, 108, *117*
shot, types of, 95–96
shroud, rigging, 65
signets, brass, 107
Sigüenza y Góngora, Carlos de, 34

silicone oil conservation material, 132
silver mines, Spanish: crucibles as evidence of La Salle's intentions, 104; French designs on Spanish, 3, 11; French survivors' work in, 129; location of, **9;** Spanish discovery of French intentions, 8
single-sheaved blocks, 64, *67*
skeletal remains, 15, 115–27
Smith, C. Wayne, 132
smoked meats, 124–25
smoking pipes, 105
Society of Jesus (Jesuits), 16, 17, 18, 90
Sokkia Corporation, 55
sounding weights, 109, *110*
Spanish authorities in New World: discovery of French colony, 6–10, 27, 34–35, 83; vs. France as first to attempt Texas colony, 145n 4; French plans for undermining, 8, 19–20, 22, 76, 128; interrogation of Thomas, 7–8; settlement at Fort St. Louis location, 28. *See also* silver mines
spoons, 102
square spikes, 76
Starved Rock, Illinois, French fort at, *23*
Stasny, James, 134
state government of Texas and project funding, 47, 48–49
Steele, Gentry, 115, 118
stereolithography technique, 120–21
stern cabin, 71
stern hold (lazarette), 71, 86
stoneware containers, 98, 99
straw packing materials, 87
structure of *La Belle*: archival resources on, 66–69, *70, 71*; compartment layout, 69–71; construction history, 66–67, *68,* 71–81, 143n 14; overview of layout, *75*; rigging elements, 64–65, *67. See also* hull
Summerlee Foundation, 49
sump pumps for water extraction, 55
sunglass timers, 109
surmarks on framing timbers, 76
swimming, sailors' lack of skill in, 116
swivel guns, 94, 95
swords, 95
syphilis, mercury for cure of, 98

tableware, 99–101
tacks, brass, 103
technology, archaeological. *See* methods and technology
teredo worm damage, 15, 40, 94, 134–35
Tessier, Capt. Pierre, 3, 4–5, 10, 72, 126
Texana Museum, 139
Texas, consequences of La Salle's failure for, 140
Texas Antiquities Committee, 142n 2
Texas Historical Commission, 38, 47, 48, 137, 142n 2
Texas Maritime Museum, 139
Texas State Cemetery, 122–23
Texas State History Museum, 131, 135